Social Welfare

The American Partnership

Jerry D. Marx

University of New Hampshire

Boston New York San Francisco
Mexico City Montreal Toronto London Madrid Munich Paris
Hong Kong Singapore Tokyo Cape Town Sydney

Series Editor: *Patricia Quinlin*
Editorial Assistant: *Annemarie Kennedy*
Marketing Manager: *Taryn Wahlquist*
Production Editor: *Michelle Limoges*
Editorial Production Service: *Omegatype Typography, Inc.*
Electronic Composition: *Omegatype Typography, Inc.*
Composition and Prepress Buyer: *Linda Cox*
Manufacturing Buyer: *JoAnne Sweeney*
Cover Desinger: *Linda Knowles*

Library of Congress Cataloging-in-Publication Data
Marx, Jerry D.
    Social welfare : the American partnership / Jerry D. Marx.
      p. cm.
    Includes bibliographical references and index.
    ISBN 0-205-34265-5 (alk. paper)
      1. United States—Social policy. 2. Social policy—Economic aspects—United States—History. 3. Social policy—Political aspects—United States—History. 4. Public welfare—United States—History. 5. Social service—United States—History. I. Title.

HN57.M276 2003
361.6'1'0973—dc21

2003043709

Printed in the United States of America

10 9 8 7 6 5 4 3   HAM   08 07 06 05

To my mother

CONTENTS

5 American Social Policy and the Industrial Boom   67

6 American Social Policy During the Progressive Era   85

7   American Social Policy in the Great Depression and World War II   107

PREFACE

The fundamental approach of *Social Welfare: The American Partnership* is to describe and examine social policy development as a partnership among the political, economic, and social sectors of American society. That is, the book focuses on the ways that all three sectors have collaborated in creating social policies and programs that respond to emerging social needs. The book is organized in three major sections: Part I, The Historical Foundation of American Social Policy; Part II, Current Services and Issues in American Social Policy; and Part III, What Can Be Done: A Process for Social Policy Development. Organized in this way, the book is a resource that can be used in undergraduate and graduate social welfare policy courses.

Many social welfare textbooks are primarily focused on the efforts of government in addressing social need. Often the assumption is that government has the primary responsibility of addressing social problems neglected or created by the American capitalist economic system. Although this may be true, American social welfare is also a history of collaborative efforts by various groups in promoting well-being. As we enter the twenty-first century, this collaboration may be increasingly required in a global economy threatened by terrorism.

This book not only looks at the contribution of all three sectors—government, business, and private nonprofit organizations—to American social welfare policy but also strives to make social policy fun and interesting for students, a group that often views the subject as tedious at best and irrelevant at worst. I suspect that many students take social welfare policy courses only because they are required. Readers may be surprised to find that social welfare policy can be relatively interesting and fun to learn.

To make the book user friendly, inserts are employed in the text to draw student attention to relevant and interesting information. For example, the book provides "Did You Know" framed inserts to provide students with interesting and amusing pieces of historical information. Furthermore, these inserts include critical analysis, ethical questions, illustrations, and case studies meant to generate personal reflection and class discussion regarding social justice, diversity, empowerment, self-determination, and other ethical issues.

In addition, the book provides short historical profiles of interesting and significant personalities in American social welfare history. These profiles are integrated into the more general historical discussion and include the many women and minorities often given little attention in traditional history. Likewise, the historical profiles include leaders from the business sector, another group that is often neglected in traditional social welfare policy books. I find that students tend to be more interested in personalities and the individual challenges they overcame to achieve historical significance than the more traditional emphasis on election results and war victories.

As previously stated, this book is organized as follows: Part I, Historical Foundation of Social Policy; Part II, Current Services and Issues in American

Social Policy (including an overview of major social programs); and Part III, What Can Be Done: A Process for Social Policy Development. This chronological sequence, I believe, promotes better understanding and retention by students. In so doing, the book provides students with a more thorough and coherent historical foundation than do most comprehensive social policy books. The historical material in these books is often minimal and disjointed, with little coverage of business and private nonprofit organizations. To develop strong professional identities, students need an awareness of the characteristics and efforts of those who have gone before them in their respective fields. Similarly, to promote effective and just social policy, professionals must have a knowledge of the historical influence of various policies on oppressed and disadvantaged populations, such as the rural and urban poor, women, gays and lesbians, and people of color.

Conversely, books that are focused primarily on social policy history typically contain relatively little material for students on advocacy and the policymaking process. Students are left asking, "What can we do now to better address these social problems?" The goal of this book, therefore, is to combine the social welfare history, current social issues, and social policy-making process material in one book. Part II of this book provides an overview of current issues and major programs in contemporary American social policy. Subsequently, Part III of the book provides students with concrete policy practice skills based in theory and research methods. That is, Part III offers students a tangible, step-by-step process for policy analysis and advocacy, emphasizing basic research and analysis methods used in policy development. The process detailed here stresses the importance of thorough problem definition, including the historical context of a problem, past research on the problem, and societal values underlying the problem. The trick, however, is to present this information in a way that is not flat, elementary, dry, or boring! Therefore, many illustrations and cases are provided to enliven the policy development process for readers.

Acknowledgments

I am indebted to the teachers, colleagues, and friends who have served as mentors during my education and career. I also thank my research assistants over the years: Maria Gagnon, Heidi Howard, Jill Ferraro, Nicole Bandera, and Judith Kowalik. Their attention to detail is invaluable in a large project such as this book. My thanks to the reviewers: Marian A. Aguilar, Texas A&M International University; Stephen C. Anderson, New Mexico State University; Kimberly A. Battle-Walters, Azusa Pacific University; Patricia K. Cianciolo, Northern Michigan University; Marcia B. Cohen, University of New England; John M. Herrick, Michigan State University. Finally, I state my love and appreciation for my family—Susan, Andy, and Becca. And I thank Bob Hebert who, for two Maine lobsters, traded me his Toshiba laptop computer, which I used to write this book!

PART ONE

The Historical Foundation of American Social Policy

1 Basic Concepts in Social Policy

John F. Kennedy talks issues with an older American.

Social Policy: A Conceptualization

Social Policy as a Field

Gilbert, Specht, and Terrell provide a simple definition for the term **policy.** According to the authors, a policy is "an explicit course of action."[1] Mayer provides a second and slightly more complex definition: a policy is the "expressed intent of an organization to influence the behavior of its members by the use of sanctions."[2]

A **sanction** is a mechanism for promoting a collective's standards. Sanctions can be regulatory, such as fines, copyrights, building codes, zoning, certification, and licensing. They can also be financial in nature, for example, taxes, grants, contracts, loans, and rewards. Sanctions can be positive, such as a bonus, or negative, such as employment termination.

A policy also has two fundamental characteristics. First, a policy is coercive or constraining for the members of the collective.[3] That is to say, a policy is binding on members of a collective, whether the collective is a nation, state, county, city, or organization. Second, a policy typically refers to decisions made at the highest level of the collective.[4] This would apply whether the collective is in the public sector, such as the federal government, or in the private for-profit sector, such as IBM, or the private nonprofit sector, such as the Girl Scouts.

Based on the preceding discussion, a **social policy** can be defined as a collective course of action, set by policymakers, involving the use of sanctions, to address the needs of some group of people. Defined as such, social policy is a broader concept than public policy in that all three major institutional sectors of society, not just government, take part in developing social policy. For the same reason, it is a broader concept than social welfare policy in that social welfare policy typically refers to programs, benefits, and services of government.[5]

This definition of social policy is consistent with the broad approach taken in this book to the examination of social policy as a field. That is, social policy is viewed here from a societal perspective.[6] In contrast to authors who equate social policy with the twentieth-century welfare state, the focus of this book is more comprehensive. Collectives such as the United States create and organize institutions, based on an underlying set of values, to maximize well-being. The outcome is social welfare. The more effective policymakers are in developing social policy, the greater the social welfare. Social policy is the means; social welfare is the end.

This comprehensive approach to the study of social policy is appropriate for social work because the profession is so broad and comprehensive. Social workers find employment not just in the public sector but also in the private nonprofit sector and even in the private for-profit sector. Social workers can be found throughout the United States in state child welfare departments, adult protective units, state correctional facilities, and mental health services. They can also be found in administrative and direct service positions in the private nonprofit sector—in organizations such as United Way, the American Red Cross, the Boy's and Girl's Clubs, and Big Brothers/ Big Sisters. Yet social workers are also employed in the for-profit sector in corporate employee assistance programs, corporate foundations and charitable giving programs, child care centers, hospitals, and nursing homes. Social workers educated in subjects such as diversity, race, culture, oppression, and group process are expected to become more valuable to corporations competing in a global economy. The fact that social work skills, perspectives, and ethics are valued and in demand across all three major sectors of our country is a tribute to social work education. It also testifies to the need for a more comprehensive education in social policy, so that social workers are prepared to successfully participate in policy development and advocacy, whether working in government, business, or the voluntary sector.

Social workers, given the frontline nature of their work, often gain first-hand knowledge of the various ways in which social policies impact vulnerable individuals, families, groups, and communities. Social workers need to increasingly bring this insight into the policy development process. After all, social workers are trained in human development. That is one of their areas of expertise. However, the true distinction of the profession of social work is its focus on individual functioning in a social environment.[7] This is the social work unit of intervention that requires a balance between the psychological and the social.[8] Schorr maintains that social workers must listen with an "inner ear" and an "outer ear."[9] The inner ear represents the psychological life of the client, whereas the outer ear is a metaphor for the social environment of the client. But surely this social environment does not consist solely of the welfare system or even the entire public sector. The social environment should refer to society itself, whether examining the United States or the entire world community. By understanding contextual factors in the broadest sense, social workers are better able to serve their clients.

This comprehensive perspective on social policy, to various degrees, builds on the work of other authors in the field. In *Becoming an Effective Policy Advocate*, Jansson strives to make social policy more relevant to social workers by examining the topic in organizational and community settings in addition to the traditional legislative context.[10] Karger and Stoesz in their book *American Social Welfare Policy: A Pluralist Approach* discuss the need to include the efforts of the voluntary sector and the corporate sector in promoting social welfare.[11] Gilbert, Specht, and Terrell in *Dimensions of Social Welfare Policy* distinguish between the economic market of capitalism and the "social market of the welfare state."[12] This social market, as described by the authors, contains both a public and private sector, the latter including voluntary and profit-oriented agencies. Iatridis takes an even broader perspective on social policy, stating that "social policy is related to the entire social system and therefore has a much broader nature than social welfare programs."[13]

Figure 1.1 is an adaptation for my purposes of a simple but very useful model of the institutional context of social policy provided by Iatridis.[14] A major theme throughout this text is that American social welfare is an outcome of the efforts of three sets of institutions: economic, political, and social institutions. Therefore, American social welfare is, broadly defined, a **partnership** among these institutional sectors. All three sectors will be discussed in more detail in the remainder of this chapter. For now, it must be stressed that throughout American history, all three sectors have collaborated to promote social welfare. The economic sector, dominated today by large corporations, produces goods and services for a profit. Yet, the American political sector has historically supported, and at times regulated, our business institutions to better promote social welfare. And the voluntary associations of our social sector, often supported by progressive leaders in business and government, have done what business could not do at a profit and what government did not have the will to do alone. At other times, voluntary associations have needed to pressure business and government to "do the right thing," thereby creating a rich history of American activism. Thus, all three sectors contribute to national social welfare. Sometimes the partnership takes the form of a coalition, a league, a federation, a contracted service, or simply a volunteer effort. National, state, or local organizations from one, two, or all three major institutional sectors may be involved. In any case, institutional collaboration ultimately is needed to maximize social welfare.

Systems Model for Social Policy

Ideological Input

To understand social policy in the United States or any country, the dominant **ideology** of the system must be made explicit. In other words, nations

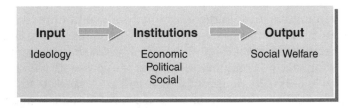

FIGURE 1.1   Systems Model for Social Policy

Source: Adapted from Demetrius S. Iatridis, *Social Policy: Institutional Context of Social Development and Human Services.* (Pacific Grove, CA: Brooks/Cole, 1994).

such as the United States, in an effort to maximize social welfare, build and organize institutions based on a set of values. A **value** is a principle or quality that is considered desirable. Values serve as criteria for making choices, including choices involved in social policy development. Since the mid-1800s, the groups considered most influential in terms of American values have been conservatives, liberals, and the radical left.

In terms of promoting social welfare, **conservatives** support a free market economy and limited government. To this group, the market is the most fair and efficient institutional mechanism for distributing society's resources. Like an "invisible hand," the marketplace guides investment and consumption decisions in maximizing societal well-being.[15] Conservatives believe that individual profit is the great motivator, that individuals left free to pursue their own self-interest in a capitalist system work for the betterment of all. To this end, the role of government should be limited to defending private property rights and maintaining social order. A more expanded role for the public sector, according to conservatives, only drains resources that could be invested in the business sector. Government resources are resources that cannot be used for creating wealth and employment in a capitalist economy.

In cases where the for-profit sector does not meet the needs of certain groups of people, conservatives prefer the use of local institutions in the social sector (see Figure 1.1). That is, for people who cannot participate in the workplace—people with disabilities, older Americans, and children, for example—conservatives typically choose to rely on support provided by the family, churches, and other private nonprofit organizations such as local United Way member agencies (Meals On Wheels, the Girl Scouts, and so forth). In addition, conservatives prefer that these voluntary efforts to support needy people be funded, when necessary, from private charitable giving. Conservatives, therefore, tend to be big promoters of philanthropy on the part of individuals, corporations, and foundations. In short, conservatives tend to value a private means to social welfare.

In contrast to conservatives, **liberals** advocate for a more regulated market and an activist government. Liberals typically agree with conservatives that the market economy is the best promoter of social welfare; however, based in part on the U.S. experience in the Great Depression, traditional liberals believe that the market economy has certain negative tendencies that should be monitored and regulated by government to maximize social welfare. These tendencies include erratic business cycles, racism, sexism, and environmental pollution. Thus, liberals support an expanded role for government in areas such as unemployment insurance, health care, affordable housing, civil rights, affirmative action, and environmental protection. This group tends to be associated with the New Deal under Franklin Roosevelt and the Great Society under Lyndon Johnson.

In summary, liberals tend to support more of a "mixed economy" in the form of European welfare states than do conservatives.[16] Therefore, liberals believe that all three major institutional sectors—political, economic, and social—need to play significant roles in promoting social welfare.

The **radical left** in the United States has consisted historically of socialists and communists. Although it is even harder to generalize about the beliefs of this group, the radical left typically supports a major reorganization of the three major institutional sectors in the United States, one that would result in a greatly reduced role for capitalists in the economic and political sectors. This might include a government-planned economy. It might also include increased workplace democracy, where workers have a much greater role in business decision making. This group tends to see the source of social problems such as poverty and racism as inherent in the capitalist economy. In other words, social problems are the result of structural defects in the capitalist economy; therefore, only fundamental reform of our current institutional structure will maximize social welfare.

Another important part of the ideological input of society, especially for social workers, is the predominant belief at a given point in history regarding the cause of poverty. During the Middle Ages, poverty was much more likely to be seen as a matter of fate. Droughts, military invasions, plagues, and the feudal class hierarchy were thought to be relatively uncontrollable determinants of poverty. At other times, the individual was considered to be the major cause of poverty. For example, for most of the 1700s and 1800s in the U.S., the immorality of the individual was blamed for poverty. If only the person could be reformed to live a more moral life, that person would be more prosperous. In this case, moral generally meant more hardworking, sober, and pious. Conservatives tend to stress this view of poverty. During other points in U.S. history, the social system was considered to be the primary cause of poverty. For instance, while America struggled with mass unemployment during the Great Depression, the institutional structure of the United States was criticized. As a result, institutional reforms such as the Securities and Exchange Commission and the Federal Deposit Insurance Corporation were passed. Liberals, and to a greater degree, leftist Radicals are more apt to emphasize this perspective on poverty.

In any case, the society's set of values, its ideology, will strongly influence the way society organizes its major institutions. In the next sections of this chapter, the current major political, economic, and social institutions operating in the United States are discussed.

Economic Institutions

Capitalism is an economic system that "emphasizes private business initiative in the pursuit of profits through the use of private property."[17] Whereas the basic economic unit under the mercantilist economic system that preceded capitalism was the nation-state, under capitalism, the basic economic unit is the individual. That is, capitalist ideology stresses individual initiative in the market economy. Three essentials of a capitalist economic system, therefore, are (1) that property is primarily privately owned, (2) this private property is used for the accumulation of private gain or profits, and (3) these private property owners and profit-seekers are primarily responsible for the level and direction of the national economy.

In addition, a central characteristic of capitalism is that it is a **market system** in which the factors of production are commodities for sale.[18] These factors of production are land, labor, and capital. In contrast to economies run by tradition (as in the feudal society of the Middle Ages) or command (as in the Soviet Union of the twentieth century), in a capitalist economy, individual men and women, operating freely in the marketplace, decide what to do with these factors of production.[19]

Further, a basic philosophy espoused by these individual capitalists is **laissez-faire.** This French term refers to "leaving things alone."[20] It underlies the basic argument that government should not interfere with the operations of the marketplace. Through the market dynamic of supply and demand, it is argued that a market economy is self-regulating and the fairest and most efficient mechanism for allocating and distributing society's resources.

Did You Know?

Did you know that it is said that a group of merchants called on the French finance minister, Colbert, who served between 1661 and 1683. Colbert thanked the merchants for their contributions to the French economy and asked them what he could do for them. The merchants replied, "Laissez-nous faire"— leave us alone.[21]

This "free-market" philosophy with its emphasis on free trade and competition characterizes the capitalist economy found today in the United States. It is an economy increasingly dominated by large corporations in contrast to small businesses. And it is an economic system that is now being spread with increasing speed throughout the world through the process of **globalization.**[22] Globalization is defined as "the integration of markets, nation-states, and technology to a degree never witnessed before."[23] What makes this trend unique are the technologies that make it possible, including computerization, digitization, satellite communications, fiber optics, and the Internet. These technologies are allowing corporations to create a global market for their goods and services, a market that increasingly reaches across national borders, defense systems, and cultures. The fall of the Berlin Wall and the Soviet Union are dramatic illustrations of this fact. This means that corporations are freer to move all or part of their business operations to countries all over the world. It means that investors can move their funds in and out of countries with lightning speed. And while globalization is creating or exacerbating certain social problems,[24] the optimists swear that all of this means a rising standard of living for all participants, including developing countries.

As the twenty-first century began, the United States was the leading national economy in the global economic system. Beginning in the 1990s, the U.S. economy experienced its longest continued expansion in modern history. The "extraordinarily robust technical progress in the computer and communication industries" was a central factor in this economic success.[25] U.S. households benefited from improved employment opportunities, real income gains, and a substantial increase in their net worth.[26] Overall unemployment rates were the lowest in thirty years, including record low rates for minorities.[27]

At the same time, some experts fear that globalization is creating a two-tiered employment system.[28] Corporations are hiring core personnel with relatively high salaries, full benefits, and comfortable working conditions. These employees typically are engaged in finance, marketing, or technology. While providing these high-paid jobs for a small number of employees, corporations are increasingly manufacturing their products with a second tier of people. This second tier of employment is part-time or temporary, in which employees receive low wages and few benefits. Thus, although the U.S. economy is a world leader in many ways, social workers will inevitably face the challenge of addressing the problematic aspects of globalization as vulnerable populations such as children, minorities, and single mothers deal with the vast technical and economic changes ahead.

Political Institutions

Americans live under a democratic system of government. The three major branches of government in the United States are the executive branch, the judicial branch, and the legislative branch. This book covers the federal level of these political institutions, meaning the presidency, the Supreme Court, and Congress. The influence of the various U.S. presidential administrations as well as the Supreme Court on American social policy and social welfare will be covered in the history section of this book. Congress will be discussed in greater detail here, because at the federal level, the context for a great deal of political advocacy by social workers is Congress.

The United States Congress is a **bicameral legislature;** that is, Congress is composed of two legislative bodies: the House of Representatives and the Senate. The House of Representatives contains 435 voting members.[29] Also, there are five nonvoting delegates representing the District of Columbia and U.S. territories and possessions. United States Representatives serve two-year terms. Each representative must be at least 25 years old, a U.S. citizen for seven or more years at the time he or she begins service, and a resident of the state from which he or she is elected.

The United States Senate contains 100 members, two from each state. Senators serve six-year terms. Each senator must be at least 30 years of age, a U.S. citizen for nine or more years, and a resident of the state from which elected.[30] Each Congress lasts two years and is numbered. For example, the 2001–2002 Congress was the 107th.

Social work advocates and advocates from other fields must regularly make contact with the staff of members of Congress.[31] House members typically have about twenty people on their personal staff. Staff size is roughly the same for all House members. In contrast, a senator's staff size is based on the population size of their state. The larger the population of the state is, the larger the staff of the senator. Senators from large states may have sixty or more staff members.[32] Personal staff members are usually divided between offices in Washington, DC, and the home state.

The personal staff of each member of Congress performs many tasks. In addition to routine clerical duties, staff members write speeches and assist with policy development. They also meet with constituents and lobbyists. For these reasons, congressional staff members are key contacts for social work advocates. Similarly, social workers involved with policy development will want to know the staff members of pertinent congressional committees. The committee staff provides support to congressional members on individual committees. The most common approach is for the Committee Chair to hire a staff to work with the committee members from the majority party in Congress. Likewise, the ranking minority party member hires a staff for the minority party members.[33]

Since the early decades of the 1800s, the **party system** and the **committee system** have been the primary means of organizing congressional work. First, let us look at the political parties in the House of Representatives. The majority party has the primary responsibility for organizing the legislative agenda. The majority party controls the selection of the Speaker of the House and its members constitute a majority on each committee. The **Speaker of the House** is the presiding officer. The Speaker along with the majority leader (and the other party leaders called *whips*) determine the issues that will get top priority during the session. In addition, the minority party elects a **minority leader** and minority whip to work with (or against) the majority party on legislation.[34]

Political parties also elect their leaders in the Senate. The majority party elects a **majority leader** and a majority whip. In similar fashion, the minority party elects a minority leader and minority whip. The majority leader with the help of colleagues performs numerous duties. These include organizing the work of the Senate, scheduling debate on policy issues, and helping to gather enough votes to pass specific pieces of legislation.[35]

As stated, the committee system is the second major arena for congressional work. In fact, most congressional work is done in committees. This work consists of various duties. Congressional committees initiate and prioritize specific policy proposals. They hold public hearings on various policy issues and conduct investigations. Committees carry out studies and publish reports. And congressional committees perform administrative oversight such as reviewing budget requests and passing judgment on presidential appointees. These congressional committees generally have the most expertise in Congress on a given policy subject. Senior members of committees have often dealt with certain issues for a number of years. Also, the staffs that support these committees are often specialists in the policy issue.[36]

Through the party system and congressional committees, and with the help of congressional office staff, Congress performs three major functions.[37] The first is **legislation** or "lawmaking" (Figure 1.2). Lawmaking involves information gathering, discussion, negotiation, and compromise. About 90 percent of bills introduced in a typical Congress never become law. In addition, lawmaking is influenced at every stage of the process by special interest groups. Special interest groups, which include the National Association of Social Workers, help draft legislation, testify at hearings, lobby members of Congress in committee and during floor debate, and pressure the president to sign or veto legislation.

The lawmaking process is governed by a set of rules and precedents. Legislation is considered at a number of points in the process. Each is a veto point. Therefore, the rules favor the status quo, rather than social change. Proponents of change must be successful at each point in the process. Furthermore, the rules work to slow the pace of lawmaking, which also favors the status quo. An example would be a filibuster, where a senator does not relinquish the floor during debate. In any case, social work advocates need to be prepared to work successfully in such an environment.

A second major function of Congress is **representation.** Each member of Congress represents two groups of citizens: his/her own congressional district or state and the nation as a whole. These interests may conflict. The individual may also have strong personal feelings on any given policy issue. No wonder politicians appear to try "to be all things to all people."

Ethical Considerations

When in conflict, what should members of Congress vote in accordance with: the prevailing opinion of their district/state or in the interests of the nation as a whole? the prevailing opinion of their district/state or their personal convictions on the policy issue?

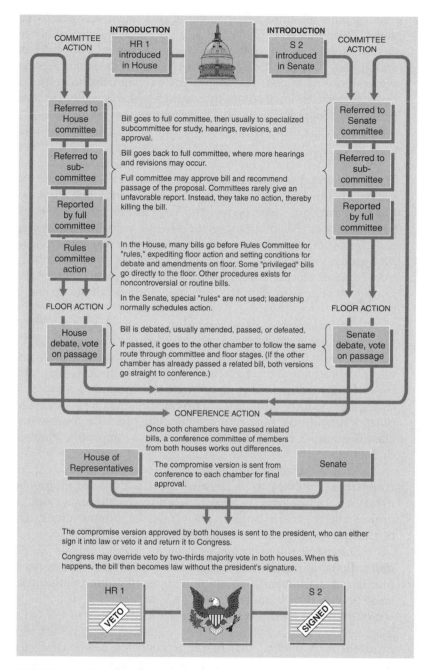

FIGURE 1.2 How a Bill Becomes Law

Source: Republished with permission of Congressional Quarterly, Inc., from *Guide to Congress,* Congressional Quarterly, 1976, p. 345, permission conveyed through Copyright Clearance Center, Inc.

Finally, the third major function of Congress is **administrative oversight.** This function is partly the result of the American public's feeling that citizens should be not only served by government but protected from it as well. Often bureaucratic agencies make expert decisions; Congress then reviews those decisions. Techniques for oversight include special investigations by congressional committees, budget hearings, Senate confirmation of presidential appointments, and impeachment.

Social Institutions

The social sector in America is referred to in various ways: the independent sector, the third sector, the voluntary sector, or the private nonprofit sector. For the most part, it will be referred to in this text as either the private nonprofit sector or the voluntary sector. This sector of American society is large. It includes churches, health and human service agencies, civic and community groups, elementary and secondary schools, arts and cultural organizations, and mutual benefit societies. In fact, the yearly budget of the American nonprofit sector exceeds the national budgets of most countries in the world.[38]

A **private nonprofit organization** is defined as an organization "that is not part of government and does not exist to make a profit."[39] As such, private nonprofit organizations are exempt from federal income tax. Nonprofit organizations are often characterized as philanthropic, charitable, or public benefit organizations. They usually exist to provide a service or promote a cause. For the most part, they are private organizations serving a public purpose. Philanthropic nonprofit organizations include those with the 501(c)3 classification. Charitable donations to 501(c)3 nonprofit organizations are tax deductible.[40]

A small percentage of nonprofits focus on aid to their members—in contrast to a "public good." These nonprofits are called **mutual benefit organizations.** Examples of these organizations include labor unions, veterans' organizations, credit unions, and fraternal organizations. Donations to mutual benefit organizations are not tax deductible.[41]

The Independent Sector, a national coalition of over 800 voluntary organizations, foundations, and corporate giving programs, reports that the number of charitable 501(c)3 organizations registered with the Internal Revenue Service nearly doubled from 1977 to 1992.[42] That is, the independent sector estimates there were 739,000 nonprofit entities in 1977, and this figure increased to 1,030,00 by 1992.[43] In 1994, the nonprofit sector had total annual funds of $568 billion. This figure represented 6.3 percent of all national income in that year. In addition, the nonprofit sector employed 9.7 million people either full or part-time in 1994.[44]

The nonprofit sector performs many roles in the United States.[45] First, and perhaps most important for social work, this sector provides a context for advancing social change. In fact, according to O'Neil, all major social movements in U.S. history started in the nonprofit sector: mental health care, women's suffrage, civil rights, consumer protection, and environmentalism.[46] Second, the nonprofit sector preserves American heritage through nonprofit historical societies, museums, and theaters. Third, this sector offers recreation to the public through organizations such as the YMCA, Girl Scouts, and Little Leagues. Fourth, the private nonprofit sector provides support to American business through its nonprofit educational and research institutions, institutions such as Harvard University. Fifth, services that cannot be delivered at a profit by the business sector are often provided in the private nonprofit sector. An example would be Habitat for Humanity's effort to build decent and affordable housing for low-income Americans. And last, this sector of society promotes the general welfare through its many health and human service agencies throughout the country. In fact, as the reader will learn more about in the subsequent history chapters, the private nonprofit sector is the birthplace of the profession of social work.

A fundamental point to remember at this point, however, is that the private nonprofit sector has historically worked closely with government to promote social welfare. For example, private nonprofit hospitals in the late 1800s received significant revenue from government.[47] In 1989, 57 percent of New York City expenditures on the poor were allocated to private benevolent institutions. This partnership continues today.[48] In 1992, of the total funds of the nonprofit sector, 31 percent came from government. This represents a larger share of total funds than were received by the nonprofit sector from private donations, which represented a little over 18 percent in that year.[49] Of interest to social workers employed in the health and human services, about 51 percent of these funds went to health services and roughly 11 percent went to social and legal services.[50]

Indeed, it is a major theme of this book that all three sectors—political, economic, and social—work in partnership to promote the social welfare. Although using a more narrow definition of "social welfare" than used in this book, Lester Salamon comments on this partnership:

> In short, by the latter 1970s, the United States had developed a complex system of social welfare protections providing significant levels of assistance not just to the poor but to the middle class as well and involving an extensive partnership between government and both nonprofit and for-profit providers.[51]

Did You Know?

Did you know, according to Lester Salamon, that the colony of Massachusetts passed a tax to help support Harvard College and paid part of its president's salary until 1791. Today Harvard University has an endowment of several billion dollars. Government does do some things right after all![52]

Outcome: Social Welfare

The term *welfare* is defined as the state of doing well, especially in respect to good fortune, happiness, health, prosperity, or well-being.[53] The concept of **social welfare** applies this definition to a collective such as a nation, state, or other group of people. As such, social welfare refers to "the state of collective well-being."[54] Although the term is also used to refer to government programs, benefits, and services, it will primarily be used here in relation to collective well-being.

Social welfare is typically measured by one or more social indicators. Indicators commonly used in the United States include the gross national product and the gross domestic product.[55] The **gross national product (GNP)** is the dollar value of the total output of all goods and services produced in the private and public sectors. The GNP includes the value of all production of U.S. entities even if they are located in foreign nations.[56] Given that a high GNP is generally associated with high employment rates and high national income, the GNP is a much-utilized indicator of national well-being.[57] The fact that the GNP includes both private and public production testifies to the fact that American social welfare is a partnership.

The **gross domestic product (GDP)** is similar to the GNP. The difference is that the gross domestic product measures the dollar value of total output of all goods and services produced within the United States by both domestic and foreign entities.[58]

The federal government produces regular updates of other socioeconomic indicators of social welfare as well. For example, as a measure of inflation, the Bureau of Labor Statistics reports changes in the **consumer price index.** This index measures the prices of a fixed market basket of some 300 goods typically purchased by an urban consumer.[59]

Although social indicators such as the GNP and the consumer price index are widely used, like most indicators they do not capture all aspects of social welfare. For example, although the GNP provides one measure of the dollar value of the total output of goods and services, it is not a very good measure of the quality of those goods and services.[60] Also, GNP does not tell us much about the distribution of goods and services in a population. Social workers often want to monitor the status of certain populations at risk: poor people, minorities, women, children, and older Americans. Therefore, social workers use other social indicators as well.

To illustrate, social workers in the health and human services tend to deal more with indicators such as unemployment and poverty rates, adult and juvenile crime rates, teen pregnancy percentages, child abuse and neglect statistics, and infant mortality. Social workers employed in the field of education are more familiar with indicators such as graduation rates, school dropout rates, literacy statistics, and school violence incidence. Similarly, social workers involved in political advocacy organizations are particularly concerned with voter registration levels and voter turnout.

What is more, when considering social welfare, the profession of social work emphasizes social justice, respect for diversity, self-determination, and empowerment of vulnerable populations. These principles are part of the ethics of the profession, and, therefore, must be included by social workers when evaluating societal outcomes. In any case, many of these measures of "social welfare" will be discussed in the chapters that follow.

CONTENTSELECT

For more information on related social work topics, use the following search terms:

Administrative oversight	Legislation	Private nonprofit
Bicamarel	Liberals	organization
Capitalism	Market system	Radical left
Committee system	Majority leader	Representations
Consumer price index	Minority leader	Sanction
Globalization	Mutual benefit organizations	Social policy
Gross domestic product	Partnership	Social welfare
Gross national product	Party system	Speaker of the House
Ideology	Policy	Value
Laissez-faire		

NOTES

1. Neil Gilbert, Harry Specht, and Paul Terrell, *Dimensions of Social Policy,* 3rd ed. (Englewood Cliffs, NJ: Prentice Hall, 1993).

2. Robert R. Mayer, *Policy and Program Planning: A Developmental Perspective* (Englewood Cliffs, NJ: Prentice Hall, 1985), p. 18.

3. Ibid., p. 17.

4. Ibid.

5. Diana M. DiNitto, *Social Welfare: Politics and Public Policy* (Boston: Allyn & Bacon, 2000), p. 2.

6. Demetrius Iatridis, *Social Policy: Institutional Context of Social Development and Human Services* (Pacific Grove, CA: Brooks/Cole 1994).

7. Florence Hollis and Mary E. Woods, *Casework: A Psychosocial Therapy,* 3rd ed. (New York: Random House, 1981), p. 27.

8. Robert Schneider and F. Ellen Netting, "Influencing Social Policy in a Time of Devolution:

Upholding Social Work's Great Tradition," *Social Work,* 44, No. 4 (1999), p. 350.

9. Schorr, 1985, as cited in Schneider and Netting, p. 351.

10. Bruce Jansson, *Becoming an Effective Policy Advocate: From Policy Practice to Social Justice* (Pacific Grove, CA: Brooks/Cole, 1999).

11. Howard Jacob Karger and David Stoesz, *American Social Welfare Policy: A Pluralist Approach,* 3rd ed. (New York: Addison Wesley Longman, 1998).

12. Gilbert, Specht, and Terrell, pp. 40–41.

13. Iatridis, p. 24.

14. Ibid., p. 21.

15. Adam Smith, *The Wealth of Nations* (New York: Penguin, 1982).

16. Ken Judge (1981), as cited in Gilbert et al., p. 41.

17. Allan Gruchy, *Comparative Economic Systems*, 2nd ed. (Boston: Houghton Mifflin, 1977), pp. 32–33.

18. Neil Heilbroner and Lester Thurow, *Economics Explained: Everything You Need to Know About How the Economy Works and Where It's Going* (New York: Touchstone, 1994), p. 15.

19. Ibid., p. 14.

20. Ibid., p. 24.

21. Ibid.

22. Thomas L. Friedman, *The Lexus and the Olive Tree* (New York: Anchor Books, 2000), p. 9.

23. Ibid.

24. Lori Wallach and Michelle Sforza, *Whose Trade Organization? Corporate Globalization and the Erosion of Democracy* (Washington, DC: Public Citizen, 1999).

25. Organization for Economic Co-operation and Development, *Economic Survey of the United States, May 2000.* Retrieved from the World Wide Web on January 10, 2001: www.oecd.org.

26. Ibid.

27. Organization for Economic Co-operation and Development, p. 10.

28. David C. Korten, *When Corporations Rule the World* (West Hartford, Connecticut: Kumarian and San Francisco, CA: Berrett-Koehler, 1995). See also Christopher Lasch, *The Revolt of the Elites and the Betrayal of Democracy* (New York: Norton, 1995) and Jeremy Rifkin, *The End of Work: The Decline of the Global Labor Force and the Dawn of the Post-Market Era* (New York: Tarcher/Putnam).

29. Stephen J. Wayne, G. Calvin Mackenzie, David M. O'Brien, and Richard L. Cole, *The Politics of American Government: Foundations, Participation, and Institutions* (New York: St. Martin's, 1995), pp. 413–414.

30. Ibid.

31. The Children's Defense Fund, *2000 Congressional Workbook: Basic Process and Issue Primer* (Washington, DC: Author, 2000), p. 27.

32. Wayne et al., p. 416.

33. Ibid., pp. 416–417.

34. Ibid., pp. 420–422.

35. Ibid., pp. 422–423.

36. Ibid., p. 428.

37. Ibid., pp. 431–448.

38. Michael O'Neill, *The Third America: The Emergence of the Nonprofit Sector in the United States* (San Francisco, CA: Jossey-Bass, 1989), p. 7.

39. Ibid., p. 2.

40. Ibid., p. 4.

41. Ibid.

42. Virginia A. Hodgkinson, Murray S. Weitzman, John A. Abrahams, Eric A. Crutchfield, and David R. Stevenson, *Nonprofit Almanac: Dimensions of the Independent Sector, 1996–1997* (San Francisco, CA: Jossey-Bass, 1996), p. 14.

43. Ibid., p. 4.

44. Ibid., p. 3.

45. D. H. Smith (1988), as cited in O'Neill, pp. 14–15.

46. O'Neill, pp. 16–17.

47. Lester M. Salamon, *Partners in Public Service: Government-Nonprofit Relations in the Modern Welfare State* (Baltimore, MD: Johns Hopkins University Press, 1995), p. 83.

48. Ibid.

49. Hodgkinson et al., p. 5.

50. Ibid., p. 7.

51. Salamon, p. 224.

52. Ibid., pp. 84–85.

53. *Random House Webster's College Dictionary* (New York: Random House, 1999), p. 1479.

54. Robert L. Barker, *The Social Work Dictionary*, 3rd ed. (Washington, DC: National Association of Social Workers, 1995), p. 357.

55. Heilbroner and Thurow, p. 57.

56. Ibid., p. 79.

57. Ibid., p. 83.

58. Ibid., pp. 79–80.

59. Campbell McConnell and Stanley Brue, *Macroeconomics: Principles, Problems, and Policies*, 14th ed. (Boston: Irwin/McGraw Hill, 1999), p. 141.

60. Heilbroner and Thurow, pp. 83–85.

2

The European Middle Ages and Early Modern Period

"The economy's never been better. Here's another potato!"

Although the potato was not actually introduced in Northern Europe until the 1700s, life in the Middle Ages, especially for the lower classes, was lived at the subsistence level.

Characteristics of Medieval Society

The period in history known as the European **Middle Ages** provides an important starting point for the evolution of social policy in the United States. Historians actually break the period up into three intervals: the Early Middle Ages from about 600 A.D. to 1050, the High Middle Ages from 1050 to 1300, and the Later Middle Ages from 1300 to 1500.[1] Society in this period is often referred to as medieval or feudal society. The feudal system at its peak is captured in the model shown in Figure 2.1.[2] Like all models, it is a simplification of reality. For one thing, the feudal system in practice varied from place to place in its specific characteristics. Yet, Figure 2.1 highlights some of the most common and important elements of this system.

The Roman Catholic Church, a monolithic institution at this period in history, was centered in Rome. The monarchy consisted of the king, noblemen or lords, and peasants, also known as **serfs.** The lord and his serfs comprised a form of social and economic organization known as a **manor.**[3] Serfs were not exactly slaves in that they commonly had more rights than a slave. For instance, serfs were allocated land, which normally could not be taken away from them. The king maintained a military force of **knights** for protection against outside invasion.

Finally, a medieval village typically contained a group of artisans and merchants, a sort of medieval business sector. An **artisan** was the term used for craftsmen who made candles, barrels, silver items, and so forth. Artisans organized themselves into **guilds,** a form of professional association. Merchants bought and sold commodities for a profit. They were traders who organized themselves into trading companies.

Guilds and trading companies were necessary to protect the interest of craftsmen and merchants for at least two reasons.[4] One is that these entities helped to limit outside competition and thereby protect the jobs and income of their members. Second, these groups had no accepted role in the feudal system. This is why they are depicted on the outer portion of Figure 2.1. The Roman Catholic Church condemned usury (i.e., the lending of money with

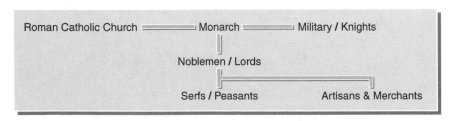

FIGURE 2.1   **The Medieval/Feudal Model**

interest), which was needed to do business. Further, the Church promoted a "just price," which was often considered unfair by merchants and artisans.

Feudalism had several other important features.[5] As suggested by Figure 2.1, the feudal society was very hierarchical. People were born into one of the social classes and usually remained there for life. And there was hierarchy in all classes. To illustrate, craft guilds were organized into three levels: master, journeyman, and apprentice. Even some serfs had a higher social status than other serfs. Conformity to this hierarchy was maintained by traditional deference to social superiors, mutual obligation, and various forms of social control, including the church and local courts.

The feudal system was not a capitalistic system. Land was not bought and sold; wealth was not accumulated by individuals the way it is in our present capitalist economy. The feudal system was a subsistence and bartering economy. It contained a market for bartering, but the market was not the central organizing mechanism that it is in today's capitalist system.[6] Tradition was much more important in guiding economic decisions.

Although it was not bought and sold as a market commodity, land was controlled by the church, kings, and lords. Serfs, in contrast, inherited the right to cultivate a piece of land. For example, serfs might work the lord's land for three days during the week, and then to sustain themselves, work a piece of land allocated to them by their lord for the rest of the week.[7]

The medieval society, like all societies, organized its institutions in an effort to maximize social welfare. Based on a fundamental principle of mutual obligation, each institution and socioeconomic group had a specific role to play.[8] The king raised an army with the assistance of his lords. More specifically, the king and higher lords granted fiefs to lesser lords in exchange for military service. The **fief** gave the lesser lord control over an area of land in exchange for military duty.[9] In addition to military duty, lords stocked food in case of famine and provided peasants with certain feasts during the year. The principle of **noblesse oblige** developed, in which it became a moral obligation for the lords to treat peasants with generosity.[10]

The Roman Catholic Church administered to the spiritual needs of people, provided legal assistance, and contributed food and shelter to the needy. Local courts, in addition to the church, enforced the rights and obligations of individuals. For instance, a lord could not take land rights from a serf without a hearing in a local court.[11] In performing its role, local courts kept records and recruited juries from the village for hearings.

Serfs, tied by birth to their allocated land, provided agricultural labor. Because they inherited the right to work their land, serfs seldom moved their residence. In fact, residency was sometimes restricted.[12] That is, peasants were not free to wander from place to place. Officials could return such individuals to their places of origin. This lack of mobility contributed to a communalism among serfs. They often owned farm tools and animals in common. Hence, the pasture where these animals grazed was called the **commons.**

Although it had many positive characteristics, the medieval period should not be romanticized the way it is in the film industry. To do so is to take for granted later increases in living standards derived from industrialism, and more specifically, capitalism. The medieval period is noted for its values of mutual obligation, solidarity, and communalism, because such values were a prerequisite for survival. However, life, especially for the lower classes, was lived at the subsistence level. During times of crop failure, it was the serf who suffered most, at times watching the starvation of family members, including children. And an average week was pitiful. Historians Edward McNall Burns, Robert Lerner, and Standish Meacham describe the medieval life of a serf:

> Dwellings were usually miserable hovels constructed of wattle—braided twigs—smeared over with mud. As late as the thirteenth century an English peasant was convicted of destroying his neighbor's house simply by sawing apart one central beam. The floors of most huts were usually no more than the bare earth, often cold and damp. For beds there was seldom more than bracken, and beyond that there was hardly any furniture. Not entirely jokingly it may be said that a good meal often consisted of two courses: one a porridge very much like gruel and the other a gruel very much like porridge.[13]

Yet, it must be emphasized that feudalism furthered the development of a strong national government in England and other parts of Western Europe.[14] Not only did feudalism lead to a strong nation-state, but also to a strong obligation on the part of the state toward the needy. And, in contrast to much of American capitalist history, the individual was not blamed for poverty and other problems during the feudal era. Famine, war, and fate were typically viewed as the source of social problems.

Transition to Capitalism

The Decline of Medieval Society

Even at its peak between 1050 and 1300, the medieval system began to experience fundamental changes in the economic, political, and social relations described earlier. The population of western Europe tripled during this time period.[15] A better food supply was a major reason for this growth. A more abundant food supply was due, in part, to climate changes that resulted in warmer and dryer weather at the time. Also, new technologies for agricultural production were increasingly employed, technologies such as the use of water mills and windmills and more effective plows.

This population explosion coincided with the **enclosure** movement in which fields were enclosed with fences and hedges.[16] A major reason for this change was the increase in the profitability, and therefore, production of wool. To produce wool, however, large tracts of land had to be turned into pastures for sheep, thereby forcing serfs from their traditional roles and lands in the feudal model.

This landless population began to seek work for wages in the villages and towns. Many were semiskilled, but many were unskilled as they searched for new ways to sustain themselves. Some peasants found work as cleaners, sweepers, or seamstresses. The evolution of the factory system, while providing work for some, caused economic hardship for many, including small craftsmen and those impacted by seasonal and cyclical unemployment. Historian Walter Trattner states:

> Subsistence...depended much less now than previously on the individual...[and more] on employment by those who owned the resources, on the factory whistle and the time clock—and on the state of the market.[17]

During this epic transition, foreign trade became more important in creating employment and national wealth. Under the mercantilist policies that were in place during the transition from feudalism to capitalism, the wealth of a nation-state was measured by the amount of gold and silver obtained through a favorable balance of trade.[18] The basic economic unit was the state in contrast to the individual under capitalism. The larger the balance of trade, the larger was the nation's independence and power. As places such as England and France became strong national entities, the colonies overseas became increasingly important as sources of gold, silver, and tradable commodities.

As a result of these economic and political changes, new social relations evolved among kings, church leaders, and emerging capitalists.[19] Merchants and bankers became more powerful members of society. These businesspeople, once relegated to peripheral roles in medieval society, began to promote the use of money, credit, interest, and rent. For example, the use of coins and national monetary systems emerged. Instead of having peasants work their fields to produce crops, lords began to ask for rent.

These capitalists began to seek limits on the power of monarchs and government in general.[20] They began to seek more freedom from regulation. Intellectuals such as John Locke, the English philosopher of the 1600s, began to speak out, describing government as a necessary evil, the power of which should be limited.

Increasing freedom was also sought in the religious world. Martin Luther, a German monk, called for reform of the Roman Catholic Church in 1517.[21] Luther objected to the corruption and basic principles of medieval Catholicism. For example, he objected to the sale of dispensations, which allowed for the annulment of marriages, and to indulgences, a remission by the Roman Catholic Church of punishment for sin. Luther also challenged the principle that people could be saved by good works. Rather, he believed that people could be saved by God's grace alone, not through priests or good works. He preferred the literal meaning of the Scriptures; he rejected everything else.

Did You Know?

Martin Luther initially meant his theses to be debated at Wittenberg University, a relatively limited arena for discussion. An unknown person translated and published his 95 theses, thus instigating the widespread "Protestant Reformation."[22]

King Henry VIII declared the English branch of the Roman Catholic Church to be a state church in 1534.[23] The most immediate reason for this action was the Pope's hesitancy to grant Henry an annulment of his marriage to Catherine of Aragon, so that he could marry another woman, Anne Boleyn. Catherine was past her childbearing age and Henry wanted a male heir to his thrown. In any case, as a result, the Church of England was established.

Parallel trends toward personal freedom, therefore, developed in the secular and religious worlds.[24] The increasingly powerful merchants, bankers, artisans, and small landowners rebelled against the monarchy. Protestant reformers and state churches challenged the Roman Catholic Church. In the process, the view of moral being began to change. Immorality was increasingly associated with the characteristics of corrupt monarchs, traits such as excessive pride, greed, laziness, lust, and wastefulness. The poor, likewise, began to be associated with many of these traits. In contrast, the moral person was autonomous, and hard working. In fact, work became the vehicle for fulfilling God's purpose on earth. Not only was the moral individual independent and industrious, this person was also frugal and acquisitive. Moral people saved; they did not waste. Although wealth was therefore a reflection of the moral lifestyle, excess wealth was expected to be used to help the poor.

This view of morality was associated, in part, with John Calvin, a French Protestant.[25] In 1559, Calvin wrote the "Institutes of the Christian Religion," probably the most theologically authoritative statement of basic Protestant beliefs to that point in history. Followers of Calvin became increasingly influential and in England, they became known as **Puritans**.

This struggle for influence, freedom, and power finally resulted in mass conflict.[26] In fact, the Early Modern period, approximately between 1560 and 1660, was a century of crisis. At the time, the common belief was that a strong national government required one unifying national faith. As a result, conflict between Catholics and Protestants was almost inevitable. In addition to religious warfare, riots by peasants erupted in protest against the enclosure of agricultural land, rent increases, and the lack of food. At this time, population increases started to create greater demand on the food supply. Many poor people starved to death as a result. Also, the poor resented the raising of their taxes by the king to pay for the religious wars.

In England, the struggle for power finally resulted in the English Civil War, beginning in 1642 and ending in 1649.[27] Small landowners, merchants, and manufacturers revolted against the social policies of King Charles I, including his oppressive taxation. The outcome of the conflict was that, during the reign of Charles II (1660–1685), England became a limited monarchy. That is, the king was forced to share policymaking power with these competing groups, an essential step in the transition to capitalism as well as democracy.

The Elizabethan Poor Law Act of 1601

The following is an excerpt from the **Elizabethan Poor Law Act of 1601.**

> Be it enacted…that the Churchwardens of every Parish, and foure, three, or two substantial Householders there…to bee nominated yeerely…under the hande and seale of two or more Justices of the Peace in the same Countie…shall be called Overseers of the poore of the same Parish, and they…shall take order from time to time…for setting to worke of the children of all such whose parents shall not…bee thought able to keepe and maintaine their children; and also for setting to worke all such persons maried, or unmaried, having no meanes to maintaine them, use no ordinary and dayly trade of life to get their living by, and also to rayse weekely or otherwise (by taxation of every inhabitant…in the said Parish) a convenient stocke of Flaxe, Hempe, Wool, Threed, Iron and other necessary ware to set the poore on worke, and also competent summes of money for, and towards the necessary reliefe of the lame, impotent, old, blinde, and such other among them being poore, and not able to worke, and also for the putting out of such children to bee apprentices…it shall and may be lawfull for the said Churchwardens and Overseers…to errect, build…convenient houses of dwelling for the said impotent poor, and also to place Inmates or more families than one in one cottage, or house.
>
> The Father and Grandfather, and the Mother and Grandmother, and the children of every poore, old, blinde, lame, and impotent person…not able to worke, being of sufficient ability, shall at their owne charges relieve and maintaine every such poore person.[28]

The Elizabethan Poor Law Act of 1601 represented the consolidation of various laws dealing with the poor as English society dealt not only with periodic crises such as the bubonic plague, war, and famine, but also with the social disorder resulting from the breakdown of medieval institutions and the rise of capitalism.[29] A primary goal of the law was to alleviate distress among the needy; yet, maintaining social control was also a major goal of the law. That is, the Elizabethan Poor Law was meant to deal with the vagrancy, theft, and rioting resulting from the enclosure movement, food shortages, and rising prices. It also recognized the legitimate need of poor peasants willing, but not able to work and sustain themselves as they were forced from their traditional agrarian roles. It was certainly difficult to blame this type of systemic unemployment on the poor.

Critical Analysis: Social Work and Social Control

Social workers have been criticized for their role in controlling the poor. Is this necessarily a negative aspect of our work? What if we rephrase the sentence to say that social workers help to maintain social order? Is this a negative role? For a profession that is supposed to promote self-determination, this appears to be a contradiction. Is it?

Trattner makes the case that the Poor Law of 1601 was rooted in the policies and practices of the medieval church at the diocese or parish level.[30] In this system, it was the parish priest who was most directly responsible for assisting the poor. With the growth of the modern nation-state, the public sector gradually assumed ultimate responsibility for its poor citizens.

In England, the **parish** referred to several things all at once.[31] First, it referred to a political subdivision of a county. Second, it pertained to the church in that subdivision. And third, the term applied to the people of that church. As previously stated, the Elizabethan Poor Law Act of 1601 was a consolidation of various laws regarding the role of local parishes in administering to the poor and needy. The various laws had been consolidated in previous legislation in 1597 and 1598, but the legislation passed in 1601 represented the last rewrite of the total law. Therefore, the 1601 act is considered the landmark legislation.[32]

The law's major characteristics included, first and foremost, the principle that the state had a responsibility to promote the social welfare of all its citizens, including the poor.[33] In so doing, the parish was the "unit of local government for poor relief."

Second, the Elizabethan Poor Law reinforced the principle of local responsibility for direct care of the poor.[34] Families were expected to care for, or pay for the care of, needy family members. Parents took care of their children, and when needed, their parents. As they got older, children assumed care of their parents and grandparents. Within each parish, public officials called **Overseerers of the Poor** were nominated among a few "substantial households" by justices of the peace. These officials, along with churchwardens, carried out such duties as collecting taxes for poor relief and making sure that the poor received care. For example, the Overseerers of the Poor and church wardens took leadership in erecting dwellings, called poorhouses, to house one or more poor individuals or families. Every household in the parish was taxed to fund these and other services for the poor. Those failing to pay such taxes could be imprisoned.

A third major characteristic of the English Poor Law was its classification of the needy into children, the **able-bodied,** and the impotent.[35] The last category included those who, for various reasons, were incapacitated. Thus, the impotent were not children and they were not able-bodied. This third category included, therefore, those who were sick, those with disabilities, and older members of the parish.

Children of poor families were apprenticed to a member of the parish to learn work skills.[36] They were often apprenticed at a very young age, as young as five or six years old. Masters could be cruel and working conditions were often harsh. Yet, the apprentice system promoted the education and future independence of poor children.

Those parish members who were poor but appeared able-bodied were thought to be less deserving of relief than children and the impotent.[37] Those considered **less eligible** often received relief funds only after the needs of the more worthy poor were met. These **undeserving poor** were more likely to receive **indoor relief.** Indoor relief was the term used to refer to services provided in an institution. Thus, the able-bodied but idle poor were more likely to be put to work in a workhouse in exchange for their support. These institutions were often prison-like in that their goal was more to prevent public disorder and serve as a deterrent to public relief than to provide human charity.[38] In fact, according to author Phyllis Day,

> All institutional arrangements—orphanages, almhouses, workhouses, and prisons—had conditions in common. Many were little more than sheds divided into warrens of rooms with little heat or insulation. There were few if any sanitation facilities, and food was inadequate and often little more than watery gruel.[39]

Furthermore, those refusing to go to the workhouse were dealt with extremely harshly. That is, vagrants not willing to work could be sent to a house of correction, whipped, branded, stoned, or put to death.[40] Dolgoff and Feldstein in *Understanding Social Welfare* emphasize the emerging institution of capitalism's need not only for land and capital but also for human labor in producing manufactured goods. This was particularly true during times of labor shortage due to disease, famine, or war. Thus,

> What began in the fourteenth century as a means of dealing with a shortage of labor for agricultural work developed by the sixteenth and seventeenth centuries into an entire philosophy that demanded that the undeserving poor (able-bodied) be controlled and dealt with punitively.[41]

In contrast to the able-bodied poor, the incapacitated poor were thought to be more deserving of relief.[42] As in the current United States, those who were too sick or too old to do substantial work were treated more humanely by society. These **deserving poor** were more likely to receive services in their home. In contrast to indoor relief, which was provided in an institution, **outdoor relief** was the term used to refer to services provided in the home. Such services included assistance with health care, food, clothing, and fuel (i.e., wood).

The principle of local responsibility for poor relief inherent in the Elizabethan Poor Law Act of 1601 was further enforced by **laws of settlement,** including the Law of Settlement of 1662.[43] Generally speaking, settlement laws stated that the poor could receive assistance only if they resided in the parish of their birth. These laws helped to decrease the number of poor peasants wandering the countryside, spreading disease, increasing local relief costs, and at the very least, causing fear among local residents. Yet, the settlement laws also made it difficult for poor peasants forced from their feudal lands to find work in growing industrial towns.

With the Elizabethan Poor Law Act of 1601, the English government became the chief enforcer of, and ultimately responsible for, poor relief. Earlier social policy that relied on voluntary contributions from local parishes to support the needy had proved insufficient.[44] However, another law passed the very same year, the Law of Charitable Uses, continued to encourage voluntary contributions by members of the parish to assist in providing relief to the poor. In fact, charitable donations funded numerous private schools, hospitals, and almshouses.[45]

The guilds established by artisans and merchants continued to be a source of private philanthropy during this time.[46] As stated previously, the guild was primarily a mutual benefit organization. Benefits included financial assistance to disabled workers and survivors of deceased workers. These benefits also included "disaster insurance" for members who, through no fault of their own, were in financial crisis. Such a crisis might be precipitated by a fire, shipwreck, robbery, flood, or even false imprisonment. In addition to member benefits of this sort, guilds also provided services to the community, including lodging to travelers and food to the needy. They even established and maintained hospitals.

A third source of private philanthropy, along with individual parish members and guilds, was the private foundation. Dolgoff and Feldstein claim that "at the time of the Reformation, there were in England at least 460 charitable foundations."[47] These foundations helped support numerous health and human services, including almshouses and hospitals.

In the late Middle Ages, England contained between 500 and 700 hospitals.[48] The hospitals of the time were often very small, serving only about twelve people at a time. Often this service was limited to providing temporary shelter to travelers and the poor. Yet, some specialized in care for the elderly and poor mothers.

The major point that needs to be emphasized here is that English social policy in the 1600s promoted private philanthropy in addition public taxation to pay for the cost of health and human services to the poor. This policy became the model on which the American colonial system was founded.

Did You Know?

Did you know that the Elizabethan Poor Law stood with only minor revisions for almost 300 years as a foundation for English and United States social policy? Also, settlement or "residency" as a factor in determining eligibility for public assistance was not legally discontinued in the United States until 1969.[49]

CONTENTSELECT

For more information on related social work topics, use the following search terms:

Able-bodied	Fief	Noblesse oblige
Artisan	Guilds	Outdoor relief
Commons	Indoor relief	Overseerers of the Poor
Deserving poor	Knights	Parish
Elizabethan Poor Law Act	Laws of settlement	Puritans
of 1601	Less eligible	Serfs
Enclosure	Middle Ages	Undeserving poor

NOTES

1. Edward McNall Burns, Robert E. Lerner, and Standish Meacham, *Western Civilizations: Their History and Their Culture,* 10th ed. (New York: Norton, 1984).

2. The characteristics of the model are based primarily on the description of this historical period by Bruce S. Jansson, *The Reluctant Welfare State* (Belmont, CA: Wadsworth, 1988), pp. 9–13.

3. Burns et al., pp. 292–294.

4. Ibid., p. 304.

5. Jansson, pp. 9–13.

6. Neil Heilbroner and Lester Thurow, *Economics Explained: Everything You Need to Know*

About How the Economy Works and Where It's Going (New York: Touchstone, 1994).

7. Burns et al., p. 294.

8. Jansson, p. 12.

9. Burns et al., p. 311. See also Phyllis J. Day, *A New History of Social Welfare,* 3rd ed. (Boston: Allyn & Bacon, 2000), p. 87.

10. Day, p. 87.

11. Jansson, p. 10.

12. Ibid., p. 11.

13. Burns et al., p. 295.

14. Burns et al., p. 311; Day, p. 89.

15. Burns et al., p. 292.

16. Walter I. Trattner, *From Poor Law to Welfare State: A History of Social Welfare in America,* 6th ed. (New York: The Free Press, 1999), pp. 6–7. See also Neil Heilbroner and Lester Thurow.

17. Trattner, p. 6.

18. Burns et al., p. 545.

19. Ibid., pp. 546–549.

20. Jansson, pp. 16–18.

21. Burns et al., p. 470–471.

22. Ibid., p. 470.

23. Ibid., pp. 480–481.

24. Jansson, p. 17.

25. Burns et al., pp. 486–489.

26. Ibid., pp. 501–507.

27. Ibid., pp. 519–524.

28. Jansson, p. 19.

29. Ralph Dolgoff and Donald Feldstein, *Understanding Social Welfare,* 5th ed. (Boston: Allyn & Bacon), pp. 48–49.

30. Trattner, pp. 5–6.

31. Dolgoff and Feldstein, p. 49; Trattner, pp. 9, 11.

32. Trattner, p. 10.

33. Ibid., p. 9.

34. Jansson, p. 19; Dolgoff and Feldstein, pp. 49–50; Trattner, p. 11.

35. Trattner, p. 11.

36. Ibid., p. 9.

37. Dolgoff and Feldstein, p. 49.

38. Trattner, pp. 11–12; Dolgoff and Feldstein, p. 51.

39. Day, p. 104.

40. Trattner, p. 11.

41. Dolgoff and Feldstein, p. 51.

42. Jansson, pp. 19–21.

43. Trattner, p. 12.

44. Ibid., p. 9.

45. Day, pp. 103–104; Trattner, p. 12.

46. Day, p. 91; Dolgoff and Feldstein, p. 41.

47. Dolgoff and Feldstein, p. 41.

48. Ibid.

49. Ibid., pp. 50–51.

3 The American Colonial Period

Abigail Adams was first lady and a leading colonial women's advocate.

Characteristics of the Colonial Economic System

Agriculture: The Small Farmer

America clearly represented a land of opportunity for many people sailing from Western Europe in the 1600s. For religious dissenters, for aspiring artisans and merchants, and for landless peasant farmers, the American colonies truly offered freedom from the oppressive constraints of Western Europe's class hierarchy, religious traditions, and central government. The colonial economy was primarily an agricultural one, more so than the English economy at the time.[1] For the castoffs of feudal England arriving in the colonies in hopes of establishing a small farm, the opportunity seemed limitless. By English standards, land was plentiful and cheap. For those willing to move westward, this land rush did not end until almost 1900.

Although colonial America was primarily a land of small farmers (called **yeomen**), *small* was a relative term. In contrast to England with its inherent limitations as an island, colonial farms in America were huge, often over 100 acres in size.[2] This meant that colonial farmers could produce for their family's use with a significant amount of produce left over for sale in the market. This colonial food supply contrasted with the previously described food riots that occurred in England between 1560 and 1660.

A relatively large food supply also resulted in a relatively high standard of living for colonial farmers.[3] American colonists consumed meat and dairy products in large quantities. Pennsylvania became known as the bread colony. Couples married early and had large families. Although infant and child mortality was high in this age, women reaching 40 years of age gave birth typically to six or seven children. Often four to five of these offspring would reach maturity. Due to their relatively generous diet, full grown, colonial males averaged two inches taller than men in England at the time.

In the colonial era, most white males living to forty or more years could expect to achieve middle class status.[4] Although one-third of white males held no significant property, most of these were young, under the age of thirty. By forty, the typical colonial farmer owned his own land and was relatively prosperous by English standards.

Historian Paul Johnson describes a common Connecticut farm in the colonial era.

> By 1750 a typical Connecticut farm owned ten head of cattle, sixteen sheep, six pigs, two horses, [and] a team of oxen. In addition the farm grew maize, wheat, and rye, and two-fifths of the produce went on earning a cash income, [was] spent on British imports or, increasingly, locally produced goods.[5]

In the south, rice was prominent in early South Carolina; however, tobacco became the main cash crop for the colonies of Virginia, Maryland, and

North Carolina, eventually spreading to Kentucky and Tennessee.[6] By the early 1600s, tobacco use was common even in Europe. In fact, the world demand for tobacco became limitless. Tobacco was so integral to the southern economy that it was used as a commodity currency for a time in some southern colonies.[7] Virginia and North Carolina tobacco farmers, after the Revolutionary War, began the development of factories to produce pipe and chewing tobacco, eventually leading to the modern southern tobacco industry.

Apprentice System: The Artisan

The opportunity afforded to artisans from Europe in the American colonies rivaled that of the small farmer.[8] There was plenty of land in America, but there was a scarcity of skilled craftsmen. Indeed, there was a shortage of all types of labor. This would soon change. Because of the demand for labor, skilled artisans in the colonies could make higher wages than their counterparts in England, and raw material was less expensive in the colonies, leading to higher profits for the craftsmen. Phyllis Day, in *A New History of Social Welfare,* claims that wages in New England, in some cases, were double what could be made at the same craft in England.[9] In addition, skilled craftsmen in the colonies attained a social status not possible in England, where status still depended much more on land and bloodlines.

For these reasons, the colonies soon attracted many skilled artisans.[10] Given the enormous forests covering America, timber was plentiful and inexpensive. Therefore, carpenters and joiners did well in the colonies. The colonies became known for high-quality furniture. The colonies also demanded the services of glassmakers and potters, due to the difficulties of profitably transporting their products across the ocean. Silversmiths found work in cities such as Boston, and shoemakers were readily employed in towns such as Lynn, Massachusetts. Women also participated in trades.[11] That is, colonial women could be found employed as bakers, brewers, tanners, printers, ropemakers, seamstresses, and even lumberjacks.

To meet the demand for skilled labor in many of these crafts, an **apprentice system** similar to that of England developed in the colonies. Those wanting to learn a trade were apprenticed to master craftsmen, typically for a period of seven years.[12] This master might be the father or brother of a young person. In any case, this master craftsman was expected to provide on-the-job training in exchange for the youth's labor. Thus, the apprentice system served as an early educational system in colonial America.

The apprentice system was also a good illustration of the partnership between the public and private sectors of the country.[13] The responsibility for the care of poor and neglected children ultimately fell to the colonial government. To provide these children with job skills, public authorities would often apprentice them to an artisan or farmer who could teach them a vocation. The children would typically live with the private family until age 18 to 21 if a male youth or until age 18 or marriage if a female. Colonial courts supervised the apprenticeship. The apprentice system, therefore, provided artisans and farmers with a cheap source of labor and the public sector with a relatively inexpensive placement for needy children.

The negative side of the apprentice system for these youth was that masters were sometimes neglectful of their responsibilities.[14] Many of the children were not fed and clothed well. Furthermore, many were not educated well, their vocational training consisting of menial labor.

Personal Profile: Benjamin Franklin

Perhaps the most successful example of an American colonial artisan was Benjamin Franklin.[15] During the last years of his life, Franklin may have been the most famous person in the world. He was rich and famous, but he was born in 1706 to a large Boston family of modest means. His father, Josiah, was an artisan, more specifically, a candlemaker. Benjamin was apprenticed to his father, and then later to his older brother, a printer. Because he did not get along with his brother, Benjamin ran away to Philadelphia at age 17. (Yes, Benjamin Franklin at one time was a homeless youth!) In Philadelphia, Franklin started his own printing business with a partner. He would later publish his own newspaper and *Poor Richard's Almanac* and become wealthy enough to retire from these businesses at age 37. In so doing Franklin became one of the first and most well-known examples of a self-made man in U.S. history. Retirement allowed him to pursue his scientific interests such as inventing the Franklin stove, the lightning rod, and bifocal glasses. In addition to his science projects, Franklin later immersed himself in politics and social projects.

Franklin's organization of the public and private sectors in promoting colonial social welfare is particularly interesting to social workers. Combining public and private financing, Franklin was instrumental in establishing Pennsylvania's first hospital. Before the hospital was built, the only medical care was provided in private homes or in prisons and almshouses. However, the homes of relatively poor colonists were often unsuitable for optimal medical care. Furthermore, colonists traveling from more rural areas to Philadelphia for medical treatment had no convenient overnight facility. Thus, the idea of a facility to centralize medical treatment and provide decent overnight care was promoted by Franklin to a skeptical colonial Assembly. In the end, Franklin brokered an agreement where the Assembly would allocate a sum of money if an equal amount could be raised through private donations. Not believing that Franklin could raise the required donations, the Assembly passed the conditional bill written by Franklin himself. Benjamin Franklin describes the agreement:

> The members who had opposed the grant, and now conceived they might have the credit of being charitable without the expense, agreed to its passage; and then, in soliciting subscriptions among the people, we urged the conditional promise of the law as an additional motive to give, since every man's donation would be doubled;...The subscriptions accordingly soon exceeded the requisite sum, and we claimed and received the public gift, which enabled us to carry the design into execution.[16]

Outside of the apprentice system, Benjamin Franklin was largely self-educated. Yet, after becoming independently wealthy, he later received honorary degrees from Harvard and Yale, among other universities.[17] This kind of social mobility was not possible in England, but illustrates the unique opportunity afforded American colonists, especially for white males.

Ethical Considerations in Policy Leadership

Benjamin Franklin was a famous author, scientist, businessman, and diplomat.[18] He played an important role in creating the United States and its democratic form of government. Yet, there is evidence that he was a womanizer and fathered at least one illegitimate child. He presented himself as a man of thrift, but while in Paris, maintained a wine collection of over 1,200 bottles. He is noted for his strict regimen for self-improvement, but bought slaves as an investment. Are such contradictions unethical? Should they have disqualified Franklin in the eyes of the public from government service? Should similar private–public contradictions disqualify someone from political leadership today?

International Trade: The Merchant, Indentured Servant, and Slave

The discovery of gold and silver by Spanish explorers in the New World, in addition to the growing English and French fishing industry in the North Atlantic, accelerated international trade.[19] Soon colonies in the Americas were needed to continue the expansion of this trade. This international trade, although initially part of a **mercantile policy** to enrich England and other European nations, was really capitalistic in its organization. That is, the English monarch issued **charters** to companies of adventures who risked their own money to establish colonies in America. These individuals invested their cash in joint stock to finance the expedition. In the Jamestown colony, for example, each investor received 100 acres of land for each share they owned. In similar ways, most of the original colonies were capitalistic enterprises run as joint-stock corporations or as proprietary companies of estate owners. Even the original Pilgrims in Massachusetts included merchants and traders looking for new opportunities in America.

Many of the English colonists who would later became successful artisans or farmers actually sailed to America as **indentured servants.**[20] About one-half million white Europeans immigrated to America as indentured servants during the colonial period. That is, they came to the colonies as non-free servants obligated to provide their labor for a period of four to seven years before they became free. This type of arrangement enabled a poor person to pay for the cost of transportation to the colonies as well as the cost of food, clothing, and shelter while getting established in America. After this period, many started their own business or farm. No less an authority than Benjamin Franklin describes the opportunity: "No man continues long a labourer for others, but gets a plantation of his own. No man continues long a journeyman to a trade, but goes among these new settlers and sets up for himself."[21]

However, many indentured servants incurred debt while getting established, and, as a result, needed to extend their number of years as indentured servants.[22] While under contract, they could not enjoy many basic liberties such as marriage and travel. And many worked twelve to fifteen hours a day, excluding Saturday afternoons and Sunday.

When compared to indentured servants, those who arrived in the colonies as slaves had a much lower quality of life. Slaves were treated as the legal property of their owners. Like livestock, **chattel slaves** were considered commodities to be bought and sold.[23] In contrast to the indentured servant, the slave's service was perpetual. Even baptism as Christians did nothing to change the servile conditions of colonial slaves. They were considered subhuman from the perspective of colonial law.

Chattel slaves were first used in Virginia in 1619, although the use of slaves in the southern colonies became large scale during the 1700s.[24] As previously stated, tobacco became one of the first economic successes of the colonies. Yet, there was a labor shortage in colonial America. Therefore, this emerging tobacco industry began to rely on slaves to supply this labor. And tobacco was not the only industry to blame. Soon, slaves would be used to support the rice economy of Carolina. Increasingly, the source of these colonial slaves was Africa. Howard Zinn, in *A People's History of the United States,* describes the conditions under which these African slaves were forced to the Americas:

> Then they were packed aboard the slave ships, in spaces not much bigger than coffins, chained together in the dark, wet slime of the ship's bottom,

choking in the stench of their own excrement.... On one occasion, hearing a great noise from below-decks where the blacks were chained together, the sailors opened the hatches and found the slaves in different stages of suffocation, many dead, some having killed others in desperate attempts to breathe. Slaves often jumped overboard to drown rather than continue their suffering.[25]

Because of the high profits of the tobacco industry and the accompanying need for labor, the number of slaves in the colonies multiplied quickly.[26] In 1714, there were less than 60,000 slaves in colonial America. Forty years later, there were 263,000. By 1790, there were close to 700,000.

New England colonies shipped fish, beef, pork, livestock, and lumber to the West Indies and southern Europe.[27] New York and Pennsylvania exported flour and wheat as well. In return, the colonies imported molasses to make rum for the fishing industry and to purchase more slaves.

Granted, colonial America was an agrarian economy for the most part. Yet, by the time of the American Revolution, it was already beginning to produce and export a significant amount of manufactured goods.[28] These items included cotton goods, soap and candles, furniture, shoes and other leather products, and iron tools. Furthermore, by 1760, about one-third of the British merchant fleet had been built in the colonies, primarily in New England. By the time of its independence, the United States of America was already a wealthy country.

Did You Know?

Not only was the United States born a wealthy country, but much of that wealth was already starting to accumulate in the hands of a few families. Howard Zinn states that in 1687, the fifty richest families in Boston owned a quarter of the wealth of the entire city. By 1770, the wealthiest 1 percent of Boston property owners, in fact, owned almost half of that city's wealth.[29]

The Responsibilities of Government in Colonial Social Policy

Land Distribution and Protection from Native Americans

One of the primary responsibilities of colonial government was land distribution. In fact, from the perspective of English colonists, and certainly not from the perspective of Native Americans, land distribution was perhaps the most successful social policy of the colonial period. Compared to England, land was incredibly easy to obtain in the colonies. Paul Johnson describes the typical procedure for acquiring land at the time:

> A settler went to the secretary of the province, recorded his entitlement, and requested a grant of land. The secretary then presented a Warrant of Survey to the surveyor-general, who found and surveyed an appropriate tract. When he reported, the secretary issued a patent, which described the reasons for the grant, the boundaries and the conditions of tenure. The owner then occupied the land and began farming.[30]

The political and economic reasons for this social policy are clear. The objective of England was to colonize the American eastern seaboard and beyond, if possible. To that end, the English government facilitated the transport of its countrymen to the New World, sending fleet after fleet of ships across the Atlantic. This was also a convenient way to rid the country of undesirables, including vagabonds, criminals, and religious dissenters. For example, between 1630 and 1660, roughly 20,000 Puritans made the voyage.[31]

This imperialistic policy of England was bound to lead to friction with the native populations of the colonial period. In the early 1600s, there was an estimated 900,000 such people in present-day Canada and the United States.[32] Between 200 to 300 different languages were spoken among them. This diversity was a barrier to united Native American resistance to English settlers when hostilities broke out.

One of the most powerful tribes was the **League of Iroquois,** which consisted of the Mohawks, Oneidas, Onondagas, Cayugas, and Senecas.[33] All shared the Iroquois language. The Iroquois lived in what is now Pennsylvania and upper New York and represent a good illustration of the cultural clash that eventually took place. The whole concept of private ownership of land was antithetical to their culture. Land, if "owned," was owned in common. Similar to the serfs of the European feudal system, land was cultivated in common. Hunting was done as a group. Food was shared. Even homes were considered a common living space among several families. In such a culture, the poorhouse was not needed.

What is more, the Iroquois culture was much less sexist than the British culture. Families were matrilineal; new husbands joined their wives' extended family. Families were organized into clans that shared the same village. Elder women in the clan appointed the men who would serve as representatives and chiefs in tribal councils. Thus, these women had the power to remove men from office if tribal policy was not satisfactory. In any case, Iroquois women played an active part in their social policy. The greatest source of contention was probably the differences in Native American and British cultures' concept of land ownership. From the British perspective, colonial America represented an opportunity for the greatest land acquisition in history. As new arrivals pushed west to obtain their private plots of land, they demanded government protection from Native American attacks. Colonial governments not meeting this social responsibility faced popular uprisings and protest from the colonists.

An example of this is Bacon's Rebellion.[34] Nathaniel Bacon, a relatively successful Virginia landowner and a leader of populist resentment against the Virginia colonial government, got himself elected to the House of Burgesses in 1676. On taking office, he attempted to organize a military unit without official approval to attack Native Americans in the western part of the state. There, a dispute over a few hogs had escalated into a guerilla war with the Doeg tribe. When government officials detained Bacon, 2,000 supporters marched into Jamestown to protest. On being released after apologizing, Bacon organized his own miniwar against the natives anyway. British troops were eventually called in to gain control over the situation. Bacon ended up dying of natural causes soon after. The important point with respect to colonial social policy is found in Bacon's "Declaration of the People" written in July of 1676. Among other things, it chastises the Virginia colonial government for not doing enough to protect western farmers from Native Americans.

Preventing Slave Revolts: Segregation and Discrimination

Not only were western farmers fearful of Native Americans, the colonial elite feared oppressed groups such as Native Americans, slaves, and poor colonists might unite in opposition to them.[35] After all, in some areas, slaves far outnumbered free people. Historian Fawn Brodie reminds us that Thomas Jefferson grew up in a community where the black population was ten times greater than the white population.[36] Jefferson was one of the colonial elite that feared a slave rebellion; he, in fact, thought such an uprising justified in the eyes of God.

> And can the liberties of a nation be thought secure when we have removed their only firm basis, a conviction in the minds of the people that these liberties are the gift of God? That they are not to be violated but with his wrath? Indeed I tremble for my country when I reflect that God is just; that his justice can not sleep for ever: that considering numbers, nature and natural means only, a revolution of the wheel of fortune, an exchange of situation, is among possible events: that it may become probable by supernatural interference! The Almighty has no attribute which can take sides with us in such a contest.[37]

And from time to time, revolts did take place. It may surprise the reader to learn that the first large slave revolt in the colonies took place in

1712, not in the south, but in New York.[38] Close to thirty slaves, mostly black, participated in the uprising. Twenty-one of them were later executed. During the mayhem, nine whites were killed.

To prevent such uprisings, colonial social policy, both north and south, encouraged discrimination and segregation. It was, fundamentally, the time-tested strategy of divide and conquer. To illustrate, Virginia passed a law in 1661 that required English (read: white) servants who ran away with black slaves to provide service for an additional number of years to the owner of the slaves.[39] In 1691, Virginia passed a law that banished from the colony any free white man or woman who married a "negro, mulatoo, or Indian man or woman."[40] Children of black-white relationships were considered illegitimate and kept within black families. In the Carolinas, laws were passed that prohibited free black colonists from entering Native American territories. Some treaties made with Native Americans included clauses requiring the return of runaway slaves. Even slaves were separated into house slaves and the more inferior field slave.[41] Furthermore, in the late 1600s, white mechanics were given preferential treatment over black colonists by the city of New York. South Carolina prohibited Charleston masters from employing black colonists and slaves as mechanics or in handicraft trades. Thus, discrimination and segregation were used as social policy mechanisms to subjugate certain populations in colonial America.

Caring for the Poor: Poverty and the Workhouse

Another responsibility of colonial government, based on the English system, was caring for the poor and sick. Despite the opportunity and prosperity of the colonies, there were still a considerable number of people in need. In any society, vulnerable children are born, sturdy adults get old and frail, some people are born with disabilities, disease is spread, and accidents happen. The colonies were no different. And like today, many people lost jobs because of seasonal and other periodic unemployment. Immigrants, who supplied a critical source of labor, needed help getting acclimated to a new environment. War veterans and widows were rendered vulnerable to poverty.

To illustrate, the populations of colonial cities such as Boston, New York, Philadelphia, and Charleston increased by 100 percent or more during the 1700s.[42] Along with that growth came large increases in poor relief costs. Boston, for example, spent about 500 pounds in 1700 on poor relief; by 1753, that figure had increased to 10,000 pounds. Later, during the French and Indian War (1754–1763), an estimated 1,000 people were forced to leave Nova Scotia and move to Massachusetts, relying on public relief to get settled. New England also had to support the families of fishermen lost at sea. Further south, close to 1,000 people in Charleston, South Carolina, died of a measles epidemic in 1772, in all likelihood, leaving hundreds of needy dependents behind.

Although colonial government was ultimately responsible, poor relief was, in practice, a partnership among government and private groups.[43] For example, several bequests from private individuals to the city of Boston were combined to pay for the construction of an almshouse. In fact, the distinction between public and private responsibilities in colonial America, and throughout American history, was often blurred. On occasion, voluntary efforts were taken over by the state. At other times, public authorities would pay private individuals or private associations to care for the poor. Like Ben Franklin and the establishment of the Pennsylvania Hospital, health and human services were many times the product of public and private funding. And the exact mixture of both state and voluntary efforts varied from colony to colony and within colonies (i.e., from county to county or from town to town).

That said, Jonathan Katz, in his study of American welfare, concludes that the colonies dealt with poor relief in one or more of four ways.[44] Outdoor relief was provided by church members to deserving people in their homes. As previously described, children from poor families were apprenticed to private individuals such as artisans or farmers. Some, especially the able-bodied poor, were given **indoor relief** in public institutions variously referred to as **poorhouses, workhouses,** or **almshouses.** And lacking other options, some public authorities auctioned off poor people to the highest bidder, a private individual who would agree to their care.

A combination of economic, religious, and historical factors made the workhouse a prominent feature of colonial social policy, especially in the larger towns and cities that could afford to build them. Workhouses were established in Boston, 1664; Portsmouth, New Hampshire, 1716; Salem, 1719; Newport, Rhode Island, 1723; Philadelphia, 1732; New York City, 1736; and Charleston, 1736.[45]

Did You Know?

Not only did the colonies use various terms for public indoor relief, but at times they used two or three terms at once. For example, the two-story brick building erected in New York City in 1736 was called the "Poor House, Work House, and House of Correction."[46] This is because colonial institutions, for the most part, were not specialized. Therefore, this little brick building probably served (I use this term loosely) unemployed people, criminals, orphans, widows, war veterans, new immigrants, elderly colonists, and psychotic individuals.

In terms of the colonial economic system, as previously discussed, America truly was a land of opportunity when compared to England. People from the lower classes in England, once in America, could obtain a small piece of land to farm within a few years. Unlike England, land was plentiful but labor was scarce. This, combined with the fact that the early colonists depended on one another's labor for survival, created a demand for able-bodied colonists to work.

This economic demand for labor was reinforced by colonial religious doctrine, most notably **Calvinism.**[47] The writing of John Calvin, the French Protestant reformer, heavily influenced the Puritans of Massachusetts Bay Colony. According to Calvinism, work represented God's calling on earth, and was, therefore, sacred. If one was apparently able-bodied, yet poverty-stricken, this was an indication that one was immoral and not destined for salvation. The able-bodied poor, as a result, were considered wicked and undeserving. Accordingly, beginning in the late 1600s, able-bodied vagabonds without vocation or property were put to work in workhouses, which combined work projects with religious instruction. The work projects, including activities such as weaving cloth and making shoes, helped meet the cost of the poor relief.[48] In so doing, workhouses were considered economically beneficial to the colony and morally therapeutic to the poor.

This colonial social policy was patterned after that of the **Elizabethan Poor Law Act of 1601.**[49] Colonial government was ultimately responsible for the poor, yet administration of poor relief was left to local government units. Consequently, the local town or county generally administered the workhouse. In New England, decisions were made at the town meeting; in the southern colonies, at the county level. Overseers of the Poor were appointed to collect taxes to pay for establishing and operating the workhouse as well as other poor relief. This relief included items such as firewood, food, and clothing.[50]

Residency requirements for public assistance similar to those found in England were established, although enforcement was often loose.[51] One reason for residency requirements was public concern regarding the cost of providing relief to the poor in any one community. Frontier settlers during times of need would make their way to more wealthy towns such as Boston and New York in search of assistance. These people were often women and children who had lost male members of the family as a result of disease or war. One way that colonial towns tried to keep their relief costs down was to "warn away" strangers looking for public assistance. Those not heeding the town's warning could be punished, including flogging, tarring and feathering (a particularly creative form of torture), or even hanging.[52] In what can be considered an early form of state public assistance, these towns eventually started to request funds from the colonial government to help meet the needs of these nonresident poor.[53] Thus, although local administration of poor relief and residency requirements were the prevailing norm in colonial America, there were exceptions including assistance paid by colonial treasuries for soldiers and others considered deserving by the colonies.

For the poor that remained in rural areas, particularly during the 1600s, the workhouse was often not an option.[54] This was because local residents could not afford to build and maintain one. In these cases, the poor were often auctioned to the lowest bidder, many times at the local tavern following a town meeting. To assist in caring for these unfortunate people, the town typically provided clothing and medical care in addition to some financial support to the winning bidder.

Another group not served in the workhouse were black colonists.[55] Part of the explanation for this is racism. Black colonists were considered by most whites to be subhuman. Furthermore, local government officials did not assist black colonists for fear that slave owners would turn them over to localities when unable to work anymore. Again, high taxes and high public assistance costs were a concern even during the colonial era.

The Founding Fathers and Social Policy

After the American Revolutionary War ended, a relatively small and elite group of men completed an institutional structure for the new nation. The **Founding Fathers**—George Washington, Benjamin Franklin, Thomas Jefferson, Alexander Hamilton, John Adams, and James Madison—did not share a totally common set of values in establishing this institutional framework. They all believed in the sanctity of private property, but there was not an absolute consensus among the group about the type of political system to be developed. Hamilton, for example, favored a permanent senate, elected for life terms.[56] Both Hamilton and Adams were elitists who did not trust the lower classes with democracy.[57]

Furthermore, the type of economic system was also a subject of intense debate. Perhaps the two strongest and most juxtaposed ideologies were held by Alexander Hamilton and Thomas Jefferson.[58] On the election of George Washington in 1789, Thomas Jefferson became Secretary of State, and Alexander Hamilton was appointed the first Secretary of the Treasury. Whereas Jefferson, the Virginia plantation owner, believed that the new nation should maintain an agrarian economy with small central government consisting of gentlemen farmers, Hamilton, the self-made New York lawyer, argued that a strong central government must promote an industrial economy. Jefferson firmly believed that an economy dominated by manufacturing would lead to the social problems previously described in England: unemployment, food shortages, landless vagabonds, and rioting. Unconvinced, Hamilton advocated for a strong central bank, the Bank of the United States, to serve as the chief fiscal mechanism for the new government. The United States government would own most of its stock and serve as the bank's major customer.

In this policy debate, Hamilton's views were more reflective of merchants and manufacturers in the northern colonies; Jefferson's views were more consistent with the farmers of the southern states.[59] Although Washington, a southerner, shared Jefferson's concerns regarding an industrial economy, he was enough of a visionary to see that capitalism and industrialization were an unstoppable wave on the American shore. Even before Washington took office, the states had issued charters to start thirty-three companies, at least some of which were involved in building bridges, turnpikes, and canals.[60] The first cotton factory was built in Beverley, Massachusetts, in 1787, and a year later, the first woolen factory was constructed in Hartford, Connecticut. Two years later, in 1789, the same year Washington was elected president, John Jacob Astor bought his first real estate in New York City.[61] Astor's real estate and fur business would grow to make him the first great American fortune, $30 million at his death.

The point is the industrial tide was rising as the nation was born. Washington, the military man, felt that an industrial economy would produce a first-class military with the requisite ships, cannons, and other military hardware to defend the new nation.[62] Therefore, the first president of the United States supported Hamilton's industrial policies, to a significant extent laying the social policy foundation for the Industrial Boom of the 1800s and the military-industrial complex of the 1900s.

Personal Profile: Thomas Jefferson

Although the views of Thomas Jefferson on industry did not ultimately prevail, his vision of the American utopia and the role of government did eventually materialize in several social policy areas. His influence on the other Founding Fathers was profound. As stated earlier, Jefferson, a Virginia plantation owner, envisioned a primarily agrarian economy with farmers serving as leaders in a democratic government. To this end, Jefferson was a leading supporter of making land acquisition easy for small western farmers.[63] Such a policy gave the common person a stake in the new democratic system of government in America in addition to facilitating the population and geographic expansion of the new nation.

Jefferson was also a leading advocate for education in America. Certainly an educated citizenry would be critical to the success of the new democracy. During his political career, Jefferson proposed the development of a statewide tax-supported system of elementary and secondary schools in Virginia.[64] Furthermore, he advocated for the institution of college scholarships for promising Virginia youth. In preparing for his death, he requested that several major achievements be listed on his gravestone. Among them was the fact that he was the "Father of the University of Virginia."[65]

Another major feature of Jefferson's utopia was the separation of church and state.[66] This ranks along with the Declaration of Independence as Jefferson's major contribution to democratic government in the United States and throughout the world. On the subject of the separation of church and state, Jefferson writes:

> Almighty God hath created the mind free.... To compel a man to furnish contributions of money for the propagation of opinions which he disbelieves and abhors, is sinful and tyrannical.... Our civil rights have no dependence on our religious opinions, any more than our opinions of physics or geometry.[67]

Unfortunately, Jefferson's vision of the American utopia did not include a strong federal government with significant social responsibility for the poor and ill.[68] His utopia, perhaps, was meant to prevent such problems, at least, on a large scale. Certainly his vision did not address the specific social needs that would be created by the growing factory system and the coming Industrial Boom. These were needs created by a national industrial system and would require national social policies.

Yet, the American Constitution does not specifically address this social responsibility.[69] Jefferson and the other Founding Fathers were apparently content to leave such responsibilities to the state and local governments and voluntary associations. As will be discussed in subsequent chapters, this colonial policy position continues to influence American social policy in the twenty-first century.

Ethical Analysis: Jefferson and Slavery

Jefferson's views on slavery were and remain controversial.[70] He, theoretically at least, supported the gradual emancipation of American slaves. In fact, he proposed federal legislation in 1784 that would have outlawed slavery in any new states.[71] Yet, Jefferson kept slaves on his Virginia plantation his whole life. In addition, evidence indicates that he fathered children by one of his slaves, Sally Hemings.[72] Was Jefferson a visionary leader regarding emancipation, ahead of his time on this social policy, or was his public position just the hypocritical rhetoric of another politician?

Personal Profile: Abigail Adams and Colonial Women

The role of the Founding Fathers in the history of the United States is familiar to many U.S. citizens. It is a staple of high-school history. What about the role of women? Why didn't the colonies produce a group of "Founding Mothers"? One rather obvious explanation is that women were often discouraged from overt participation in colonial policy development.[73] It was not considered an appropriate role for women. Due in part to her critical statements about the government in the Massachusetts Bay Colony, Anne Hutchinson was banished from the colony in 1638 (and later killed by Native Americans while trying to resettle). Also, the ability to communicate with one another is critical to political organizing and advocacy. Yet, while most white men in the colonies could read by 1750, most of their female counterparts could not. After the Revolutionary War, New Jersey was the only state to grant women the vote. Realizing its unique position among the states, it rescinded that right in 1807. Like today, without the power of votes, citizens are not taken seriously when policies are developed. Such was the case for colonial women.

There were exceptions. Women were more politically active in southern and western frontier communities that were just getting started. Given the relative scarcity of men in these towns, women's participation was needed. Also in times of crisis, women were more apt to openly participate in public affairs. For example, women were politically active in the Revolutionary War.[74] **Daughters of Liberty** groups were formed in opposition to certain British policies such as the British tax on tea. These groups encouraged colonial women to boycott British goods, to buy American products, and make their own goods when possible.

Abigail Adams was also an exception.[75] She was one of the first well-known women's advocates in U.S. history. Born in Weymouth, Massachusetts, in 1744, Abigail Smith grew up the daughter of a minister. In 1764, she married John Adams, who would become the second president of the United States. Although she was married to Adams for fifty-four years, it was not always a happy life for Abigail, who experienced depression at times. Her husband was often away on political business, leaving Abigail to raise their five children and manage their farm in Quincy.

Despite these domestic responsibilities, Abigail stayed active in her husband's, and, therefore, the country's political life, particularly through her many letters. She even corresponded with other political leaders such as Thomas Jefferson. She was known for her intellect and, in contrast to her husband, for her charming personality. Because of this and her privileged political position, she was listened to more than most colonial women. She spoke for women's rights in a number of areas, including a woman's right to choose whom she marries, to limit the number of children she has, and to take legal action against an abusive husband. In her famous "Remember the Ladies" letter to her husband in March of 1776, Abigail saw an opportunity to advocate for women:

> In the new code of laws which I suppose it will be necessary for you to make, I desire you would remember the ladies, and be more generous to them than

your ancestors. Do not put such unlimited power in the hands of husbands. Remember, all men would be tyrants if they could. If particular care and attention are not paid to the ladies, we are determined to foment a rebellion, and will not hold ourselves bound to obey the laws in which we have no voice of representation.[76]

The Growth of the Private Nonprofit Sector in Colonial America

The Central Role of Organized Religion and the First Amendment

Much of the **private nonprofit sector** that developed in the United States can be considered a direct result of organized religion.[77] As previously described, the **Puritans,** a group of religious nonconformists first landing on the coast of present-day Massachusetts in 1620, brought their version of the English poor relief system to America.[78] When able, families were expected to care for their needy members. The church was seen as an extended family. Church officials aided poor families in providing basic health and human services to their needy members. Overseerers of the Poor were elected to collect taxes to fund relief of poor parish members.

Over time, religion in America became more diverse with numerous groups becoming influential. These included the Quakers, Anglicans, Baptists, and Catholics. These religious groups gradually developed an increasingly sophisticated network of education and health and human services for their individual denominations.[79] In addition, ethnic, trade, and other social groups started a wide variety of organizations to assist their members as well as the community at large. These self-help networks evolved into our current private nonprofit sector or voluntary sector.

By the colonial period, the growth of this sector was already evident.[80] Private nonprofit charitable organizations helping the poor and otherwise needy included the Scots Charitable Society (1657); the Friends Almshouse of Philadelphia (1713); the Ursuline Sisters' New Orleans Orphanage (1729); the Saint Andrew's Society of Charleston, South Carolina (1730); the Episcopal Charitable Society of Boston (1754); and the Charitable Irish Society of Boston (1767). Private groups of this sort complemented the efforts of public officials to help the poor and ill. More precisely, they became an integral part of the poor relief system.

The passing of the **First Amendment** to the Constitution ensured that the growth of the private nonprofit sector would continue. In fact, the First Amendment provides the legal foundation for this sector of American society.[81] The amendment provides for freedom of religion, freedom of assembly, freedom of speech, and the right to petition government over grievances.

As such, it established the principle at the federal level that government is inherently different than religion. Recall that in England and other parts of western Europe during the late Middle Ages, there was a close connection between the state and religion. A national religion was believed to promote a strong, united country. However, in the United States, Thomas Jefferson and the rest of the Founding Fathers believed that government should not be used to prevent citizens from congregating and exercising their distinctive faith.

Furthermore, the First Amendment meant that government should not be used to prevent people from associating and speaking out in accordance with their shared values on more secular issues.[82] This had great significance for the ongoing development of voluntary associations, including voluntary health and welfare organizations. These were organizations of people with similar values who wanted to address certain unmet health and human service needs in their community. Not surprisingly, the profession of social work originated in this sector of society.

The Influence of American Philanthropy

The growth of the private nonprofit sector was fueled by **American charitable giving.** The Puritans, believing in predestination, viewed wealth as a sign that the individual was destined for salvation.[83] An individual's work was considered God's calling on earth. The harder the individual worked, the more prosperous he/she would become. The more prosperous an individual became, the more moral he/she must be. Thus, charitable giving was an outward sign of morality on the part of God's chosen people. In any case, the Puritans viewed charitable works as an obligation of all people.[84]

By the mid-1700s, in contrast to the Puritan belief in predestination and salvation only through the grace of God, there was a growing belief that living a charitable life could increase one's chances of salvation. This belief was encouraged by the **First Great Awakening,** which began in the late 1720s.[85] The First Great Awakening was essentially a religious revival movement emphasizing faith, repentance, and regeneration. As such, it featured a conversion experience, commonly referred to as being "born again." Based in large part on the religious writings of Jonathan Edwards and communicated to the masses by such gifted preachers of the day as John Wesley, and more importantly, George Whitefield, the central message of the movement was that the individual has a free will.[86] That is, the individual's salvation depended on his/her willingness to live a moral life on earth. Hence, charitable giving to needy community members became an investment in one's own salvation, a good deed that was good for the donor as well as the donee. The First Great Awakening, therefore, gave poor colonists, including black and other minority colonists, hope for salvation. In so doing, the movement popularized philanthropy.[87]

By the 1700s, numerous colonists were beginning to amass fortunes, thereby enabling them to become philanthropists.[88] In addition to Benjamin Franklin, Thomas Bond, who deserves the most credit for founding the Pennsylvania Hospital, Benjamin Rush, a physician, and Stephen Girard, a businessman, became known for their charitable efforts. This increased charitable giving, in turn, helped fund the growth of charitable agencies in the nonprofit sector of the country. Many of these agencies would eventually recruit health and human service volunteers and employees, pioneers in the profession of social work.

Trattner draws this conclusion:

> While, from the outset, the public was responsible for providing aid to the needy who, in turn, had a right to such assistance, as soon as they could afford to do so, private citizens and a host of voluntary associations also gave generously to those in distress—orphans, widows, debtors, needy mariners, the religiously oppressed, new residents of communities who were not covered by the poor law, and others who could not care for themselves. In view of the antagonism later thought to exist between public assistance and private charity, this cooperative approach to the problem is one of the more noteworthy aspects of American colonial history.[89]

CONTENTSELECT

For more information on related social work topics, use the following search terms:

Almshouses
Apprentice system
Calvinism
Charters
Chattle slaves
Daughters of Liberty
Elizabethan Poor Law Act
  of 1601

First Amendment
First Great Awakening
Founding Fathers
Indentured servants
League of Iroquois
Mercantile policy
Poorhouses
Private nonprofit sector

Puritans
Residency requirements
Workhouses
Yeomen

NOTES

1. Paul Johnson, *A History of the American People* (New York: HarperPerennial, 1999), p. 93.
2. Ibid., p. 94.
3. Ibid.
4. Ibid., p. 95.
5. Ibid., pp. 94–95.
6. Arthur M. Schlesinger, Jr., *The Almanac of American History* (New York: Barnes & Noble, 1993), p. 34.

7. Ibid., p. 35.
8. Johnson, p. 68.
9. Phyllis J. Day, *A New History of Social Welfare*, 3rd ed. (Boston: Allyn & Bacon, 2000), p. 133.
10. Johnson, pp. 68–69.
11. Howard Zinn, *A People's History of the United States* (New York: Harper Colophon, 1980), p. 109.

12. Bruce S. Jansson, *The Reluctant Welfare State* (Belmont, CA: Wadsworth Publishing, 1988), p. 30.

13. Walter I. Trattner, *From Poor Law to Welfare State: A History of Social Welfare in America,* 6th ed. (New York: The Free Press, 1999), p. 112.

14. Ibid.

15. Schlesinger, p. 89; Carl Van Doren, *Benjamin Franklin* (New York: Penguin, 1991), pp. 194–196.

16. Van Doren, p. 195.

17. Schlesinger, p. 89.

18. Van Doren, pp. 91, 129; Johnson, p. 164; Schlessinger, p. 89.

19. Johnson, pp. 22–24, 54, 102.

20. Johnson, pp. 27, 58, 95; Dolgoff and Feldstein, p. 62.

21. Van Doren, p. 216.

22. Johnson, pp. 27, 58.

23. Ibid., p. 73.

24. Zinn, p. 23; Johnson, pp. 27–28, 38.

25. Zinn, pp. 28–29.

26. Johnson, p. 74.

27. Ibid., pp. 74–75.

28. Ibid., pp. 92–93, 108.

29. Zinn, p. 49.

30. Johnson, pp. 57–58.

31. Ibid., p. 54.

32. Ibid., p. 47.

33. Zinn, pp. 19–20.

34. Ibid., pp. 39–41.

35. Ibid., pp. 34–37.

36. Fawn M. Brodie, *Thomas Jefferson: An Intimate History* (New York: Bantam, 1975), p. 41.

37. Brodie, pp. 199–200.

38. Zinn, p. 35.

39. Ibid., p. 31.

40. Ibid.

41. Ibid., p. 35.

42. Zinn, p. 49; Trattner, pp. 30–32.

43. Ralph Dolgoff and Donald Feldstein, *Understanding Social Welfare,* 5th ed. (Boston: Allyn & Bacon), p. 64. See also Michael B. Katz, *In the Shadow of the Poorhouse: A Social History of Welfare in America,* 10th ed. (New York: Basic Books, 1996), p. 11.

44. Katz, p. 14.

45. Ibid., p. 15.

46. Zinn, p. 49.

47. Trattner, pp. 22–23.

48. Dolgoff and Feldstein, p. 65.

49. Katz, pp. 14–15.

50. Day, p. 134.

51. Trattner, pp. 19–21. See also Dolgoff and Feldstein, p. 63.

52. Day, p. 135.

53. Trattner, pp. 21–22.

54. Ibid., p. 18.

55. Ibid., p. 23–24.

56. Johnson, p. 218.

57. Ibid., pp. 218, 232.

58. Ibid., pp. 214–215.

59. Ibid., 215.

60. Ibid., 227.

61. Schlesinger, p. 155.

62. Johnson, p. 227.

63. Brodie, p. 154.

64. Ibid.

65. Ibid., p. 604.

66. Ibid., p. 155.

67. Ibid.

68. Jansson, pp. 38–39.

69. Ibid.

70. Brodie, p. 302.

71. Ibid., p. 230.

72. Ibid., pp. 293–294.

73. Zinn, pp. 108–109.

74. Ibid.

75. C. A. Akers, *Abigail Adams: An American Woman* (New York: Addison Wesley Longman, 2000). See also E. B. Gelles, *Portia: The World of Abigail Adams* (Bloomington, IN: Indiana University Press, 1992) and J. Whitney, *Abigail Adams* (Westport, CT: Greenwood Press, 1947).

76. Akers, p. 48.

77. Michael O'Neill, *The Third America: The Emergence of the Nonprofit Sector in the United States* (San Francisco: Jossey-Bass, 1989), p. 20.

78. Trattner, p. 17.

79. Ibid., p. 35.

80. O'Neill, p. 99; Trattner, p. 35.

81. O'Neill, p. 30.

82. Ibid., pp. 29–30.

83. Schlesinger, p. 40; Johnson, pp. 43–44.

84. Schlesinger, p. 40.

85. Trattner, pp. 36–38.

86. Johnson, pp. 112–113.

87. Trattner, pp. 36–38.

88. Ibid., p. 33.

89. Ibid., p. 36.

4 American Social Policy, Westward Expansion, and the Civil War

TECUMTHA.

Tecumseh was a brilliant speaker who tried to unite various American Indian tribes in opposing American westward expansion.

Westward Expansion

Economic Motivations: Land Ownership

The Founding Fathers believed that the new nation was destined for greatness due to a great extent to its abundance of God-given natural resources. Much of those natural resources lay to the west of the Appalachian Mountains. Thus, to become a great world power, public leaders such as Washington, Hamilton, and Jefferson believed that western territories had to be acquired and settled. A major social policy of the young nation, therefore, was to expand westward, settling the western regions of the United States as rapidly as possible. This social policy was later expressed in an 1845 magazine article by the term **manifest destiny.** The editor of that magazine, John L. O'Sullivan, claimed that it was "our manifest destiny to overspread the continent allotted by Providence for the free development of our yearly multiplying millions."[1]

As stated before, Jefferson was a leading proponent of making land acquisition easy for small western farmers.[2] Such a policy gave the common person a stake in the new democratic system of government in America while facilitating the population and geographic expansion of the nation. Although parts of the United States were beginning to industrialize, the opening of the west to farmers extended and prolonged Jefferson's vision of a utopian agricultural society, full of opportunity and free of European social problems. Jefferson's **Louisiana Purchase** in 1803 was a gigantic step toward the achievement of his vision, acquiring vast territories west of the original thirteen colonies.[3] The agreement with France allowed the United States to roughly double its geographic size for about $11 million. The purchased land would eventually become thirteen states: Louisiana, Arkansas, Missouri, Minnesota, Kansas, Iowa, Nebraska, Colorado, Montana, North Dakota, South Dakota, Oklahoma, and Wyoming.

Western territories that could not be purchased were acquired by other means such as war. The Mexican War, for example, fought between 1846 and 1848, enabled the American government to claim land all the way to the Pacific Ocean.[4] These new lands were organized as territories until reaching a population of about 60,000. At that point, the territory could be admitted to the union as a new state.

For most territories, attracting 60,000 was not a difficult goal to reach. Established states and territories hoping to become states offered land to aspiring farmers at little or no cost. This was a means of attracting immigrants and poor city dwellers to sparsely populated regions. Earlier, in the 1700s, the colonial governments in Maryland and Virginia had enticed Pennsylvania farmers to move to their colonies by offering land at low prices.[5] The **Homestead Act of 1862** offered farmers 160 acres of public land at $1.50 an acre or for free after five years of residence.[6] Later, after the Civil War, Governor Joshua Chamberlain of Maine, the last frontier on the Atlantic seaboard, offered free land to Swedish immigrants to encourage them to settle in northern Maine, which they did in New Sweden in 1870.[7]

The federal government also auctioned large tracts of public land in the west to the highest bidder. Unfortunately for the poor, the highest bidder was usually a person of wealth, a speculator, or a company. To assist poor settlers, the federal government lowered the down payment cost of land and eventually reduced the size of the auctioned tracts from 320 acres to 160 acres to 40 acres. And preemption laws allowed squatters to buy their land at public auctions.[8]

Social policies promoting easy land acquisition combined with open immigration policies to populate the west at an astounding rate. About 250,000 immigrants landed in America between 1790 and 1820.[9] During the early 1800s, the pace of immigration accelerated greatly. About 60,000 immigrants arrived in 1832, 105,000 in 1842, and 372,000 in 1852. Due in part to these high immigration rates, the population of many American cities grew considerably. Between 1820 and 1860, the population of Boston increased from 43,000 to 178,000. The population of New Orleans went from 27,000 to 169,000, and that of New York City grew from 124,000 to 1,080,000. In fact, during these early years of the new nation, the population doubled about every 24 years. Many headed west, drawn by the policy lure of inexpensive land and a chance to start their own farm or small business.

The American Government and Its Policy of Indian Removal

The westward expansion of the United States was one of the epic events of the 1800s. The rush by settlers to obtain land in the West was actively promoted by the American government. The outcome was astonishing from the perspective of European Americans and devastating for Native Americans. Consider these statistics.[10] In 1790, there were close to 4 million citizens of the United States. By 1830, there were 13 million "Americans." By 1840, 4.5 million had crossed the Appalachian Mountains. In contrast, in 1820, 120,000 Native Americans lived east of the Mississippi River. By 1844, about 30,000 lived east of the Mississippi. That is a 75 percent reduction in the Native American population!

This vanishing of the Native American is due in part to assimilation into the rapidly growing European American population.[11] However, a significant part of the cause is due to the policy known as **Indian Removal**.[12] To clear the land for agriculture and manufacturing, American political leaders supported the forced removal of Native Americans to the western frontier. Along with slavery, Indian Removal remains one of the most ethically controversial social policies in American history. However, most Americans of European descent, rich and poor, supported the policy at the time.

The policy, in many cases, was carried out in something like the following sequence.[13] First, Native Americans were promised security and land by the American government if they would move westward. A treaty was typically signed for this purpose. As Andrew Jackson stated, the treaty was supposed to be valid for "as long as grass grows or water runs."[14] Later, European Americans would move into the new Native American territory. The inevitable result was conflict. Native Americans, defending their rights, would often kill one or more of the new settlers. Consequently, the American government would demand that the "murderers" be turned over to American officials. When the Native Americans refused, the United States military would invade the Native American territory. In the end, another treaty was signed requiring Native Americans to move westward again, vacating the disputed land.

These forced migrations are infamous in Native American history due to the death and suffering that resulted. At least in some cases, these relocations, essentially death marches, were contracted out by the American government to private organizations.[15] Concerned with costs, these private entities, as in the 1836 case of the Creek march, did not supply adequate food, clothing, shelter and medical attention. As a result, many of the 15,000 Creeks died of starvation or sickness. The Cherokee march, presided over by President Martin Van Buren in 1838, is still referred to by Cherokees as the **Trail of Tears.** An estimated 4,000 of the 17,000 Cherokee people perished during the relocation.

If the Native American tribe chose not to move west, it was forced to abide by state law.[16] In states such as Alabama, Georgia, and Mississippi during the Jackson Administration, these laws stripped the tribe of its culture, while discriminating against its people. These states did not recognize the tribe as a legal unit, even outlawing tribal meetings. The chief of the tribe was stripped of any formal power. At the same time, these Native Americans were subjected to military duty and state taxes, while being denied legal representation and the right to vote.

Chief Black Hawk spoke for many Native Americans on surrendering to U.S. authorities in 1832.

> I fought hard. But your guns were well aimed. The bullets flew like birds in the air, and whizzed by our ears like the wind through the trees in the winter. My warriors fell around me.... The sun rose dim on us in the morning, and at night it sunk in a dark cloud, and looked like a ball of fire. That was the last sun that shone on Black Hawk.... He is now a prisoner to the white men.... He has done nothing for which an Indian ought to be ashamed. He has fought for his countrymen, the squaws and papooses, against white men, who came year after year, to cheat them and take away their lands.[17]

Personal Profile: Chief Tecumseh

Chief Tecumseh (or Tecumtha) was a leader in the fight against the policy of Indian Removal.[18] Born in 1768, Tecumseh was the preeminent Native American leader in the northwest by the age of 27.[19] He was a brilliant speaker who tried to unite various tribes in opposing American westward expansion. In so doing, he developed the greatest Native American military alliance in history.[20] In the War of 1812, Tecumseh fought on the side of the British, eventually becoming a Brigadier General in the British Army.[21]

At one point in his life, Tecumseh almost decided to assimilate into the white culture.[22] He met and fell in love with a white American named Rebecca Galloway. She taught him English, the Bible, and Shakespeare. After Tecumseh proposed to her, Rebecca said that she would be willing to marry him if he would give up his Native American lifestyle and live as a white man. Tecumseh took a month to make his decision, but decided that he could not leave his people. He never saw her again.

Tecumseh was shot and killed as a British Officer at the Battle of the Thames.[23] The following Tecumseh quote captures his perspective on the American policy of Indian Removal:

> These lands are ours; no one has a right to remove us because we were the first owners; the Great Spirit above has appointed the place for us on which to light our fires; and here we will remain. As to boundaries, the Great Spirit above knows no boundaries, nor will his red people know any.[24]

Personal Profile: Andrew Jackson

Andrew Jackson, although closely associated with Indian Removal, is considered one of the great American presidents.[25] In addition to being a hero in the War of 1812 against the British, he was the first nonaristocratic, self-made man to become president. This, combined with his social policies in support of Indian Removal and in opposition to national banks, made him extremely popular among small farmers, craftsmen, and laborers. His views on government reflected the populist values of Thomas Jefferson and built mass support for the Democratic Party (which had formerly been called the Republican Party during Jefferson's era.).

Jackson's military record made him a national hero among most Americans. In the Battle of New Orleans, the final battle of the War of 1812, Jackson's troops killed about 2,000 of Great Britain's most experienced soldiers, whereas the American force lost only sixteen men.[26] However, Jackson's military conquests were not limited to the British. In the Battle of Horseshoe Bend in 1814, Jackson's army defeated a Creek force of 1,000, killing 800 of them while suffering few casualties.[27] His military conquests of the Seminoles and Spanish in

Florida during the Seminole War of 1818 resulted in American acquisition of that territory.

As in Florida, Jackson's military victories typically produced new land for American land speculators, farmers, plantation owners, merchants, and industrialists.[28] Thus, he became a hero to many. Yet, these victories were often defeats for Native Americans who were forced to move west or give up their culture to assimilate.

Ethical Analysis: Native American History

Does the fact that American political leaders such as Jefferson and Jackson saw the potential greatness of a new nation, a nation that did in fact become a world leader, justify the oppression of Native American culture? Some might argue that Native American tribes made war on each other and were not, historically speaking, total innocents or passive victims. Some might argue that giving Native American tribes the choice of assimilation or moving west was humane under the historical circumstances. Do you agree?

Jackson is also known for instituting the **spoils system** in American politics. Upon his landslide election in 1828, Jackson proceeded to replace as many government employees as possible from the previous administration. Some historians claim that Jackson's action helped return government to the common people of America, in contrast to a government of aristocrats.[29] In so doing, he helped to preserve and strengthen representative democracy in America. However, reformers during the Progressive Era (1880–1920) would later advocate against the spoils system and political patronage in favor of the civil service system and professional public administration.

Finally, President Andrew Jackson may be the first great critic of corporations in American history.[30] It was during the "Age of Jackson" that corporations began to emerge as a dominant power in society, foreshadowing the Industrial Boom later in the century. Jackson attacked the Second Bank of the United States, a private institution that held monopoly-like power in its relation to the federal government. Many felt the bank primarily served the interest of wealthy aristocrats, had too much influence on American government, and was not accountable enough to the American public. Jackson's efforts put an end to "the Bank."

Jackson also initiated changes in the way corporations were started.[31] Previously, corporations were chartered by government. Politicians, susceptible to bribery, determined which individuals could start a corporation, and just as importantly, which individuals could not. Jackson Democrats called for general laws of incorporation which opened up the process to greater numbers of aspiring Americans. Connecticut was the first state to pass and implement the new policy when it passed the Hinsdale Act in 1837. Other states followed, leading to the system that the United States has today.

As the forms of business organization became more complex to facilitate large-scale industry, the distinctions and inequities between capitalists (i.e., corporate owners) and labor (those working for wages) became a social problem. The Democrats, led by Jackson, were the first major political party to advocate for average workers laboring in the growing industrial system. For example, Jackson Democrats around the country began to push for shorter workdays for industrial laborers.[32] In places such as Massachusetts, it was not unusual to find common laborers working between 11½ and 13½ hours per day. Democrats began to push for a 10-hour workday. Whigs, the name of the other major political party at the time, opposed the policy proposal, stating: "To work only ten hours in summer…is to waste life."

The Civil War

Economic Conflict: Industrial versus Agrarian Economies

Several influential factors contributed to the Civil War. First was the rivalry between two different economic systems.[33] The northern states were rapidly developing as industrial regions requiring free markets, free labor, and inexpensive land. In contrast, the southern states maintained an agricultural economy, specifically a slave-powered plantation system of cotton, rice, and tobacco. This economy also needed labor and land. Thus, a fundamental economic conflict between north and south was ready to climax.

This conflict was present right from the very birth of the United States.[34] Jefferson's Declaration of Independence had established an expectation for many that the end of slavery was near. However, in order to develop and pass the Constitution for the new nation, a short-term compromise was made that prohibited the Congress from abolishing or restricting the slave trade until 1808. In fact, the words *slavery* and *slaves* were not permitted in the Constitution; it was that much of a taboo subject for southern leaders. The clause in the Constitution that prohibited Congress from passing any law that restricted the slave trade did so without mentioning the word: "The Migration or Importation of such Persons as any of the States now existing shall think proper to admit, shall not be prohibited by the Congress prior to the Year one thousand eight hundred and eight."[35]

In order to establish a unified nation in the first place, this compromise was made.[36] In a congressional debate on emancipation that occurred soon after the Constitution was ratified, southern leaders maintained that they did not even want to discuss the topic of slavery publicly, that without slavery the economy of the South would cease to exist.

The debate on whether national economic policies should promote industry or agriculture, as discussed earlier, was demonstrated in the personal differences between Alexander Hamilton and Thomas Jefferson, two leading cabinet members competing for influence with George Washington.[37] Hamilton pushed for commerce and industry, whereas Jefferson advocated for an agrarian culture. This fundamental conflict in national policy continued into the mid-1800s when the Lincoln administration was forced to confront the matter.

By this time, the southern economy was even more dependent on slave labor than during the colonial era.[38] To illustrate, in 1790, one thousand tons of cotton was produced yearly in the nation. This production required 500,000 slaves. After the invention of the cotton gin in 1794, the production of cotton greatly expanded. By 1860, when Lincoln took office, the southern economy was producing one million tons of cotton annually, and it depended on four million slaves.

Political Conflict: Slave versus Free States

Lincoln and many other leaders in the Republican party believed that if slavery was contained in the southern states that existed during his time, slavery would eventually die out.[39] That is, because of the depletion of soil in southern states and the growing population of slaves born in the United States, slave plantations would be forced to expand into more western regions of the country. The very survival of the southern agricultural economy depended on it. At the same time, the land and other resources of the western territories were needed for the growing industrial system. The very future of northern capitalism depended on it.

Therefore, the economic conflict between northern and southern states was the core of the political debate over whether or not new western states would be admitted to the union as slave or free states.[40] Whether new states entered the union as free or slave states would determine which major economic system, industry or agriculture, controlled Congress and the nation's future.

Various social policies such as the **Missouri Compromise** maintained a sensitive balance between free and slave states. However, soon after Abraham Lincoln was elected president at the head of a new Republican Party that pledged to oppose the extension of slavery into western states, the Civil War exploded.[41] During the war, Lincoln's main objective was to save the Union, whether slavery ended or not. In a reply to a critical editorial by Horace Greeley in the New York Tribune, Lincoln wrote:

> My paramount object in this struggle is to save the Union, and is not either to save or to destroy slavery. If I could save the Union without freeing any slave

I would do it, and if I could save it by freeing all the slaves I would do it; and if I could save it by freeing some and leaving others alone I would also do that.[42]

As proof of his immediate objective, Lincoln's **Emancipation Proclamation of 1863** did not end slavery in states loyal to the Union; it emancipated slaves only in those southern states still fighting against the Union. Thus, the policy served also as a military strategy meant to help win the war and preserve the Union.[43] That said, historian David Herbert Donald, in his award-winning biography of Lincoln, maintains that Lincoln knew that a war fought to preserve the Union was a war fought to contain slavery. And as stated previously, if slavery could be contained to the existing southern states, Lincoln and other national policy leaders believed it would eventually wither away totally.[44]

Did You Know?

Did you know that Abraham Lincoln was a marvelous storyteller with a great sense of humor? During his presidential campaign, the opposition ridiculed his physical appearance. The *Houston Telegraph* wrote:

> Lincoln is the leanest, lankest, most ungainly mass of legs and arms and hatchet face ever strung on a single frame. He has most unwarrantably abused the privilege, which all politicians have, of being ugly.[45]

What made Lincoln appealing, though, was his self-deprecation. He told audiences that

> He felt like the ugly man riding through a wood who met a woman, also on horseback, who stopped and said: "Well, for land sake, you are the homeliest man I ever saw." "Yes, madam, but I can't help it," he replied. "No, I suppose not," she remarked, "but you might stay at home."[46]

Social Conflict: The Role of Northern Abolitionists, Women, and Religion

If the Civil War was the result of these economic and political battles, certainly it was the result of an intense social conflict as well. Not to be discounted, the dispute over the morality of slavery was also a major "cause" of the Civil War. Many groups, including business, women, and religious leaders, were active in the **Abolition Movement.** As early as 1790, members of the Quaker Church from New York and Pennsylvania petitioned the House of Representatives to put an end to the slave trade.[47] Although southern leaders and sympathizers developed elaborate arguments to justify the morality of slavery, abolitionists maintained that it directly contradicted the founding principles of the nation. It was a crime against man and God. To promote abolition, William Lloyd Garrison started publishing a newspaper, the *Liberator,* in Boston on January 1, 1831.[48]

Two years later, in 1833, several other events took place as the Abolition Movement gathered momentum.[49] John Greenleaf Whittier advocated abolition in his publication, *Justice and Expediency,* while in St. Louis, Elijah P. Lovejoy began publishing an abolitionist newspaper, *The Observor.* In December of 1833, both the American Anti-Slavery Society and the Female Anti-Slavery Society were organized in Philadelphia. Lucretia Mott, one of the foremothers of the profession of social work, helped organize the Female Anti-Slavery Society and became its first president.

Later, in 1841, the former slave, **Frederick Douglass,** gave his first speech against slavery in Nantucket, Massachusetts.[50] Douglass would later start his own abolitionist newspapers, write two autobiographies, and serve as an advisor to President Lincoln.[51] Starting around 1840 and continuing to about 1861, individuals, including Douglass and Harriet Tubman, began developing a secret network of supporters to assist slaves in escaping to free states in the north. This was the famous **Underground Railroad.**[52]

Did You Know?

Did you know that two of the three men responsible for founding the American Anti-Slavery Society were businessmen? Arthur and Lewis Tappan, wealthy New York City merchants, led the organizational effort along with the famous minister Theodore Weld.[53]

Personal Profile: William Lloyd Garrison

Garrison was one of the great social critics in American history, a radical reformer who promoted abolition, women's rights, and pacifism. From a social work standpoint, he was on the right side of most big social issues, but he managed to get on the wrong side of almost everyone he met. He was irresponsible, belligerent, and vindictive, liked by few people, hated by many.[54] In fact, he was attacked by an angry mob in Boston in October of 1835 for preaching that all men, including black Americans, were created equal. He was consequently jailed for his own safety.[55] Yet, he courageously promoted social justice as he saw it in the *Liberator* for thirty-five years.[56] In so doing, he became a leading advocate in the moral fight against slavery. His famous manifesto in the first issue of the *Liberator* read as follows:

> I will be as harsh as truth, and as uncompromising as justice. On this subject, I do not wish to think, or speak, or write, with moderation. No! No! Tell a man whose house is on fire to give a moderate alarm; tell him to moderately rescue his wife from the hands of the ravisher; tell the mother to gradually extricate her babe from the fire into which it has fallen—but urge me not to use moderation in a cause like the present. I will not retreat a single inch— AND I WILL BE HEARD.[57]

Personal Profiles: Women in the Abolition and Women's Rights Movements

A case can be made that several women active in the Abolition Movement and the Women's Rights Movement were, in many ways, foremothers of the social work profession. Social work as a profession did not come of age until the 1920s.[58] Women of the 1800s in America were the first to obtain college degrees, but their professional choices were limited to a very few occupations such as teaching and nursing. Women of this century did not have universal suffrage and were discouraged from active participation in politics. Yet, women wanting to influence social policy and promote social justice found ways to use their education and experience in the great social movements of the 1800s. Later in the century, women with these interests became involved in settlement house work and the emerging social work profession. But, during the first half of the nineteenth century, these female leaders became social advocates within the Abolition and Women's Rights Movements.

As stated earlier, Lucretia Mott was an organizational leader and first president of the Female Anti-Slavery Society. After the Civil War, she helped to provide education and other support to former slaves and campaigned for black suffrage.[59] Born in Nantucket, Massachusetts, on January 3, 1793, Lucretia attended several schools, including the Nine Partners Boarding School, where she became an assistant teacher after several years of outstanding academic performance.[60] She later became a full-time teacher and eventually a Quaker minister, while raising six children.[61] She became famous as a social reformer. Not only was she an outspoken proponent of abolition, she also persistently advocated for women's equality and religious freedom. Delivering the opening and closing speeches, Lucretia was a leader in organizing the First Women's Rights Convention at Seneca Falls, New York, in 1848, and was later elected president of the American Equal Rights Association in 1866.[62] Her nontraditional views and outspoken style prompted the *Boston Recorder* to derisively describe her as "another prominent spouter on the platform."[63]

Another woman to speak out publicly against slavery was Lucy Stone. Born in 1818 in West Brookfield, Massachusetts, Lucy was the first woman in Massachusetts to earn a college degree.[64] She graduated from Oberlin College in 1847.[65] By 1848, she was already regularly lecturing for the Anti-Slavery Society.[66] Like the other prominent women activists of her generation, Lucy also advocated for women's rights. She wore bloomers for several years (very unlady-like!) and when she was married in 1855, she kept her own name, not wanting to compromise her individuality. During the ceremony, Lucy and her husband, Henry Blackwell, did a reading protesting the sexist marriage laws of the time.[67] In 1869, she helped found the American Woman Suffrage Association and edited the association's newspaper.[68]

Elizabeth Cady Stanton met her future husband at an antislavery meeting.[69] For their honeymoon, the couple sailed to England to attend a world antislavery convention.[70] A graduate of Emma Willard's female seminary in Troy, New York, Elizabeth actively rejected the notion that men were socially and intellectually superior to women. She was a coleader with Lucretia Mott in organizing the First Women's Rights Convention in Seneca Falls, New York.[71] At this convention, she helped draft the Declaration of Sentiments, which included a woman's right to vote.[72] In 1854, Elizabeth was the first woman to be asked to speak before the New York state legislature, where she addressed the topic of discrimination against women.[73] Twelve years later, in the face of America's sexist values, Stanton ran for Congress as an Independent. Although she only received twenty-four votes, she made her point. Along with her close friend, Susan B. Anthony, Elizabeth helped organize the National Woman's Suffrage Association.[74] She later served as president of the combined National Woman's Suffrage Association and the American Woman Suffrage Association.[75] In addition to all of this, she edited a feminist newspaper, wrote the Woman's Bible addressing sexism in the Bible, published her autobiography, and raised seven children.

For African American women born into slavery, education was more difficult to obtain. Sojourner Truth, for example, was illiterate.[76] However, she found a way to publish her autobiography and become a noted public speaker for abolition and women's rights. She made her famous "And a'n't I a Woman?" speech at the Third Women's Rights Convention in Akron, Ohio, in 1851.[77] During the Civil War, after Lincoln decided to enlist African Americans, Sojourner helped to recruit black soldiers into the Union Army. In addition, she worked as a nurse and teacher in refugee camps for recently freed slaves. After the war ended, Sojourner worked to find employment for freed slaves.[78]

The following is a quote from her powerful speech at the Third Women's Rights Convention:

I have ploughed, and planted, and gathered into barns, and no man could head me! And a'n't I a woman?... I have borne thirteen children, and seen most all sold off to slavery, and when I cried out with my mother's grief, none but Jesus heard me! And a'n't I a woman?[79]

Post–Civil War: Free but Segregated

Many African Americans were freed from slavery as a result of the Union Army's victory in the Civil War. However, there were few social programs to facilitate the transition to freedom. Support provided included **Freedmen's Camps**.[80] These camps, run by the Union Army, provided former slaves with food, clothing, health care, and work details. The **Freedmen's Bureau Act** established the Bureau of Refugees, Freedmen, and Abandoned Lands.[81] Authorized to establish courts in southern states, the Freedmen's Bureau provided legal assistance to freed slaves. For instance, the Bureau helped ensure that contract labor between former slaves and landowners was clearly written and honored. The Freedmen's Bureau also distributed confiscated and abandoned land to freedmen and refugees.[82] The establishment of the Bureau was controversial because many people believed that the federal government had no authority over welfare matters. Partially as a result, no doubt, of this belief, the Bureau depended on private philanthropy and was terminated in 1872.

Several pieces of legislation gave African Americans increased citizenship.[83] Ratified in 1865, the **Thirteenth Amendment** to the Constitution outlawed slavery, the **Fourteenth Amendment** in 1868 granted African Americans citizenship, and the **Fifteenth Amendment** (1870) gave African American males the right to vote. Furthermore, the **Civil Rights Act of 1875** outlawed discrimination against black citizens in public facilities.

Unfortunately, U.S. policy over time allowed property confiscated during the war to revert to the heirs of the Confederate owners.[84] Also, abandoned plantations were leased to northern whites or former planters. Some land was sold at auction, but few black Americans could afford to buy it. In the end, a wealthy few individuals gained control over large tracts of land, whereas most southerners, black and white, became poor tenant farmers. The result: the black slave of southern landowners before the war became the black "serf" for southern landowners after the war.

Other civil rights of African Americans were maintained in former Confederate states through the presence of Union troops.[85] To settle a dispute over the results of the 1876 presidential election, the Republican candidate, Rutherford Hayes, agreed to pull remaining Union troops out of the South. This marked the end of the **reconstruction** of the South.[86] Soon discriminatory laws called **black codes** and the **Ku Klux Klan** surfaced to subjugate and segregate African Americans. The result was a policy of apartheid in the American southern states, a system that would remain unchallenged until the Civil Rights Movement of the 1960s.

CONTENTSELECT

For more information on related social work topics, use the following search terms:

Abolition Movement	Freedmen's Camps	Reconstruction
Black codes	Homestead Act of 1862	Spoils system
Civil Rights Act of 1875	Indian Removal	Thirteenth Amendment
Emancipation Proclamation	Ku Klux Klan	Trail of Tears
Fifteenth Amendment	Louisiana Purchase	Underground Railroad
Fourteenth Amendment	Manifest destiny	
Freedmen's Bureau Act	Missouri Compromise	

NOTES

1. Arthur M. Schlesinger, Jr., ed.,*The Almanac of American History* (New York: Barnes & Noble, 1993), p. 249.

2. Fawn M. Brodie, *Thomas Jefferson: An Intimate History* (New York: Bantam, 1975), p. 154.

3. Schlesinger, 1993, p. 178.

4. Marcus Cunliffe, *Testing a Union 1788–1865*, ed. Schlesinger, 1993, p. 148.

5. Paul Johnson, *A History of the American People* (New York: HarperPerennial, 1999), p. 91.

6. Ibid., p. 491.

7. Charles Shain and Samuella Shain, eds., *The Maine Reader: The Down East Experience from 1614 to the Present* (Jaffrey, NH: Godine, 1997), p. 183.

8. Bruce Jansson, *The Reluctant Welfare State: American Social Welfare Policies—Past, Present, and Future* (Pacific Grove, CA: Brooks/Cole, 1997), p. 83.

9. Marcus Cunliffe, p. 148.

10. Howard Zinn, *A People's History of the United States: 1492–Present* (New York: HarperPerennial, 1995), p. 124.

11. Johnson, p. 270.

12. Zinn, p. 124; Jansson, 1997, p. 85.

13. Zinn, p. 128.

14. Ibid., p. 132.

15. Ibid., pp. 141–142, 146.

16. Ibid., pp. 131–132.

17. Ibid., p. 129.

18. Albert Britt, *Great Indian Chiefs: A Study of Indian Leaders in the Two Hundred Year Struggle to Stop the White Advance* (Freeport, NY: Books for Libraries Press, 1969), p. 127.

19. Alvin M. Josephy, Jr., *The Patriot Chiefs: A Chronicle of American Indian Leadership* (New York: The Viking Press, 1961), pp. 145–146.

20. Ibid., pp. 153–154.

21. Charles H. L. Johnston, *Famous Indian Chiefs: Their Battles, Treaties, Sieges, and Struggles with the Whites for the Possession of America* (Freeport, NY: Books for Libraries Press, 1971), p. 332.

22. Josephy, pp. 146–147.

23. Ibid., pp. 171–172.

24. Britt, p. 140.

25. Schlesinger, 1993, pp. 219–220.

26. Ibid., p. 219.

27. Zinn, pp. 126, 128.

28. Ibid., p. 125.

29. Arthur M. Schlesinger, Jr., *The Age of Jackson* (Boston: Little, Brown and Company, 1945), p. 47.

30. Ibid., pp. 74–75.

31. Ibid., pp. 336–337.

32. Ibid., pp. 342–343.

33. Jean Strouse, *Morgan: American Financier* (New York: HarperPerennial, 2000), p. 89; David Herbert Donald, *Lincoln* (New York: Touchstone, 1996), p. 234.

34. Joseph J. Ellis, *Founding Brothers: The Revolutionary Generation* (New York: Knopf, 2001), pp. 82, 84, 89.

35. Ibid., p. 84.

36. Ibid., pp. 84–85.

37. Johnson, pp. 214–215.

38. Zinn, p. 167.

39. Donald, pp. 234–235.

40. Jansson, p. 90.

41. Donald, p. 191.

42. Donald, p. 368.

43. Zinn, p. 187.

44. Donald, p. 368.

45. Paul F. Boller, Jr., *Presidential Campaigns* (New York: Oxford University Press, 1985), p. 107.

46. Donald, p. 190.

47. Ellis, p. 81.

48. John L. Thomas, *The Liberator: William Lloyd Garrison* (Boston: Little, Brown, and Company, 1963), pp. 127–128.

49. Schlesinger, 1993, p. 229.

50. Gregory P. Lampe, *Frederick Douglass: Freedom's Voice, 1818–1845* (East Lansing, MI: Michigan State University Press, 1998), p. 1.

51. William S. McFeely, *Frederick Douglass* (New York: Norton, 1991), pp. 146, 182, 273.

52. Schlesinger, 1993, p. 239.

53. Ibid., 229.

54. Thomas, pp. 3, 7.

55. Russell B. Nye, *William Lloyd Garrison and the Humanitarian Reformers* (Boston: Little, Brown, and Company, 1955), pp. 86–87.

56. Thomas, p. 3.

57. Ibid., p. 128.

58. John H. Ehrenreich, *The Altruistic Imagination: A History of Social Work and Social Policy in the United States* (Ithaca, NY: Cornell University Press, 1989), p. 53.

59. Harriet Sigerman, *Biographical Supplement and Index*, ed. Nancy F. Cott, *The Young Oxford History of Women in the United* States, vol. 2 (New York: Oxford University Press, 1995), p. 108.

60. Otelia Cromwell, *Lucretia Mott* (Cambridge, MA: Harvard University Press, 1958), pp. 3, 18.

61. Cromwell, p. 18; Sigerman, p. 108; Dorothy Sterling, *Lucretia Mott* (New York: The Fem-

inist Press at the City University of New York, 1992), p. 13.

62. Sigerman, p. 108.

63. Cromwell, p. 120.

64. Alice Stone Blackwell, *Lucy Stone: Pioneer of Woman's Rights* (Norwood, MA: The Plimpton Press, 1930), pp. 7, 73.

65. Sigerman, p. 157.

66. Blackwell, p. 76.

67. Ibid., pp. 103, 171, 166–169.

68. Sigerman, p. 158.

69. Judith Nies, *Seven Women: Portraits from the American Radical Tradition* (New York: Viking, 1977), p. 71.

70. Sigerman, p. 153.

71. Nies, pp. 61, 70.

72. Sigerman, p. 153.

73. Nies, pp. 85, 87.

74. Sigerman, p. 153.

75. Nies, pp. 61, 91; Sigerman, p. 154.

76. Nell Irvin Painter, *Narrative of Sojourner Truth: A Bondswoman of Olden Time, with a History of Her Labors and Correspondence* (New York: Penguin, 1998), p. vii.

77. Sigerman, p. 165.

78. Painter, p. xi.

79. Sigerman, p. 165.

80. Jansson, p. 93.

81. Donald, p. 563.

82. Jansson, p. 94.

83. Zinn, pp. 193–194.

84. Ibid., p. 192.

85. Ibid., pp. 198–201.

86. Mayer, p. 300 in Schlesinger, 1993; Zinn, pp. 194, 198.

5 American Social Policy and the Industrial Boom

Perhaps the most famous American labor organizer, Mother Jones gained respect and notoriety among union men for her great speaking skills and direct participation in the dangerous strikes.

The Industrialization of America

Economic Developments

The Civil War facilitated the industrialization of the United States in many ways. Before the war, the nation still had a postcolonial economy, importing most of its manufactured goods from Britain.[1] This changed during the Civil War. Not only did the war create a nation of free and mobile labor, it also hastened the development of an industrial infrastructure.[2] The growth of railroads, telegraphs, iron mills, and coal mines helped the Union forces to win the war. Soldiers needed transporting; generals needed to communicate with troops; and guns and ammunition needed to be manufactured. In the process, new fortunes were created.

If the colonial era represented America's birth and childhood, the 1800s represented its adolescence: tempestuous, rapid growth, increasing strength, and finally, maturity.[3] The railroad was, perhaps, the most significant factor in this development. The completion of a transcontinental railroad in 1869 enabled industry to use the natural resources of western territories.[4] In addition, the railroads allowed western farmers and ranchers to sell their wheat and beef to the growing industrial cities in eastern and Midwestern parts of the United States, cities filling up with new immigrants.[5] Towns sprang up all along the growing network of railroads, thus further facilitating the settling of the western United States. With these benefits associated with the railroad, the federal and state governments were eager to subsidize railroad entrepreneurs such as Cornelius Vanderbilt, E. H. Harriman, and Leland Stanford.[6] And eastern banks, led by J. Pierpont (J. P.) Morgan, were eager to finance them.[7] Vast fortunes were made by all of these men. According to an 1889 magazine article entitled "The Owners of the United States," the average annual income of American families in the United States was less than $500, whereas the average yearly income of the wealthiest 100 men was over $1 million.[8]

Did You Know?

In 1911, J. P. Morgan ordered himself a new Rolls Royce, custom-equipped with an electric cigar lighter, silver flower vases, mother-of-pearl trays, brass fittings, a clock, hat racks, velvet carpets, leather hassocks, silk curtains, a long trumpet horn, and his initials on the doors. The automobile cost $7,275 at the time. Morgan liked it so much that he bought himself a second one and sent a third one to a friend.[9]

There were other significant factors associated with the Industrial Boom. The absence of a large federal government in the United States, in comparison to European nations, allowed ambitious businessmen much room for industrial initiative, creativity, expansion, and conquest. Soon a stronger federal government would be needed to protect the public interest and regulate the emerging industrial giants, huge corporations led by names such as Carnegie and Rockefeller. But from the end of the Civil War to the presidency of Theodore Roosevelt, America industrialized at full speed with few regulations on business competition. This winner-take-all capitalism provided ample opportunity and motivation for industrial entrepreneurs to start and build businesses.[10]

Another significant factor in the Industrial Boom was the liberal patent laws in the United States, laws that encouraged inventions that further increased American industrial and agricultural productivity.[11] Alexander Graham Bell invented the telephone in 1876; three years later, Thomas Edison invented the electric light bulb. Barbed wire, simple as it seems, and the refrigerated railroad car were inventions that facilitated the cattle-raising and the meat-packing industries.

Furthermore, there were plenty of energy sources to fuel industrial growth. Coal needed in the huge steel mills of Andrew Carnegie was in ample supply. As a result, Carnegie steel was a central ingredient in building or rebuilding the railroads, factories, bridges, and skyscrapers of industrial centers such as Chicago, Detroit, and Cleveland. By 1900, the United States was the third leading producer of steel in the world.[12] In the 1830s, Chicago was little more than a village with pastures; by 1900 it was a city with over a million people. Meanwhile, in Cleveland, John D. Rockefeller entered the oil refining business with an eye on the vast oil reserves of northern and western Pennsylvania.[13] By 1870, he had incorporated the Standard Oil Company of Ohio.[14] An oil-based kerosene from Rockefeller's refineries, at the time, provided a low-cost illuminant for American as well as foreign homes and businesses. On incorporation, Rockefeller's company already produced 10 percent of petroleum refining in the United States, a market share that would eventually grow to monopoly proportion.[15]

With government policies promoting land ownership and railroad development, the agricultural economy of the western states also flourished during the last half of the nineteenth century.[16] By 1900, the United States was the leading exporter of agricultural products in the world.[17] However, as a result of the Civil War, it was an agricultural system reflecting, and made subservient to, the major tenets of a capitalist industrial economy.

Personal Profile: Andrew Carnegie

Andrew Carnegie was one of the leading barons of American industrialism. He immigrated to the Pittsburgh area from Scotland in 1848.[18] Although he started out at age 14 working twelve hours a day in the cellar of a cloth mill, the young Carnegie was impressed with the contrast in economic opportunity between his old home in Scotland and his new home in Pennsylvania.

This opportunity in a country experiencing the early stage of industrial development, as well as his outstanding success in the game of capitalism, made him a firm believer in the "survival of the fittest" ideology. During his business career, Carnegie transitioned from working as a telegraph clerk, to working for the railroads, to owning his own iron companies, to heading a steel-production empire.[19] Along the way, he became a self-made millionaire and philanthropist. His career was not typical, but for healthy, white males of the time, his perspective on American economic opportunity was typical:

> Our public lands of almost unlimited extent are becoming settled with an enterprising people. Our dense forests are falling under the ax of the hardy woodsman. The Wolf and the Buffalo are startled by the shrill scream of the Iron Horse where a few years ago they roamed undisturbed. Towns and cities spring up as if by magic.... Our railroads extend 13,000 miles. You cannot supply iron fast enough to keep us going. This country is completely cut up with Railroad Tracks, Telegraphs, and Canals.... Pauperism is unknown. Hundreds of labor-saving devices are patented yearly.... Everything around us is in motion.[20]

The Ethics of Industrial Capitalism

As discussed earlier, the last half of the nineteenth century in America was an economic free-for-all. With the removal of Native Americans, the abolition of slavery, an abundance of land and natural resources, and a relatively weak but proindustrial federal government, the United States has been likened to the feudal era where nobles established great kingdoms through fierce and bloody battle with their peers.[21] Out of the economic battle that followed the Civil War and the "Indian" wars emerged a few industrial barons heading large armies of laborers. Men such as Carnegie and Rockefeller were the biggest victors in the struggle. As in war, this industrial battle contained few rules. Some rules were broken; many rules were made up over time. Did these men deserve their wealth? Did the nation as a whole benefit from their industrial activity? Did they have any responsibility to those who lost in the struggle: bankrupted small businessmen, injured laborers, and oppressed women and minorities?

Social Need: Poor Wage Labor and Growth of the Union Movement

During the 1800s, the United States developed into a leading world industrial power. Millions of immigrants arrived in search of jobs, land, and opportunity. Relative to Europe, America offered higher wages and hope for social advancement.[22] From the perspective of social welfare, this history should not be minimized. Many poor immigrants did, in fact, improve their lives. A few such as Andrew Carnegie even became rich. But some immigrants remained or eventually became needy, victims of a young industrial power with little regulation and few safeguards. This should also be emphasized. Dramatic industrial growth was followed by periods of recession. The country faced economic crises in 1819, 1837, 1857, 1873, 1884, and 1893.[23] In 1837, 50,000 people in New York City were unemployed.[24] An estimated 200,000 nationwide were left unemployed by the economic crash in 1857.[25] About 40,000 of these 200,000 unemployed people were concentrated in New York City. During these crises, rallies and protests by angry unemployed citizens, at times, turned into riots. Out of desperation around the end of the Civil War, about 12,000 women in New York City worked as prostitutes.[26]

Eastern industrial cities were crowded, their poor populations suffering the worst during hot summers and freezing winters.[27] These rapidly growing cities lacked adequate supplies of food, water, and sanitation. Their streets were often filled with garbage. Outbreaks of disease were disastrous. During the first week of July 1877, 139 infants died in Baltimore.

Furthermore, those immigrants lucky and healthy enough to work in a factory were subject to oppressive heat, polluted air, dangerous machinery, and long hours.[28] In fact, some worked essentially from sunrise to sunset. The long hours and dangerous machinery led to many accidents that disabled workers, rendering them worthless to industrial managers. Again, poverty and dependency were the result. What is more, industrial laborers, many coming from traditions of pride in craftsmanship as the sons and daughters of artisans, began to realize that their labor was no longer valued. They were expendable parts of the industrial machinery. Social status went to the owners and managers of capital, not to the common laborer. In his famous history, *The Robber Barons,* Matthew Josephson describes the change:

> In hard times, the manufacturers were not responsible for the souls of their hired hands, like the manorial lords of the Middle Ages; few measures of safety were provided in mines and mills where hundreds and even thousands were killed and maimed annually. Little heed was paid to the quarters in which workers and their families resided, the food they ate or the water they drank.... With the passing of time, toward 1890, 10 percent of the population of our great cities was housed in slums as terrible as those of the wretchedest places of the Old World. And in the neighborhood of the big manufacturing works, stockyards, and mines, the unlovely shacks of laborers, communities clustered, like the cottages of servants and hired hands in feudal times.[29]

Given all of this, factory laborers started organizing themselves into trade unions. And they started defending themselves in a factory system that often exploited them. For instance, during 1835 and 1836, there were an estimated 140 labor strikes, protesting work conditions in the factories of eastern cities.[30] Before the Civil War, many of the strikes took place in the textile mills of New England.[31] During the Civil War, strikes continued all over the nation. Often, these strikes resulted in the organization of labor unions. By 1864, about 200,000 workers in the United States were unionized.[32]

Of interest to social workers, a profession primarily of women, is that women were very active in the union movement.[33] In 1825, for example, a women's union, the United Tailoresses of New York, went on strike to seek higher wages. Three years later, female mill workers went on strike in Dover, New Hampshire. Women mill workers, just down the road in Exeter, New Hampshire, went on strike when they discovered that factory management was setting the clocks back to secretly increase the length of the workday.

In Lowell, Massachusetts, female textile workers lived in dormitories and worked from 4 a.m. to 7:30 p.m., and they were charged for the dorm room.[34] In 1834, they went on strike because of a wage cut. Two years later, they again went on strike to protest a raise in their dorm charges. Each time, the women were unsuccessful in getting their demands met by factory management. Each time, the strike leaders were fired.

Looking at old photos of mill workers of the time, their faces, hands, and clothes dirty from work in the factories, one may be tempted to conclude that people of the 1800s were callous and brutish, accustomed to hard work and harsh conditions. Yet, these people shared the same needs, desires, and sensitivities as workers of today. For instance, 500 men and women petitioned the Amoskeag Manufacturing Company in New Hampshire not to cut down a beautiful elm tree to clear space for another mill.[35] These were not industrial robots; they were employees concerned about their health and work environment.

Political Response: Immigration and Antilabor Policies

Throughout the 1800s, the United States government continued to welcome more immigrants. This policy met industry's need not only for labor but for cheap labor. In the view of industrial leaders, worker wages were a cost of business that needed to be kept low. Thus, America welcomed millions of European immigrants to work in its expanding factory system, to compete with each other for jobs, thereby minimizing wage demands. During the 1880s, 5½ million immigrants arrived; in the 1890s, another 4 million made their way to the United States.[36]

Although promoting increases in the supply of labor, U.S. policy during the 1800s was antagonistic to the union movement. U.S. courts and political leaders tended to support the needs of industrial owners and management at the expense of the needs of common laborers.[37] Trade unions were considered by U.S. courts to be "conspiracies" to restrain trade, and thus illegal.[38] One judge in New York referred to trade unions as "artificial combinations" not needed in America. The judge believed foreigners to be primary supporters of the American union movement. (Given the millions of immigrants pouring into the United States to work in factories, the judge's perception represents a keen awareness of the obvious.)

During the Civil War, Union troops forced striking workers back to the mills.[39] African Americans were often used to break strikes by Irish workers in New York, fostering a racist competition between these groups. Similarly, the **Contract Labor Law of 1864** generated cheap labor with which to break strikes. The law allowed businesses to sign contracts with foreign workers. Under the agreement, the company paid the worker's cost of emigration in exchange for twelve months of labor. These aspiring workers were then used to replace existing factory workers.

After the Civil War, strikes and organizing continued by laborers in industries such as textiles, coal mining, steel, and the railroads.[40] Federal troops, meaning the U.S. infantry and/or national guard, were often called in to break up strikes. State militia and local police were also used. In some cases, like the 1892 strike at Andrew Carnegie's Homestead steel mill, the industrial leaders employed hundreds of armed Pinkerton guards, a private army for hire, to break the strike.[41] Both strikers and guards were killed in the Homestead strike, a particularly bloody labor war that lasted five months and ended only when government troops overwhelmed the strikers.

The result of these promanagement, antilabor policies was a national labor surplus, particularly during the frequent recessions.[42] During these economic downturns, the desperate economic competition among poor workers fostered racism and violence. But laborers continued to organize unions in an effort to promote the value of labor and defend their mutual interests in the new industrial system. As a sympathetic Abraham Lincoln stated at one point in his life:

> Labor is prior to, and independent of, capital. Capital is only the fruit of labor, and could never have existed if labor had not first existed. Labor is the superior of capital, and deserves much the higher consideration.[43]

Personal Profile: Mother Jones

Perhaps the most famous labor organizer in American history was a woman named Mary Harris Jones, better known as "Mother Jones."[44] She was an educated woman, graduating in 1859 from Toronto Normal School, a teacher's college. Yet, she only worked as a teacher for less than one year. Her real interest was helping poor workers—men, women, and children. After the death of her husband, a union organizer, and her four children from yellow fever in 1867, she moved to Chicago to become a dressmaker. She began to get more involved in the movement to organize labor, eventually participating in the

Pittsburgh railroad strike of 1877, the Haymarket Riot of 1886, and the Pull-man strike of 1894. She unofficially joined the Knights of Labor in 1879, be-cause they did not officially admit women. Jones gained respect and notoriety among union men for her great speaking skills and direct partici-pation in the dangerous strikes. Later, she was a leader in the organizing of the United Mine Workers and the Industrial Workers of the World.

Although much of her labor organizing involved miners, she also orga-nized the famous **March of the Mill Children** in 1903.[45] To protest the ex-ploitation of children in the workplace, she recruited an army of child laborers and led them in a march from Kensington, Pennsylvania, to Oyster Bay, New York, where President Theodore Roosevelt vacationed. The chil-dren held signs that read: "We want time to play." The following quote of Mother Jones might serve as an inspiration for social workers engaged in social advocacy: "Pray for the dead, but fight like hell for the living."[46]

The Antipauper Movement

Political Contributions: The Poorhouse and the Growth of Public Institutions

The nineteenth century was an era of epic events: westward expansion, the Civil War, immigration, and industrialization. It was also an era of great na-tional movements: the **Abolition Movement,** the Women's Rights Move-ment, the Temperance Movement, and the Antipauper Movement. The last movement of the century, the Antipauper Movement, is of special interest to social workers because much of the origin of the social work profession is found in the Antipauper Movement.

During the 1800s, immorality was still believed by many Americans to be the cause of individual poverty and other social problems such as alcohol-ism.[47] In some ways, this was a reasonable conclusion, given the major role of American churches in caring for the poor. Each profession has its perspec-tive and religion deals with morality. The lasting influence of Calvinism in Protestant America maintained that the poor were not working hard enough at God's calling. It was also a reasonable conclusion for many Americans, be-cause the nation, in contrast to Europe, offered many opportunities for rela-tively high-wage jobs and land ownership.

The **Second Great Awakening** began in America in the late 1780s, last-ing into the 1830s.[48] This second great Protestant religious revival, once again, rejected the Calvinist notion of predestination, the belief that personal salvation is gained only through the grace of God. With predestination, wealth and philanthropy were an indication that you were one of God's chosen people. In contrast, the Second Great Awakening preached that all people could be saved and that all Christians should practice benevolence.

This religious crusade, no doubt, had an influence on the great social movements that took place later in the 1800s, including the Antipauper Movement.[49] Helping to "save the poor" became a widespread responsibility.

The Antipauper Movement that eventually developed included an increase in the number of poorhouses.[50] According to historian Michael Katz, author of the social history *In the Shadow of the Poorhouse,* the American poorhouse had several goals.[51] One was to prevent starvation. A second goal was to deter pauperism. (Note that a **pauper** is one who is extremely poor, especially one dependent on public assistance or charity.) In so doing, a third goal, minimizing public relief costs, might be achieved. A fourth goal was to rehabilitate the poor person. Again, immorality, particularly in the case of apparently able-bodied paupers, was assumed to be the cause of their poverty. And a fifth goal was to prevent pauper children from becoming pauper adults.

Supporters of the poorhouse believed that all of the above goals with the possible exception of preventing starvation could be achieved better through a public institution like the poorhouse than through outdoor relief (i.e., home-based services).[52] To achieve these goals, the poorhouses combined religious instruction with work projects.[53] Women weaved garments. Men chopped wood and did various public works.

Yet, the fundamental philosophy underlying the poorhouse was flawed.[54] Like the public assistance programs of the twentieth century, the primary goals of the system were conflicted. That is, preventing starvation is an act of compassion, based on religious and ethical principles. In contrast, the goal of "deterring pauperism" required a punitive approach to service provision. Public relief needed to be an unattractive option to the workplace, based on the ongoing need of industrialism for labor and the concern of the general public for low taxes.

However, the belief in the merits of "indoor relief" led to an increase in the number of public institutions in the United States during the 1800s.[55] In addition, during this time, America's public institutions became more specialized. Previously, not only did the poorhouse serve unemployed but able-bodied people, it also housed people with mental illness and other disabilities. Older Americans, too old to work, and young children, too young to work, were also a part of the clientele at poorhouses.

Thus, the old poorhouse system contained many different people, reflecting the many different causes of poverty, not just immorality. The difficulty of meeting the needs of this varied a group became obvious to social reformers. Therefore, social advocates began to lobby government policymakers for more specialized institutions. These included separate institutions for people with mental illness, for criminals, for delinquent and neglected youth, and for the "deaf, dumb, and blind."[56]

There were several positive aspects of the growth of these specialized public institutions.[57] First, they separated people according to categorical needs. The indiscriminate public reliance on poorhouses for all needy people was ineffective and unethical. Second, more specialized rehabilitation services were developed. This included a rehabilitation approach to correctional facilities. Third, specialized public institutions, in many cases, were safer than the previous system. Vulnerable older people and poor children, for instance, were not mixed with criminals.

The negative aspects of these public institutions were not inherent in the system, but rather acquired over time due to political patronage and a lack of adequate public support.[58] More specifically, the administration of these public institutions was too often incompetent and corrupt. Hiring and contracts were often based on political patronage in contrast to professional expertise. At the same time, many institutions were chronically underfunded by government, which in turn contributed to a shortage of trained staff. Some state mental health institutions were intended to be located in beautiful rural areas with meditation, gardening, religious instruction, recreation, and work projects, but poor administration and funding prevented such quality. As a result, those with financial resources went to private facilities.

Personal Profile: Dorothea Dix

Dorothea Dix, another foremother of the social work profession, was born in Hampden, Maine, in 1802.[59] Her field research, publication, and legislative advocacy resulted in the founding or enlarging of thirty-two hospitals for people with mental illness.[60] At least some of the inspiration for her social advocacy derived from her own periodic physical and mental health problems. While teaching in Massachusetts in 1836, she suffered a nervous and physical collapse. Her doctor told her, if she did recover, she should never teach again.[61] Her interest in mental health services was furthered that very same year while vacationing in England when she became acquainted with Dr. Samuel Tuke, a mental health specialist.

On arriving back in the United States, Dorothea taught a Sunday School class in a Cambridge, Massachusetts, jail, where she discovered that most of the female convicts were mentally ill and living in horrible conditions.[62] That year, 1841, she began a remarkable crusade for better hospitals and prisons, beginning in Massachusetts with passage of the Massachusetts Hospital Bill in 1843.[63] She later traveled about 60,000 miles nationwide between 1843 and 1847 to directly observe public institutions and advocate for better conditions for those with mental illness. Her advocacy efforts culminated in the passage of federal legislation providing funding and millions of acres of land for the construction of more hospitals for people with mental illness.[64] The fundamental point of her advocacy was that people with mental illness needed medical care based in a humane setting and on the latest scientific information.[65]

Social Contributions: The Growth of Private Nonprofit Agencies

The 1800s also witnessed the growth of private nonprofit agencies to assist the needy. These voluntary efforts were an extension of the colonial role of the church in providing for the poor. During the early 1800s, business and professional leaders in New York (1817), Philadelphia (1817), Baltimore (1820), and Boston (1835) established a **Society for the Prevention of Pauperism** in their respective cities.[66] These organizations were noteworthy for their attempt to analyze the causes of pauperism and possible ways to prevent it. They also encouraged the use of **district visitors** to visit and advise poor families in each district of the city. After 1840, **provident associations** and associations to improve the condition of the poor employed similar strategies to help the poor.[67]

The **city mission movement,** which followed the Second Great Awakening, was another voluntary effort, dependent on philanthropy, and often inspired by religious beliefs.[68] In the mid-1800s, as the inner-city became more industrialized, the more established business and professional classes tended to relocate to the outskirts of the city, building new churches in their new neighborhoods. Recent immigrants were left in the old, poorer neighborhoods of the inner city. The city mission was a way for the wealthier families to reach out to these foreigners concentrated in the core of the city, fast becoming slums. The missions were often set up and funded by the wealthier churches. In contrast to these more established congregations, immigrant families were not expected to rent a pew in church or wear expensive clothes.

The city missions provided religious education and other services to poor, immigrant families.[69] Religious education included Sunday Schools for children. Teaching good Christian (read: Protestant) morals early was the nineteenth-century version of preventative care. Given the widespread belief that poverty was the result of immorality, it was the means by which to prevent future poverty and dependency. Alternative education classes were also established for very poor or unruly children. Other services of city missions typically included food, shelter, employment referrals, and for working women, child care. To this extent, the city missions were a forerunner of the later settlement houses established by social workers.

Personal Profile: Charles Loring Brace

Charles Loring Brace is perhaps the most famous city missionary in American history. Born in Litchfield, Connecticut, in 1826, Brace attended Yale and then studied theology, intending to become a preacher.[70] However, after touring Europe, he returned to New York to become a city missionary, working with homeless boys. Charles explained his decision to his father this way:

> If I am only a city missionary with $200 a year, or anything else mean, but really doing good, you should be contented. I want to raise up the outcast and homeless, to go down among those who have no friend or helper, and do something for them of what Christ has done for me.[71]

In 1853, he was asked to head a "mission to the children."[72] The new mission was called the **Children's Aid Society.** As part of the mission, Brace started an industrial school in the basement of a church for vagrant children.[73] In the following year, he established the Newsboys' Lodging House, a dorm-like house where homeless boys could get a bed, bath, and meal. He later opened similar services for girls.

Furthermore, Brace is most known for his **placing out** of homeless children with farmers and other families in western states.[74] This was an 1800s' version of foster care in that Brace typically retained guardianship of the children to deter possible abuse or neglect. Brace did a regular fund-raising canvass of various Protestant churches in New York City and throughout the country to support his efforts.

By 1872, in its twentieth year, the Children's Aid Society operated twenty-one industrial schools and fifteen night schools, serving about 9,000 children per year.[75] In addition, it served 12,000 boys and girls in its lodging houses and provided homes for 3,000 children. Brace later described the Children's Aid Society and his work as follows:

> The principles on which this charity was founded, thirty-three years ago, have been more and more confirmed by the experience of the leading nations. The ideas which we then preached to dull ears are now received cordially in this country, in England, and on the continent of Europe. They have become a part of the settled principles of the century. These were: the absolute necessity of treating each youthful criminal or outcast as an individual, and not as one of a crowd; the immense superiority of the home or family over any institution in reformatory and educational influence; the prevention of crime and pauperism by early efforts with the children, and the vital importance of breaking up inherited pauperism by putting almshouse children in separate homes, and most of all, the immense advantage of 'placing out' neglected and orphan children in farmers' families.[76]

Other organizations founded during the century, in addition to denomination services such as Catholic charities, included the YMCA in 1851, the YWCA in 1866, the Salvation Army in 1880, and the American Red Cross in 1881.[77] The YMCA, in particular, was well supported by local businessmen, many of whom, no doubt, had used its services in making the earlier transition from rural areas to the city.[78]

The Development of Charity Organization Societies

As these private nonprofit organizations began to proliferate, members of the business and professional class increasingly felt that the entire health and human service system needed to be more professionally run, based on the latest information in the social sciences.[79] In so doing, these groups began to challenge a health and human service system primarily based on religion. Where philanthropy had been inspired by religious beliefs related to personal salvation, in the latter half of the 1800s, business and professional leaders began to see philanthropy as a matter of social responsibility and enlightened self-interest. If the American system of democracy and capitalism was to continue to flourish, upper-income groups needed to assume more civic responsibility. Wealthy industrialists needed to give something back to the community. The "haves" needed to give to the "have-nots." And it all needed to be done more effectively and efficiently. Thus, philanthropy became more secular and the health and human service system began to reflect a secular humanism not seen in earlier times.

This call for more professionalism in health and human services was also part of a trend in government, where business and professional groups were growing increasingly critical of government run by political patronage.[80] Patronage, which also effected public relief services, was considered to be filled with fraud, and, therefore, a waste of taxes. It was also thought to lead to a sense of entitlement from the perspective of the poor, which concerned community leaders worried about the mounting costs of public poor relief.[81] Instead of people receiving jobs or services based on their political support at election time, these critics called for a more professional system based on technical expertise, empirical information, and rational planning. Like Dorothea Dix and state mental health hospitals, other health and human services needed to be predicated on the latest scientific information. Thus, philanthropy became more scientific, and health and humans services began to reflect the concept of **scientific philanthropy.**[82]

Charity organization societies, based on scientific philanthropy, began to emerge to better coordinate and deliver services to the needy. Buffalo, New York, gets credit for the first official American charity organization society. It was started there in 1877 by the Reverend S. Humphrey Gurteen, who had visited the London Charity Organization Society.[83] To better inform the public, Gurteen authored the *Handbook of Community Organization*, which offered practical advice on establishing charity organization societies.[84]

Although Gurteen imported the concept from Europe, the founding and growth of the charity organization societies in America were the result of a partnership among business and professional leaders in urban communities.[85] For instance, the New York Charity Organization Society, headed by Josephine Shaw Lowell, the most prominent American writer on scientific charity, listed among its supporters such noted business leaders as William Waldorf Astor, Andrew Carnegie, J. P. Morgan, and Mrs. Cornelius Vanderbilt. In fact, local business leaders often served as trustees on the boards of the charity organization societies. Historian Walter Trattner quotes one (unidentified) enthusiast: the "same wisdom which has given this generation its wonderful industrial capacity will preside over the administration of charity."[86]

Did You Know?

To solicit support for his Charity Organization Society in Buffalo, the Reverend Gurteen compared society's indiscriminate giving to paupers to a growing monster, a Frankenstein no less, that might evoke sympathy, but would eventually destroy its maker (in this case, society).[87]

Aiming to be more scientific, professional, and business-like, the charity organization societies emphasized individual needs assessment, case histories, case conferences, service referrals, interviewing skills, as well as community service coordination.[88] The point about service coordination needs to be emphasized. In the beginning at least, these organizations did not directly deliver services.[89] Instead, they provided a community organization function for the many direct service agencies in the community. To accomplish this role, the charity organization societies kept a registry of relief applicants, a history of services provided to various individuals and families, and a list of the many health and human services. After collecting information on the relief applicant, a referral to an appropriate agency was then made.

Friendly visitors, primarily female volunteers from the business and professional classes, did home visits to investigate and document family needs.[90] This was to cut down on indiscriminate giving, which was thought to promote idleness, destroy character, and lead to poverty. In contrast to impulsive, emotional giving, the goal of this more rational philanthropy was to "restore the recipient of charity to the dignity of as much self-sufficiency and personal responsibility as he could manage."[91]

During the home visits, friendly visitors aimed to establish a personal relationship with the family. This personal service is in contrast to the old poorhouse and jail system, which were often just warehousing the needy in neglectful and inhumane conditions. It was also hoped by members of the business and professional community that a personal connection between the rich and poor would better class relations, given the rising popularity of socialism and communism during the Industrial Revolution.[92]

Furthermore, home visits allowed the volunteer to collect information on the individual needs of the family and set up a case conference with other civic-minded leaders from the community.[93] These case conferences allowed community leaders to better determine what services were required by the individual. At the same time, the conferences enabled business and professional leaders to identify and fund services needed in the community.

Home-based service also allowed the friendly visitor to do role modeling of appropriate behavior for various reasons, some related to health and safety, some related to morality.[94] However, in contrast to previous forms of relief such as the city missions and organizations such as the Salvation Army, the charity organization societies aimed to separate health and human services from religion.[95] At this point in American history, being simply moralistic, as the friendly visitors were, yet not requiring a religious conversion to receive aid was another step toward professionalization.

In retrospect, charity organization societies had their negative characteristics.[96] At its worst, the friendly visitor approach was essentially middle- and upper-income people telling poor immigrants the right way to live, while providing little or no material relief. In addition, friendly visitors were not only friendly role models but investigators determining the deserving and undeserving poor. As such, they probably felt like spies to some immigrant families. In any case, the charity organization societies had difficulty finding enough volunteers to fill the role of friendly visitor. They also seemed to be better at managing than eradicating or preventing poverty, and were, therefore, attacked by American socialist and communist critics as irrelevant.

A Critique of Charity Organization Societies

Some critics might claim that the charity organization societies were the "managed care" of the late 1800s. The societies emphasized relief of a short duration and cost containment. In this case, cost containment came in the form of determining those deserving and undeserving of assistance, preventing duplication of community services, and, in general, keeping the cost of poor relief as low as possible. Were the charity organization societies too cold and business-like or just practical and efficient, given limited community resources?

Be that as it may, charity organization societies certainly were an improvement over the old poorhouse system and helped to professionalize American health and human services. The origin of the profession of social work, in part at least, can be traced to the charity organization societies, which pioneered in the development of casework and community organization in the health and human services. Ironically, their emphasis on research, documentation, and technical skills led to the conclusion that part-time volunteers were not adequate. As a result, charity organization societies later helped to establish professional social work education programs at such universities as Indiana University, Ohio State, Bryn Mawr, the University of Minnesota, and Columbia University.[97] These societies also helped initiate the growth of Community Chests, the predecessor of the modern United Way system.[98]

CONTENTSELECT

For more information on related social work topics, use the following search terms:

Abolition Movement
Charity organization societies
Children's Aid Society
City mission movement
Contract Labor Law of 1864

District visitors
Friendly visitors
March of the Mill Children
Pauper
Placing Out

Scientific philanthropy
Second Great Awakening
Society for the Prevention of
    Pauperism
Temperance Movement

NOTES

1. S. L. Mayer, "Forging a Nation: 1866–1900," Arthur M. Schlesinger, Jr., ed., *The Almanac of American History* (New York: Barnes & Noble, 1993), p. 302.

2. Ron Chernow, *Titan: The Life of John D. Rockefeller, Sr.* (New York: Vintage Books, 1999), p. 71.

3. Mayer, p. 303.

4. Ron Chernow, pp. 98–99.

5. Mayer, p. 302.

6. Paul Johnson, *A History of the American People* (New York: HarperPerennial, 1999), pp. 532–533.

7. Mayer, p. 300.

8. Jean Strouse, *Morgan: American Financier* (New York: HarperPerennial, 2000), p. 215.

9. Ibid., p. 636.

10. Mayer, p. 300.

11. Johnson, pp. 531–532; Mayer, p. 303.

12. Mayer, p. 303.

13. Chernow, p. 78.

14. Ibid., p. 132.

15. Ibid., pp. 132, 297.

16. Johnson, p. 532.

17. Mayer, p. 303.

18. Matthew Josephson, *The Robber Barons* (New York: Harcourt Brace, 1962), p. 41.

19. Ibid., pp. 42, 103.

20. Carnegie quote in Josephson, p. 42.

21. Ibid., p. 80.

22. Ibid., pp. 361–362.

23. Strouse, p. 24.

24. Howard Zinn, *A People's History of the United States: 1492–Present* (New York: HarperPerennial, 1995), p. 220.

25. Strouse, pp. 73–74; Zinn, p. 222.

26. Zinn, p. 235.

27. Ibid., pp. 235, 240.

28. Josephson, p. 362.

29. Ibid., pp. 362–363.

30. Zinn, pp. 224–225.

31. Josephson, p. 364.

32. Zinn, p. 230.

33. Ibid., p. 223.

34. Ibid., pp. 223–224.

35. Ibid., p. 224.

36. Ibid., p. 261.

37. Josephson, p. 367.

38. Zinn, p. 218.

39. Ibid., pp. 230, 233.

40. Zinn, p. 241; Josephson, p. 370.

41. Josephson, pp. 370–371.

42. Zinn, p. 261.

43. Lincoln quoted in Loewen, *Lies My Teacher Told Me* (New York: Touchstone, 1996), p. 200.

44. Judith Nies, *Seven Women: Portraits from the American Radical Tradition* (New York: The Viking Press, 1977), pp. 98–105.

45. Ibid., p. 111.

46. Ibid., p. vii.

47. Bruce S. Jansson, *The Reluctant Welfare State: American Social Welfare Policies—Past, Present, and Future* (Pacific Grove, CA: Brooks/Cole, 1997), pp. 66, 68–69.

48. Michael B. Katz, *In the Shadow of the Poorhouse: A Social History of Welfare in America,* 10th ed. (New York: BasicBooks, 1996), p. 62.

49. Jansson, p. 63.

50. Ibid., p. 67.

51. Katz, pp. 23–24.

52. Ibid., p. 23.

53. Jansson, p. 67.

54. Katz, pp. 33.

55. Jansson, p. 69.

56. Ibid., pp. 69–70.

57. Ibid., p. 71.

58. Ibid., pp. 71–72.

59. Harriet Sigerman, *Biographical Supplement and Index,* Nancy F. Cott, ed. *The Young Oxford History of Women in the United States,* vol. 2 (New York: Oxford University Press, 1995), p. 50.

60. James Leiby, *A History of Social Welfare and Social Work in the United States* (New York: Columbia University Press, 1978), p. 67; Helen E. Marshall, *Dorothea Dix: Forgotten Samaritan* (Chapel Hill, NC: University of North Carolina Press, 1937), p. 245.

61. Marshall, p. 48.

62. Ibid., pp. 53, 60–62.

63. Ibid., pp. 95–99.

64. Ibid., pp. 130–148.

65. Leiby, p. 68.

66. Ibid., pp. 43–44.

67. Leiby, p. 112; Walter I. Trattner, *From Poor Law to Welfare State: A History of Social Welfare in America,* 6th ed. (New York: The Free Press, 1999), p. 93.

68. Leiby, pp. 76–77.

69. Ibid., p. 77.

70. Emma Brace, *The Life of Charles Loring Brace: Chiefly Told in His Own Letters* (New York: Charles Scribner's Sons, 1894), pp. 1, 8, 34, 154.

71. Brace, pp. 153–154.

72. Ibid., p. 156.

73. Ibid., pp. 166–169, 186, 252.

74. Brace, pp. 172–173; Leiby, pp. 83–84.

75. Brace, p. 328.

76. Ibid., p. 432.

77. Michael O'Neill, *The Third America: The Emergence of the Nonprofit Sector in the United States* (San Francisco: Jossey-Bass, 1989), p. 101; Leiby, pp. 78, 159.

78. Leiby, p. 78.

79. Trattner, p. 91; Leiby, pp. 90–93.

80. Leiby, pp. 90–93.

81. Trattner, p. 90.

82. Leiby, p. 114.

83. Leiby, p. 114; Trattner, p. 92.

84. Katz, p. 75.

85. Katz, p. 78; Leiby, pp. 90–91, 117; Trattner, pp. 94–95.

86. Trattner, p. 94.

87. Katz, pp. 76–77.

88. Katz, p. 78; Leiby, p. 115.

89. Jansson, p. 139; Trattner, p. 93.

90. Jansson, p. 139.

91. Leiby, p. 114.

92. Trattner, p. 93.

93. Leiby, p. 115.

94. Jansson, p. 139.

95. Leiby, p. 114.

96. Katz, pp. 79, 83–85.

97. Jansson, p. 140.

98. Eleanor Brilliant, *The United Way: Dilemmas of Organized Charity* (New York: Columbia, 1990), p. 19.

6

American Social Policy During the Progressive Era

Grace and Edith Abbott were progressive reformers and pioneer social workers.

The Economic Context

The Growth of Giant American Corporations

The period in American history from about 1900 to 1920 is known as the **Progressive Era** (although there is no precise beginning and end to the era).[1] It was a time of major reforms in the economic, political, and social institutions of the nation. The Adam Smith model of a capitalist economy based on small business competition was increasingly overshadowed by the influence of large-scale industry. The enormous industrial growth that followed the Civil War featured unregulated competition among individual entrepreneurs based on the ideology of Social Darwinism—survival of the fittest.[2] Yet, as the nineteenth century came to an end, many liberal reformers believed that American institutions needed better coordination, collaboration—even regulation. These reformers, firsthand witnesses to the Industrial Revolution, came to understand both the positive and negative social welfare aspects of an industrial economy.[3] To better promote social welfare, new, more civic-minded organizations needed to be created. Social cooperation needed to supplement individual initiative and competition. In the end, Progressive reformers were remarkably successful in achieving these objectives.

The industrialization of America, as previously stated, held both positive and negative outcomes for social welfare in America. In the decade of the 1880s, the value of manufacturing output in the United States almost doubled, growing from about $5 billion to $9 billion. By 1900, the United States was the undisputed industrial power of the world.[4] The mass production of food in the Chicago stockyards amazed the rest of the world.[5] Between 1875, when Andrew Carnegie opened his new million-dollar steel mill, and 1890, steel production in the United States increased fifty fold. By 1916, businessmen such as Cornelius Vanderbilt, E. H. Harriman, and Leland Stanford had built 254,000 miles of railroads, a national transportation system that represented one-third of the world's total railroad system.[6] At the same time, John D. Rockefeller's Standard Oil Company, one of the world's first multinational corporations, supplied 90 percent of the oil used in the United States and 80 percent of the world's supply.[7]

These business leaders were not the only ones to profit from this industrial growth, although they certainly profited the most. Workers and consumers benefited as well. Millions of unskilled European immigrants continued to come to the United States, taking jobs in these giant industries. By 1920, the railroads alone employed over 2 million workers.[8] Although factory work was miserable, wages were generally higher in America than Europe.[9] In addition, the United States offered a greater possibility to the worker of eventually transitioning from the factory to their own business or farm. At any rate, American workers experienced significant increases in their real incomes (i.e., inflation-adjusted) and standard of living during the late 1800s and early 1900s.[10]

Furthermore, mass production often resulted in lower prices for American consumers. For example, from the time Rockefeller's Standard Oil Company incorporated in 1870 until 1890, the price of kerosene used in heating and lighting dropped from 23.5 to 7.5 cents per gallon.[11] Due in part to increased mechanization and mass production, food also dropped in price, while becoming more diverse and plentiful for consumers.[12] Mass production of farm machinery by businessmen such as Cyrus McCormick (reaper) and John Deere (plow) greatly increased agricultural productivity. Many successful business owners, people such as the Armour brothers and Adolphus Busch, also found better ways to use farm and ranch products in mass-producing consumer goods.

A Critical Analysis of Government and the Railroads

As discussed, the railroads played a central role in the development of the new nation. Business leaders such as Cornelius Vanderbilt, E. H. Harriman, and Leland Stanford became millionaires while developing this national transportation system. Yet, the federal and state government heavily subsidized these business owners. That is, the railroad companies received huge tracts of land at no or low cost from the public sector in building these railroads.[13] The business sector cannot take total credit for this national development. It was a public–private collaboration that illustrates the positive role that government can play in the United States. That said, what about those who claim that government is a necessary evil? Is it true that government does nothing well? Is it wise to limit the federal government to roles such as national security? Can you think of other roles that government must play to effectively promote social welfare—roles not lucrative enough for business and too complex for voluntary associations?

Populations at Risk

The high standard of living of the United States compared to the rest of the world at the beginning of the twentieth century cannot be taken for granted. Private, for-profit organizations in the economic sector contributed undeniably to American social welfare. Yet, the presidential election of 1912 trumpeted the call for reform.[14] Theodore Roosevelt, essentially splitting the Republican vote with William Howard Taft, ran for president at the head of a reform party, the Progressive Party, comprising reformers, social workers, feminists, intellectuals, sympathetic businessmen, and Republicans loyal to

Roosevelt. The Democrats also ran a reform candidate, Woodrow Wilson. Although the Democrats won the election, even the Socialist candidate, Eugene Debbs, did well, attracting nearly 900,000 votes.[15] Clearly, reform was in vogue!

Did You Know?

This was the campaign in which Theodore Roosevelt, on his way to make a speech, was shot by a would-be assassin in the rib, the bullet stopping close to his right lung.[16] Apparently feeling well enough to make the speech anyway, Roosevelt proceeded to make an hour and a half speech before going to the hospital. This effort was from a man who suffered from bronchial asthma all his life.[17]

Social reformers documented many problems in America. Poverty existed, and not just among laborers in industrialized regions of the country. In fact, historian James Patterson, in his study of poverty in America, states that the highest incidence of poverty in America at the time was found in the agricultural economy of the southern states.[18] Yet, much of the reform of the Progressive Era targeted the poverty-related problems of industrial centers.

Decent housing for poor industrial laborers, for example, was a major social problem during the Progressive Era. At the time, the poorer neighborhoods of the largest industrial cities, places such as New York's Lower East Side, had the most crowded conditions in the world.[19] To illustrate, the Lower East Side of New York City contained 330,000 people per square mile, compared with 175,000 people per square mile in London at its worst. According to the famous social worker and eyewitness Jane Addams, industrial cities such as Chicago had grown so fast that much of the housing when built was considered temporary, and, therefore, of poor quality.[20] However, as it turned out, poor families lived for years in these dwellings, sometimes several families crowded into housing meant for single families. Many tenements were wooden and had no fire escapes. Sometimes the only running water was a backyard faucet. Garbage was piled in boxes located in the streets, where young children played. There were few, if any, housing codes.

What is more, Addams, in her book *Twenty Years at Hull-House,* tells of the unhealthy tenement activities of immigrant families, many of them from rural European regions and unused to city living.[21] Some slaughtered sheep in their basements; others sorted rags retrieved from city dumps; still others baked bread beneath the pavement of filthy city streets.

In addition to unhealthy living conditions, new problems associated with the mass production of food were discovered. Upton Sinclair, in his influential 1905 book about the Chicago stockyards entitled *The Jungle,* vividly alerted the public to the problem of food impurities due to the use of diseased cattle, illegal animals, and other foreign matter in the mass production of meat products.

> Up to a year or two ago it had been the custom to kill horses in the yards—ostensibly for fertilizer; but after long agitation the newspaper had been able to make the public realize that the horses were being canned. Now it was against the law to kill horses in Packingtown, and the law was really complied with—for the present, at any rate. Any day, however, one might see sharp-horned and shaggy-haired creatures running with the sheep—and yet what a job you would have to get the public to believe that a good part of what it buys for lamb and mutton is really goat's flesh![22]

The harsh and dangerous working conditions in slaughterhouses, other factories, and various mines continued to be a social problem as the 1800s came to an end. Based on the **scientific management** of the day, work projects were reduced to simple, repetitive tasks that any unskilled immigrant could learn quickly.[23] And it was still common to see a worker repeat the same simple task for twelve hours, six days per week. These long hours doing repetitive work with dangerous machinery contributed to many industrial accidents. To illustrate, 35,000 workers were killed and 700,000 injured in industrial accidents in 1914.[24] This is not to mention those left permanently disabled. Jane Addams tells of her experience in Chicago:

> During the same winter three boys from a Hull-House club were injured at one machine in a neighboring factory for lack of a guard which would have cost but a few dollars. When the injury of one of these boys resulted in his death, we felt quite sure that the owners of the factory would share our horror and remorse, and that they would do everything possible to prevent the recurrence of such a tragedy. To our surprise they did nothing whatever, and I made my first acquaintance then with those pathetic documents signed by the parents of working children, that they will make no claim for damages resulting from "carelessness."[25]

As indicated by the preceding passage, the use of child labor in dangerous factory settings also became a public issue during the Progressive Era. Some children worked as many as eighty hours per week in U.S. factories.[26] Most were only between the ages of 10 and 15. What is more, many of these children worked for years in these factories while turning over most, if not all, of their wages to their parents.[27] Again, Upton Sinclair provides an excellent illustration, this time of the bleak, mind-numbing factory work done by an immigrant youth:

> [A man at the packing plant] showed the lad how to place a lard can every time the empty arm of the remorseless machine came to him; and so was

decided the place in the universe of little Stanislovas, and his destiny till the end of his days. Hour after hour, day after day, year after year, it was fated that he should stand upon a certain square foot of floor from seven in the morning until noon, and again from half-past twelve till half-past five, making never a motion and thinking never a thought, save for the setting of lard cans.[28]

Harsh as factory conditions were, the alternative for most immigrant families was unemployment and poverty, while their children slipped into juvenile delinquency as members of turn-of-the-century street gangs. Note, though, that it was increasingly difficult to blame many of these social problems on the individual. Although individual immorality was still associated by community leaders with social problems such as prostitution, alcoholism, and gambling, issues such as impure food, unsafe housing, and dangerous factories were increasingly viewed during the Progressive Era as institutional failures, as problems in the environment of the individual.[29]

Political Context

Political Machines and the Patronage System

The political patronage system in the United States was also perceived by Progressive Era reformers to be a problem. **Political patronage** was a distributive system where political parties provided jobs and services to individuals in return for the individual's political support.[30] Such patronage was particularly evident in the major urban areas in the East and Midwest. In these areas, sophisticated political organizations, called **political machines,** aggressively pursued the support of new immigrants. In so doing, local politicians became familiar with the needs of individual families in the district. A social exchange[31] took place where needy immigrants, thankful for the help of local politicians, voted to keep their benefactors in office. Continued political support by the immigrants led to further favors by elected officials. These "favors" included food baskets on holidays, money for a casket or wedding, contracts for public construction projects, government jobs, or leads to jobs in the business sector.[32]

The positive view of political patronage as practiced in the United States in the late 1800s and early 1900s emphasized its social welfare aspect. The millions of poor immigrants in the major industrial cities needed assistance getting established—at times, even surviving. The major political parties, especially the Democrats, provided this assistance, often in a timely manner before other sources of support responded, if at all. A spokesperson for **Tammany Hall,** the famous New York political machine, described the support this way:

If a family is burned out, I don't ask whether they are Republicans or Democrats, and I don't refer them to the Charity Organization Society, which
would investigate their case in a month or two and decide they were worthy
of help about the time they are dead from starvation. I just get quarters for
them, buy clothes for them if their clothes were burned up, and fix them up
until they get runnin' again. It's philanthropy, but it's politics, too—mighty
good politics.[33]

Political patronage, though, was not confined to the big industrial cities. It took place at the national level as well. In fact, while in office in the
early 1860s, Abraham Lincoln scheduled time each week to talk with a succession of people seeking jobs and other favors.[34] And Theda Skocpol, a
noted Harvard sociologist, emphasizes the fact that federal pensions for
Civil War veterans and their families became a patronage prize for both
Democrats and Republicans in Congress, resulting in ever-expanding program costs.[35]

Social reformers of the Progressive Era, therefore, grew increasingly
concerned with fraud, abuse, and escalating costs associated with patronage
politics.[36] These reformers, many of them middle- and upper-income members of business and professional groups, frequently cited public outdoor
relief at the local level (i.e., local government aid outside of institutions) and
soldiers' pensions at the federal level as illustrations of the negative consequences of patronage. Stories such as New York City politicians paying close
to $200,000 for three tables and forty chairs fueled the incentive for reform.[37]

The Social Response

Progressive Reform

The Progressive Era social reformers, viewing themselves as political moder-
ates, addressed the previously described social problems primarily through
government regulation.[38] In contrast to the Populist Movement of the 1890s
that advocated for farmers in the Midwest and South, the Progressive
agenda focused mostly on urban issues. In addition, much of the reform took
place at the state and local level.

Progressive reformers did not advocate for a great deal of federally
funded social services because they feared that federal relief programs
would be used by national political parties as patronage prizes, much the
way Civil War pensions had been used to attract and reward voters.[39] These
pensions had become a kind of social security program for soldiers and their
families with ever-expanding benefits. Middle- and upper-class reformers of
the Progressive Era did not trust that spending on other federal social programs would not escalate also, due to the corruption of patronage-oriented

political parties and the lack of professionally trained public administrators in Washington, DC. In fact, the federal government of the United States at the time was very small by European standards. Social reformers did not feel that the federal government bureaucracy could fairly and efficiently manage nationwide social services.

Progressive Era activists, therefore, used government regulations to pursue social change. One set of reforms involved safety regulation.[40] Fire codes were passed to address unsafe housing in urban neighborhoods. Upton Sinclair's influential writing led to the passage in 1906 of the Meat Inspection Act and the Pure Food and Drug Act.[41] And increasingly, work conditions at factories were regulated.

Furthermore, by 1923, fifteen states and the District of Columbia had passed minimum wage laws for women workers, and by 1921, forty-one states had instituted or improved laws that regulated the maximum number of hours that female workers were allowed to work per day.[42] One of the social issues at the time was that young women were jeopardizing their health and safety by working all night in factories, and then instead of sleeping, doing housework during the day.[43]

Another major area of reform focused on political patronage. Concerns about America's patronage democracy led to advocacy for greater professionalization and citizen participation in government.[44] As opposed to the patronage system of exchanging government jobs for votes, social reformers called for the increased use of a civil service system of government employment based on professional merit.[45] At the federal level, the Pendleton Civil Service Act was passed in 1883. The legislation established a commission that began the process of filling civil servant jobs based on merit.

Increased regulation of so-called morality issues was also part of the Progressive agenda.[46] That is, social reformers during the Progressive Era continued to believe that some social problems were caused by character deficits and immorality. As a result, many local governments began to place restrictions on gambling, prostitution, and alcohol sales.

Social reformers also took on the corporations during this period of increased activism.[47] As discussed earlier, business leaders in the 1800s faced few government regulations in the competition for industrial supremacy. However, as the capitalistic game unfolded, journalists began to publicize the growing power of big industry over the little guy—the small business owner and the common laborer. Journalists such as Ida Tarbell began to feature stories in magazines on the ways business leaders had built their industrial empires, emphasizing business practices that seemed unfair and unethical to the general public.[48]

To counter the growing power of corporations in America, the federal government passed legislation to regulate banking and industry. The Sherman Antitrust Act, for example, was passed in 1890 to regulate business monopoly and promote free competition. (The legislation, however, was initially ineffective due to weak support from several presidents and the Supreme Court.)[49] In addition, the Federal Reserve Act was passed in 1913. This act established regional reserves of money in the U.S. banking system.[50] Other legislation established the **Federal Trade Commission** in 1915 to further regulate anticompetitive practices by corporations.[51]

Social work was also impacted by the Progressive agenda. Reformers of the era called for increased licensing and accreditation of professions such as medicine, law, and nursing.[52] In accordance with the times, the New York Charity Organization Society started a summer training course in 1898, an initiative that led to the development of the New York School of Philanthropy, which later became the Columbia University Graduate School of Social Work.

Did You Know?

Before the Progressive reform movement, many medical schools in the United States were considered "diploma mills."[53] Just 23 of the 155 medical schools in 1910 required more than a high school diploma for admission. Some did not even require a diploma. A research report funded by the Carnegie Foundation for the Advancement of Teaching uncovered the problem, and donations from John D. Rockefeller did much to upgrade the quality of medical education in America.

The Progressive reformers, although primarily focused on regulation, did institute a limited number of government social programs. **Workmen's compensation,** for instance, was adopted in most states by 1920.[54] This legislation was the product of a coordinated effort on the part of various groups. That is, the reform had broad support not only from workers and social advocates but also from business leaders. Workers sought quicker settlements and more adequate compensation for injuries. At the same time, business leaders wanted to mitigate the high legal costs and rising insurance premiums resulting from the law suits of individual workers. Thus, this coalition of stakeholders in individual states across the country was able to successfully advocate for and pass workmen's compensation laws.

Between 1911 and 1919, most states also enacted **mother's pensions.**[55] These pensions, a forerunner of Aid to Dependent Children, provided money to poor, single mothers to help them in caring for their children. Although usually not a requirement of the legislation, most single mothers at this point in history were, in fact, widows. The alternative to mothers' pensions, reformers argued, was foster care, orphanages, or unsupervised children roaming the streets. Jane Addams, the settlement house activist, supported the concept of mother's pensions, but most social workers and other charity leaders initially opposed the proposal.[56] There were several reasons for this opposition, one being the general Progressive Era aversion to public spending on outdoor relief. Another reason concerned professional "turf" in that support for widows and children had traditionally been the domain of private agencies. Furthermore, Mary Richmond, the charity organization society spokesperson, opposed mother's pensions, because she did not want to confuse "pensions" with "relief." That said, supporters of the legislation felt the benefits outweighed the potential costs of the program.

Social reformers in the Progressive Era successfully advocated for other services that benefited women and children. Based on a recommendation made at the 1909 White House Conference on Child Dependency, the **Children's Bureau** was established in 1912.[57] Although it did not provide much funding for direct services, the Bureau did conduct research and disseminate information on women's health and child development. Key issues addressed by the bureau included child labor, infant mortality, birth rates, child diseases, and juvenile courts. In addition, the Children's Bureau successfully advocated for the passage of the Sheppard-Towner Infancy and Maternal Protection Act, an act that created federally subsidized maternal health information clinics.[58] Public health nurses provided much of the information and basic services of the clinics. (Recognizing the social work aspects of the job, many of these nurses took courses in schools of social welfare.)

In addition to these government services, activists in the Progressive Era created many of the most well-known nonprofit agencies in the United States today.[59] These voluntary organizations included many health and human services: Goodwill Industries (1902), Big Brothers (1903), the Boys Clubs of America (1906), the YWCA (1906), Big Sisters (1908), the Boy Scouts (1910), the Camp Fire Girls (1910), and the Girl Scouts (1912).

The Social Advocacy of Women and the Settlement Houses

The driving force behind much reform during the Progressive Era was the grassroots political advocacy of women.[60] Discouraged from official roles in government, women increasingly influenced government by creating significant roles for themselves in the private nonprofit sector. That is, through creation of their own voluntary associations, women effectively advocated for social changes of relevance to themselves. In addition to some of the nonprofit organizations just listed, the General Federation of Women's Clubs (founded in 1890) was a national advocacy network, starting at the local community level, which was very influential in passing many of the reforms of the Progressive Era. The **National Congress of Mothers,** started in 1897, was another advocacy organization heavily involved in reform efforts during the Progressive Era. This organization later became the well-known Parent–Teacher Association or PTA.

Of most interest to social workers was the community organizing and social advocacy of the various **settlement houses.** The first settlement house, Toynbee Hall in London, England, was a residence for Oxford University men in a poor section of the city. Run by an Anglican priest, the Rev. Samuel Barnett, this "settlement in the slums" was an outpost from which to teach students social responsibility in accordance with Christian social ideals.[61]

Using Toynbee Hall as a model, American settlement houses were private nonprofit organizations, established in poor, inner-city neighborhoods to promote the social welfare of community residents. In cities such as New York and Chicago, the vast majority of these residents were poor immigrants. Women—including several famous social workers—became the dominant force in American settlements, eventually comprising 70 percent of settlement residents.[62] Jane Addams, Edith Abbott, and Grace Abbott were all settlement house residents who became identified as social workers. Although often inspired by religious conviction, settlement leaders moved beyond their city mission predecessors to further emphasize scientific methods.

During the Progressive Era, the settlement houses became prominent leaders in social research and advocacy. Although the first American settlement house was established in 1886 in New York, the most famous early settlements were Chicago's **Hull House,** founded by Jane Addams and Ellen Starr in 1889, and New York City's **Henry Street Settlement,** established by Lillian Wald in 1895.[63] (Because Lillian Wald was a nurse, the Henry Street Settlement was initially called the Nurse's Settlement.) By 1900, there were 100 settlement houses in existence.[64] Ten years later, about 400 settlements were operating in the United States.

These settlement houses (along with social work educators such as Eduard Lindeman)[65] were significant influences on the community organization and group work methods in the emerging profession of social work. Like charity organization societies of the time, settlement houses were founded on the principle of scientific philanthropy. Observation, information gathering (or in today's terms, "data collection"), and documentation were believed to be prerequisites to social advocacy and change. In fact, residence, research, and reform were the three "Rs" of settlement house work.[66] While acknowledging the worth of the individual, for the most part, settlement leaders targeted their reform efforts on the social environment of immigrant neighborhoods in the large industrial cities. In so doing, their goal was the prevention of poverty and class conflict while promoting the health and welfare of industrial communities.

Leaders of the settlement houses criticized the casework approach of charity organization societies for not being more social reform-minded. Yet, radicals in the labor movement considered the settlement houses to be too conservative in terms of social reform.[67] Settlement leaders such as Jane Addams accepted the capitalist base of the American industrial system. After all, life in the United States was better for most immigrants than the life they left in Europe.[68] The settlement houses, therefore, aimed to promote social integration, facilitating the functioning of immigrant groups as they adapted to industrial life. Where radicals in the Socialist and Communist Parties emphasized the struggle among classes, settlement leaders, for the most part, encouraged cooperation among classes in promoting social welfare.[69] Addams, for one, believed that the most effective anecdote to rapid and disorganized industrial growth was better coordination among key community stakeholders. In short, the mission of the settlements was to make the existing system better, not to replace it.

Although there was variation among settlement houses, the reader might be surprised at the range of activities organized at some settlements. Hull House, the most prominent example, first started a kindergarten, which helped to establish a positive relationship with immigrant parents and children in the neighborhood.[70] The kindergarten was followed by a public kitchen, called a "coffee house," and a gymnasium, adapted from a former saloon.[71] Due to the limited amount of activity space in the crowded urban neighborhoods, settlements such as Hull House were particularly valued by immigrants as a space to hold club meetings, public discussions, lectures, dances, and other social activities. As a result, Hull House became the social center of the neighborhood, constantly filled with activity. Eventually, other services were added including a "boarding club" for young women, a nursery, and a post office branch.[72] In fact, services commonly found at the settlement houses around the United States included employment referral, visiting nurses, arts and crafts courses, libraries, penny savings banks, art galleries, and music halls.[73]

In providing space for various clubs, lectures, and public discussions, the settlement house workers were able to see and hear the needs of the various neighborhood immigrant groups. Settlement workers at Hull House, for instance, spent much time advocating for needy individuals.[74] This made the settlements attractive sites for young professionals interested in social research and advocacy, especially young, well-educated women wanting a socially significant career. The medical research of physician and Hull House resident, Dr. Alice Hamilton, examined the spread of typhoid in the tenement buildings.[75] Hamilton and Florence Kelley, a lawyer and fellow Hull House resident, were also active in industrial research, and consequently, the fight for occupational disease laws, eight-hour workday maximums for women, and labor restrictions for children. Consistent with the settlement philosophy, careful research typically preceded the call for reform.

Thus, settlement leaders became active in the various social reforms of the Progressive Era. Given the significant amount of social legislation passed during the Progressive Era, the community organization and social advocacy efforts of settlement house leaders must be considered a success.[76] Yet, settlement leaders were aware of their limitations as voluntary charitable organizations.[77] Leaders such as Jane Addams recognized the importance of coordinated effort among various community stakeholders, both public and private, in promoting social welfare. In fact, settlement houses served as a means of communication among various groups.[78] Sometimes these were diverse immigrant groups with different languages but common problems. Sometimes these groups were in opposition regarding some community problem. At other times, the groups trying to communicate were public officials and needy immigrants seeking services.

The settlement leaders, therefore, often worked in partnership with other groups in conducting research, initiating community improvements, founding other social organizations, and advocating for social legislation.[79] These groups included city and state government officials, trade unions, progressive business leaders, and other nonprofit associations. To illustrate, in 1899, long before Ralph Nader's consumer movement, settlement leaders such as Florence Kelley worked with other reformers in creating the **National Consumers League,** an organization that used consumer pressure in advocating for child labor laws, minimum wages, and shorter work days for women, as well as safer consumer products.[80] With respect to trade unions, settlement house leaders collaborated with other reform groups to establish the National Women's Trade Union League in 1903. Furthermore, regarding minorities, a number of settlement reformers supported the founding of the **National Association for the Advancement of Colored People (NAACP) in** 1909 and the **National Urban League** in 1911. In helping to organize the NAACP, Lillian Wald hosted the National Negro Conference at the Henry Street Settlement in 1909.[81]

Did You Know?

Florence Kelley became a resident of Hull House while fleeing a violent domestic situation.[82] In late December of 1891, after being hit and spit on by her husband, Florence packed up her three children and belongings and moved to Chicago, becoming a resident of Hull House within a week of her arrival.

At times settlement leaders worked in coalitions with other groups. At other times, a community project started by one group was handed over to another group for future operation. In one instance, a landlord gave Hull House a free lease on a tract of city property with four buildings.[83] Hull House was allowed to keep the rent from the property. When Hull House leaders asked the landlord for permission to tear down one building and move the other three to make a playground, the landlord consented. Hull House operated the playground for ten years, at which time it turned over the playground to the city. Thus, all three sectors—for-profit, nonprofit, and public—contributed to the establishment and maintenance of a critically needed resource for parents and children.

Their focus on collaboration eventually led settlement house leaders to join forces with the charity organization societies, further contributing to the emergence of social work as a profession.[84] A significant event in this evolution of the profession was the 1905 merger of the settlement house journal, *The Commons,* with the New York Charity Organization Society's journal, *Charities.* And in 1909, Jane Addams became the first settlement house leader to be elected president of the National Conference of Charities and Corrections, the most prominent national conference at the time for social workers.

Did You Know?

Did you know that Jane Addams was voted in public opinion polls the most "exemplary" American?[85] Can you imagine a social worker receiving that honor today? Her father had been a prosperous businessman in Illinois, and perhaps the biggest ethical influence on her life. In addition to establishing her Chicago settlement, Hull House, Addams helped found the American Civil Liberties Union in 1920 and was a leader in national and international peace efforts. For this latter work, she received the Nobel Peace Prize in 1931.

Personal Profiles: The First Generation of Professional Social Workers

The generation of Americans born in the mid-to-late 1800s was the first to come of age in the industrial era. Like Susan B. Anthony, Elizabeth Cady Stanton, and other women born in the early 1800s, many of this generation were well-educated women with few career options.[86] Other than nursing and teaching, most professions were closed to them. Settlement houses and charity organization societies became settings in which women could apply their college education to a significant cause. In contrast to their immediate predecessors, members of this generation were the first to identify themselves as professional social workers. Indeed, this generation did much to firmly establish social work as a profession.

In addition to Jane Addams, several women stand out in early social work history. Mary Richmond, born in 1861, is one such woman.[87] Orphaned as a child and sickly throughout her life, she became a spokesperson for the national charity organization societies while serving as head of the Baltimore Charity Organization Society, beginning in 1891, and then the Philadelphia Society for Organizing Charity, starting in 1900. In these positions, Mary became involved in the formal training of friendly visitors and other agency staff. Her 1897 paper, "The Need of a Training School in Applied Philanthropy," helped to initiate the 1898 summer training program that became the first school for social workers, the previously described New York School of Philanthropy. In fact, Richmond was recruited by the New York Charity Organization Society to teach in the initial summer workshops. In 1909, she became head of the Charity Organization Department at the newly established Russell Sage Foundation. Her teaching, research, writing, and practice experience culminated in her 1917 book, *Social Diagnosis,* the first definitive textbook on social casework theory and method.

Julia Lathrop was another early leader in social work. Born in 1858 in Rockford, Illinois, Julia attended Rockford Female Seminary, just as her friend Jane Addams did. She later graduated from Vasser in 1880.[88] She began working at Hull House in 1890, advocating for children and people suffering from mental illness. In so doing, she was appointed in 1892 to the Illinois Board of Charities, which provided oversight of the various almshouses, hospitals, and institutions serving those with mental illness.[89] Julia assisted in the organization of the social work curriculum at the Chicago School of Civics and Philanthropy, which was founded in 1907 and would become the University of Chicago School of Social Service Administration.[90] She later participated in the founding of the National Commission for Mental Hygiene in 1909 and became Chief of the Children's Bureau in 1912.[91] Five years later, Lathrop was elected president of the National Council of Social Work.

Two sisters, Grace and Edith Abbott, were also prominent pioneers in the profession of social work. Both were born in Grand Isle, Nebraska, Edith in 1876, Grace in 1878.[92] Both graduated from the University of Chicago. Edith earned a Ph.D. in Economics, and Grace graduated with a Master of Philosophy degree in Political Science.

Grace and Edith were active in all the great social issues of the day. Grace was appointed secretary of the White House Conference on the Care of Dependent Children in 1918 and became head of the Children's Bureau in 1921, succeeding Julia Lathrop.[93] For her social work, she was awarded the Gold Medal from the National Institute of Social Sciences in 1931, the institute calling her "by far the most important social worker in public life today."[94] Because her career spanned the Progressive Era and the New Deal, she later was able to take part in developing the Social Security Act.[95]

Edith Abbott distinguished herself as a social researcher investigating the labor conditions of women and children for the Bureau of Labor Statistics. In conducting this research, Edith published nineteen volumes of findings.[96] In 1920, she became an Associate Professor of Economy at the

University of Chicago Graduate School of Social Service Administration, where she later became dean of the school and editor of its prestigious journal, the *Social Service Review*.[97]

Edith's influential 1931 book *Social Welfare and Professional Education* established the foundation for professional social work education by arguing that schools of social work needed to be affiliated with universities.[98] In so doing, social work students would receive an education based in science. In addition, and consistent with the focus of this book, Edith was a proponent of a broad perspective in social work education and practice:

> There are great reaches of territory...the great fields of public charitable organization, of law and government in relation to social work, of social economics, of social insurance, and modern social politics—all of which are required if the social worker is to be an efficient servant of the state.[99]

Business Charitable Contributions: The Growth of Community Chests and Service Clubs

Like the settlement houses, the charity organization societies during the Progressive Era were concerned about community organization and collaboration. One result of this concern was the **community chest,** now called United Way. That is to say, United Way of America traces its origin to the Charity Organization Society of Denver in 1887.[100] Considered to be the first federated fund-raising organization in American history, the Denver charity organization society centrally organized fund-raising for several community charities. Although Denver's religious leaders took the lead in establishing the organization, community business people also supported the effort.

Subsequently, the community chest model became very popular among business leaders around the country for several reasons.[101] Business leaders saw private philanthropy as a preferred option to the higher taxes and political patronage associated with public agencies. Others participated for religious reasons or for social status. Still others may have provided support in hope that business charitable contributions would diffuse the social criticism of radicals and the press at the time.

Another major reason for the popularity of community chests with the business sector was that community chests reflected the concept of scientific philanthropy.[102] This is because the chests provided a vehicle by which to assess community needs and services systematically. Businesses as single entities lacked these community assessment and evaluation skills. Requests for support by local health and human service agencies could be investigated and evaluated for credibility in a manner similar to the charity organization society's investigation of individual need. The financial and other technical skills of local business leaders were utilized in doing so. This systemic perspective of the community chests allowed business and professional leaders to identify duplication of effort and opportunities for partnerships among various health and human services. Thus, community chests were an instrument for coordination of charitable efforts.

The community chests provided business groups with a vehicle for community organization in another way as well. The federated fund-raising drive proved to be an efficient, well-organized method of raising support for needed health and human services.[103] Instead of responding to multiple requests for donations throughout the year, the federated campaign solicited funds in a single community-wide drive.

In addition to the efficiency gained through a single campaign, local businesses derived direct benefit in other ways. Services funded by the community chests enhanced community living conditions, thereby helping local businesses attract skilled labor. Furthermore, community chests relieved business of providing certain industrial welfare services directly. That is, company employees often utilized the services delivered by nonprofit members of the community chests. Labor absenteeism and turnover were reduced as a result.[104]

Business and professional groups also made charitable donations to community projects through an expanding array of local service clubs.[105] In 1910, Rotary International was started as a federation of sixteen local clubs. The Rotary was followed by the Kiwanis in 1916 and the Lions in 1917. Although local clubs were given flexibility in their giving programs, these groups typically targeted their donations to a selected group in need. For instance, the Rotary focused its donations on children, especially boys and crippled children. The Kiwanis also emphasized needy children, whereas the Lions assisted blind people. In addition to mutual aid societies and fraternal organizations such as the Masons, Odd Fellows, Eagles, and Loyal Order of Moose, these service clubs provided social workers with grassroots resources by which to help the needy.

Business Charitable Contributions at the National Level

As American business became national in scope, so too did its philanthropy. During the Progressive era, wealthy families increasingly established their own foundations to make donations in a rational and business-like manner.[106] By 1920, there were about 120 such foundations in the United States. Among these were the Russell Sage Foundation, created in 1907; the Rockefeller Foundation, established in 1913; and the Commonwealth Fund, started in 1918. Most foundation money went to education or health.

Industrial leaders such as Andrew Carnegie and John D. Rockefeller took business charitable giving to a new scale during this period. Concerned about the social unrest caused by the growing gap between the rich and the poor, Carnegie took the lead in encouraging wealthy Americans to increase their charitable giving during their lifetimes.[107] Rockefeller, for one, was significantly influenced by Carnegie's writing on the subject of wealth and philanthropy.

In a two-part essay published in June and December of 1889 entitled, "Wealth" (later amended in reprints to read, **The Gospel of Wealth**), Carnegie made the novel argument that the individual millionaire is a trustee of surplus wealth for those less fortunate.[108] By surplus wealth, he meant wealth in excess of that needed by the individual and his/her family to live in a moderate manner. According to Carnegie, it was the responsibility of the rich individual, given their exceptional talents, to personally administer this wealth during his/her lifetime for the common good. (Note that Carnegie's "Gospel" assumes the individual gained their wealth through merit.)

Both Carnegie and Rockefeller adhered to the prevailing belief among middle- and upper-class Americans, including those in charitable organization societies, that indiscriminate giving fostered idleness and dependency.[109] As a result, they managed their charitable giving in a very systematic way, reflecting good business practice and scientific charity. For example, Carnegie systematically contributed to the founding of an estimated 2,800 public libraries in the United States and abroad. A firm believer in meritocracy, Rockefeller focused much of his philanthropy on education-related projects. His large charitable donations were the most significant factor in the founding of the University of Chicago and Spelman College, the prestigious black women's college in Atlanta.

In addition to Carnegie and Rockefeller, other wealthy industrialists such as John Hopkins and Leland Stanford gave substantial sums of money to educational institutions. (Although another business leader, J. P. Morgan, also gave to education, he concentrated much of his philanthropy on museums such as the Metropolitan Museum of Art and the American Museum of Natural History.)[110] Consistent with the Progressive Era's focus on systemic causes of poverty, at least some business leaders viewed giving to education as a way to prevent poverty by enhancing "human capital" in America.[111] (Note, though, that the poor individual could still be blamed for not getting or using his/her education.)

A Critical Examination of American Philanthropy

Business philanthropists such as Carnegie and Rockefeller sought to promote equal opportunities, not necessarily equal outcomes.[112] This is a reason why they gave relatively little to poor relief. Carnegie, in fact, believed that private philanthropy should promote equal opportunities, particularly for those able and motivated to take advantage of such support to better themselves and their standard of living. Not wanting to undermine individual initiative in the job market, business leaders such as Carnegie felt giving to libraries and education promoted initiative for the aspiring. In contrast, Carnegie believed that public aid should focus on those not likely to become financially independent due to age, disabilities, and so forth. What do you think? Does this philosophy seem prudent in a market economy? Does it respect the dignity of all people?

Rockefeller was a leader in American philanthropy in numerous ways.[113] He gave the majority of his donations to the field of medicine. And as indicated, he was in the forefront of giving to education and black American causes. In fact, on at least one occasion, Rockefeller contributed money to a black man to buy his wife out of slavery. Yet, it was his method of giving that was most notable, helping to set a precedent for future American philanthropy. Rockefeller would purposely donate enough money to initiate a large project, but not enough to fund the entire project. In so doing, he hoped to promote the collaboration of other community leaders and philanthropists in supporting the cause. This strategy also prevented a charitable cause from becoming totally dependent on his money. Rockefeller's history of giving to Spelman College is a good illustration of this approach to philanthropy. He could have funded the college by himself, but insisted that it continue to do broader fund raising as it grew and expanded over the years.

A second way Rockefeller promoted collaboration and cooperation in American philanthropy was his charitable giving to a central agency that would then distribute his donation to various local organizations.[114] As in the United Way model of today, this method used the expertise of other professionals in distributing funds to needed and reputable projects. As Rockefeller's wealth and fame grew, he was overwhelmed by requests for donations to various causes. There was no way a single individual could investigate the credibility of each solicitation. Therefore, Rockefeller, a Baptist, used the American Baptist Home Mission Society among other conduit organizations to distribute his charity.

Andrew Carnegie and John D. Rockefeller, products of the Industrial Revolution and the Progressive Era, were two of the greatest business philanthropists in American history. In his lifetime, Carnegie made $350 million in charitable donations; Rockefeller gave away $530 million.[115] Furthermore, Rockefeller's son contributed another $537 million in direct donations and $540 million through various Rockefeller philanthropic organizations.

Ethical Considerations: Rockefeller and Charity

John D. Rockefeller is considered to be one of the great innovators in American business management and philanthropy.[116] He was a pioneer in American industrial planning and large-volume production, creating one of the first multinational corporations. Mirroring his business management, Rockefeller was one of the first to bring planning and professionalism to philanthropy, emphasizing collaboration in developing large-scale nonprofit institutions.

At the same time, Rockefeller is remembered for his unprincipled business practices at a time of few government regulations. In fact, much of the federal antitrust legislation passed in the United States to regulate big business was prompted by his method of using large corporate size to gain advantages, including secret railroad rebates, over smaller competitors. Therefore, was

> Rockefeller's philanthropy a way to alleviate his own guilt and promote a good reputation? As historian Ron Chernow puts it, was Rockefeller's charity a "spiritual double-entry bookkeeping" where a virtuous deed balances a prior sin?[117] Should leaders of charities accept donations of money made in a dubious manner?

CONTENTSELECT

For more information on related social work topics, use the following search terms:

Children's Bureau	NAACP	Progressive Era
Community chest	National Congress of	Scientific management
Federal Trade Commission	Mothers	Settlement houses
Gospel of Wealth	National Consumers League	Tammany Hall
Henry Street Settlement	National Urban League	Workmen's compensation
Hull House	Political machines	
Mother's pensions	Political patronage	

NOTES

1. Robert D. Putnam, *Bowling Alone: The Collapse and Revival of American Community* (New York: Simon & Schuster, 2000), p. 367; Theda Skocpol, *Protecting Soldiers and Mothers: The Political Origins of Social Policy in the United States* (Cambridge, MA: Harvard University), p. 265; James Leiby, *A History of Social Welfare and Social Work in the United States* (New York: Columbia University Press, 1978), p. 136.

2. Leiby, p. 137.

3. Putnam, pp. 384–385, 368, 395; Bruce S. Jansson, *The Reluctant Welfare State: American Social Welfare Policies—Past, Present, and Future* (Pacific Grove, CA: Brooks/Cole, 1997), p. 116.

4. Paul Johnson, *A History of the American People* (New York: HarperPerennial, 1999), p. 531.

5. Matthew Josephson, *The Robber Barons* (New York: Harcourt Brace, 1962), p. 285.

6. Johnson, p. 535.

7. Ron Chernow, *Titan: The Life of John D. Rockefeller, Sr.* (New York: Vintage Books, 1999), p. 259.

8. Johnson, p. 535.

9. Josephson, p. 361.

10. Putnam, p. 370.

11. Chernow, p. 258.

12. Johnson, pp. 361, 530–531; James T. Patterson, *America's Struggle Against Poverty: 1900–1994* (Cambridge, MA: Harvard University Press, 1995), p. 11.

13. Josephson, pp. 52, 78.

14. Paul F. Boller, Jr., *Presidential Campaigns* (New York: Oxford University Press, 1985), pp. 191–192.

15. Nick Salvatore, *Eugene V. Debs: Citizen and Socialist* (Chicago: University of Illinois Press, 1982), p. 264.

16. Boller, p. 195.

17. David McCullough, *Mornings on Horseback* (New York: Simon & Schuster, 1981), pp. 90, 367.

18. Patterson, pp. 10–11.

19. Walter I. Trattner, *From Poor Law to Welfare State: A History of Social Welfare in America*, 6th ed. (New York: The Free Press, 1999), pp. 164–165.

20. Jane Addams, *Twenty Years at Hull-House* (New York: Penguin Putnam, 1961), p. 65.

21. Ibid., p. 194.

22. Upton Sinclair, *The Jungle* (New York: The New American Library, 1960), p. 100.

23. Gary Dessler, *Organization and Management* (Reston, VA: Reston Publishing, 1982), pp. 154–155.

24. Howard Zinn, *A People's History of the United States: 1492–Present* (New York: Harper-Perennial, 1995), p. 320.

25. Addams, p. 132.

26. Zinn, p. 318.

27. Addams, pp. 163–164.

28. Sinclair, pp. 75–76.

29. Jansson, p. 116.

30. Skocpol, p. 83.

31. P. M. Blau, *Exchange and Power in Social Life* (New York: Wiley & Sons, 1964), p. 6; A. Heath, *Rational Choice and Social Exchange* (New York: Cambridge University Press, 1976), p. 2.

32. Skocpol, pp. 97–98.

33. Skocpol, p. 97.

34. David Herbert Donald, *Lincoln* (New York: Touchstone, 1996), p. 311.

35. Skocpol, pp. 105–106, 117.

36. Ibid., pp. 265–267.

37. Putnam, p. 374.

38. Jansson, pp. 110, 119; Skocpol, p. 266.

39. Skocpol, pp. 262, 266–267.

40. Jansson, p. 119.

41. Richard Wade, "Expanding Resources: 1901–1945," Arthur M. Schlesinger, Jr., ed. *The Almanac of American History* (New York: Barnes & Noble, 1993), p. 413.

42. Skocpol, p. 374.

43. Addams, p. 135.

44. Skocpol, p. 71; Jansson, p. 125.

45. Addams, p. 205; Mayer, "Forging a Nation: 1866–1900, Arthur M. Schlesinger, Jr., ed., *The Almanac of American History* (New York: Barnes & Nobles, 1993), pp. 351–352.

46. Jansson, pp. 118–119, 125.

47. Ibid., p. 119.

48. Chernow, p. 159.

49. Mayer, pp. 348–350; Chernow, p. 227.

50. Jean Strouse, *Morgan: American Financier* (New York: HarperPerennial, 2000), p. 627.

51. Chernow, p. 617.

52. Jansson, pp. 125, 140.

53. Chernow, pp. 491–492.

54. Skocpol, pp. 290–293.

55. Jansson, pp. 120–121.

56. Skocpol, pp. 425–426, 430.

57. Phyllis J. Day, *A New History of Social Welfare,* 3rd ed. (Boston: Allyn & Bacon, 2000), p. 239.

58. Skocpol, pp. 317, 510.

59. Putnam, pp. 386–387.

60. Skocpul, pp. 318, 329, 332–333; Putnam, p. 386.

61. Leiby, p. 127; Michael B. Katz, *In the Shadow of the Poorhouse,* 10th ed. (New York: BasicBooks, 1996), p. 164.

62. Leiby, pp. 128–129.

63. Leiby, p. 128; Harold B. Hunting, *Lillian Wald: Crusading Nurse* (Freeport, NY: Books for Libraries Press, 1945), p. 13; Clare Coss, ed., *Lillian D. Wald: Progressive Activist* (New York: The Feminist Press, 1989), p. xv.

64. Trattner, p. 175.

65. Leiby, pp. 186–187.

66. Trattner, p. 171.

67. Ibid., pp. 167–168.

68. Ibid., p. 165.

69. Addams, p. 141.

70. Ibid., p. 70.

71. Ibid., pp. 87–90, 98–99.

72. Ibid., pp. 90, 112, 199.

73. Trattner, p. 176.

74. Addams, p. 111.

75. Addams, pp. 134–136, 196–198; Moira Davison Reynolds, *American Women Scientists: 23 Inspiring Biographies* (Jefferson, NC: McFarland, 1999), p. 27.

76. Trattner, p. 171.

77. Addams, pp. 204–205.

78. Ibid., pp. 111–112.

79. Addams, pp. 150, 188, 199; Leiby, p. 129.

80. Dorothy Rose Blumberg, *Florence Kelley: The Making of a Social Pioneer* (New York: Augustus M. Kelley, 1966), p. 168; Skocpol, pp. 383, 404; Trattner, pp. 179–181.

81. Coss, p. xvi.

82. Kathryn Kish Sklar, *Florence Kelley and the Nation's Work* (New Haven: Yale University Press, 1995), pp. 168–172.

83. Addams, p. 191.

84. Trattner, p. 182.

85. Jansson, p. 117.

86. Trattner, pp. 172–173.

87. Leiby, pp. 121–123; Trattner, pp. 255–258.

88. Sigerman, pp. 94–95; Addams, pp. 32–38.

89. Sigerman, p. 95; Addams, pp. 83–84.

90. Sigerman, p. 95; Jansson, p. 140; Trattner, p. 241.

91. Addams, pp. 124, 163–164, 204.

92. Sigerman, pp. 9–10; Lela B. Costin, *Two Sisters for Social Justice: A Biography of Grace and Edith Abbott* (Chicago: University of Illinois Press, 1983), pp. 28, 39.

93. Sigerman, p. 10; Costin, pp. 113, 120–124.

94. Costin, p. 285.

95. Sigerman, p. 10.

96. Costin, pp. 101–102.

97. Ibid., pp. 64–66, 236.

98. Trattner, pp. 242–243.

99. Costin, p. 184.

100. Eleanor Brilliant, *The United Way: Dilemmas of Organized Charity* (New York: Columbia, 1990), p. 19.

101. Leiby, pp. 171–173.

102. Ibid., pp. 114–115, 172–174.

103. Ibid., p. 173.

104. Heald, 1988, p. 173.

105. Leiby, p. 171.

106. Leiby, pp. 170–171; Chernow, p. 491.

107. Chernow, p. 313.

108. Joseph Frazier Wall, *Andrew Carnegie* (New York: Oxford University Press, 1970), pp. 805–808.

109. Wall, pp. 805–808; Chernow, pp. 240–241, 302, 313–314.

110. Strouss, pp. 494, 560, 617.

111. Chernow, p. 469; Demetrius Iatridis, *Social Policy: Institutional Context of Social Development and Human Services* (Pacific Grove, CA: Brooks/Cole, 1994), p. 130.

112. Chernow, p. 469; Wall, p. 808.

113. Chernow, pp. 50, 241–242, 487.

114. Ibid., p. 241.

115. Ibid., p. 566.

116. Ibid., pp. 227–228, 238–242.

117. Ibid., p. 55.

7 American Social Policy in the Great Depression and World War II

New Deal policy advisor and social worker Harry Hopkins speaks at a 1936 charitable conference with Eleanor Roosevelt.

The Economic Context

The Second Industrial Revolution

America in the 1920s was a prosperous nation. Savings during the decade quadrupled.[1] A housing boom enabled millions of Americans to own their own home. By 1924, about 11 million families were homeowners. Automobiles, electricity, radio, and mass advertising became increasingly influential in the lives of average Americans. Automobiles, once a luxury for rich Americans, now gave industrial workers and farmers much greater mobility. Electricity put an end to much of the backbreaking work in the American home. Electric refrigerators, irons, stoves, and washing machines eventually became widespread.[2] On the farm, electric tools such as electric saws, pumps, and grinders made farmers more productive. By 1922, radios were common sources of news and entertainment for American families. With improvements in transportation and communication came increases in the mass advertising industry. In addition to all of this, corporations increasingly offered workers fringe benefits and stock-sharing opportunities.[3]

The Great Depression

The overall prosperity of the United States in the 1920s overshadowed the chronic poverty of certain vulnerable populations. These were the same populations that had always been at risk in American history: children, older Americans, minorities, female-headed families, people with disabilities, and workers with unstable or low-paying jobs. According to James T. Patterson, author of *America's Struggle Against Poverty: 1900–1994,* about one-fourth of the population in southern rural areas consisted of poor sharecroppers and tenant farmers.[4] Over a third of these small farmers were African Americans.

This is what Patterson refers to as the *old poverty.*[5] The *new poverty* began with the famous stock market crash of 1929 and the onset of the Great Depression. This is when many middle- and upper-income families first experienced poverty in America. These were hard-working people who fully shared the values and ideals of the American dream, people who had enjoyed the strong economy of the 1920s and had bought the homes, refrigerators, and automobiles. The sudden and severe downturn of the American economy left many of these people in shock and denial. Some became suicidal.

Between 1929 and 1933, unemployment in the United States jumped from 3.2 percent to 24.9 percent, almost a quarter of the official labor force.[6] This represented 12.8 million workers.[7] Unemployment in some cities was as high as 80 percent, eight out of ten workers.[8] During this period, consumer spending declined 18 percent, manufacturing output dropped 54 percent, and construction spending plummeted 78 percent. Eighty percent of production capacity in the automobile industry came to a halt.

By 1932, many politicians, businessmen, and journalists started to contemplate the possibility of massive revolution in the United States.[9] In fact, thousands of the most desperate unemployed workers began raiding food stores. Reminiscent of the food riots during the breakdown of the feudal system in Europe, this looting became widespread by 1932. Demonstrations by the poor demanding increased relief often resulted in fights with the police. In places like Harlem, the **sit-down strike** became part of the strategy during these relief demonstrations. A Pittsburgh priest named Father James R. Cox attracted 60,000 people to a protest rally; 12,000 of these followers later joined Cox in Washington to protest in front of President Herbert Hoover. When 5,000 war veterans demonstrated in Washington in the spring of 1932, Hoover sent none other than General Douglas MacArthur and Major Dwight Eisenhower to break up the rally. One observer describes the treatment of the veterans:

> The police encircled them. There was some brick-throwing. A couple of police retaliated by firing. A…man was killed and another seriously wounded.... To my right…military units were being formed.... A squadron of calvary was in front of this army column. Then, some staff cars, and four trucks with baby tanks on them, stopped near the camp. They let the ramps down and the baby tanks rolled out into the street.... The 12th Infantry was in full battle dress. Each had a gas mask and his belt was full of tear gas bombs.... They fixed their bayonets and also fixed the gas masks over their faces. At orders, they brought their bayonets at thrust and moved in. The bayonets were used to jab people, to make them move.... The entire block was covered by tear gas. Flames were coming up, where the soldiers had set fire to the buildings [housing protesters] to drive these people out.[10]

The Political Response

Franklin D. Roosevelt and the New Deal

One observer pointed out to Franklin D. Roosevelt (FDR) on taking office that, given the present crisis, he would be either the worst or the greatest president in American history. Roosevelt is said to have responded: "If I fail, I shall be the last one."[11]

By the time Franklin Roosevelt was elected in 1932, the traditional ideologies and institutions of the United States were in a state of upheaval.[12] Americans who had grown up promoting the ideology of the "deserving and undeserving poor" and the stigma of poor relief were now standing in line for relief. Private nonprofit organizations such as community chests, although valiant in their effort, were overwhelmed with requests, unable to meet the needs of their communities. State and local governments, ultimately responsible for their poor throughout American history, now looked for financial assistance.

What was needed was an expanded institutional partnership between the federal government and the other sectors of American society in promoting social welfare. In the past, the federal government had been active in other areas such as railroad development and war veteran pensions. However, the American belief, as earlier expressed by President Franklin Pierce to Dorothea Dix, was that the federal government should not be involved in providing poor relief.[13] But now the size of this national crisis required a national solution. The federal government was in the best position to initiate and coordinate national efforts among public, private, and nonprofit sectors of society. As the crisis deepened, progressive leaders and average Americans increasingly demanded that the federal government take greater responsibility in relieving and preventing poverty.

Did You Know?

One of the more radical policy proposals to address the Great Depression was put forth by Senator Huey Long from Louisiana and a second by Dr. Francis Townsend from California.[14] Long (who was later assassinated) proposed a "share the wealth" program where millionaires would be taxed to fund pensions for anyone over 60 years of age. The cost of the program was projected to be $3.6 billion, a colossal amount of money at the time. Townsend proposed a special sales tax to pay every American citizen over 60 (except convicted felons) $200 per month. The total cost of the proposal was estimated to be $2.4 billion. About 25 million people signed petitions in support of Townsend's plan.

Consequently, the Roosevelt administration established a two-tier federal system of insurance and relief programs. But to diffuse the social unrest throughout the nation, he took immediate action to address unemployment. He did so by establishing several federal agencies and programs.[15] One was the **Federal Emergency Relief Administration** (FERA), which was created by the Federal Emergency Relief Act in 1932. As its name suggests, FERA was given primary responsibility for managing the effort to distribute federal relief funds to individual states. The relief funds were used to sustain unemployed families during the immediate crisis. The **Civilian Works Administration** (CWA) was actually part of FERA. This federal program created jobs in public works. These public sector jobs included road repair, the digging of drainage ditches, and the maintenance of local parks. The **Public Works Administration** (PWA), created in 1933, also focused on public works. However, in contrast to the CWA, it focused on complex public works such as dams and airports. Another program started in 1933 was the **Civilian Conservation Corps** (CCC). The target population of this program was unemployed youth. That is, the CCC provided jobs for youth in various parks. The U.S. Army was used to supervise the youth. Furthermore, Congress passed the Wagner-Peyser Act in 1933. This legislation provided federal funding to individual states to develop employment offices. Only twenty-three states had such services before 1933. And finally, though not directly job-related, emergency food programs were set up to prevent starvation. For instance, surplus agricultural goods were distributed to the poor. Also, a relatively small-scale "food stamp" program was established for needy federal workers.

Federal reforms during the FDR administration also included reforms to stabilize the economic sector.[16] These included creation in 1933 of the National Recovery Administration. This controversial program, which was declared unconstitutional by the Supreme Court in 1935, temporarily threatened capitalist ideology by directly intervening in the "supply and demand" workings of the market. More precisely, this federal initiative sought to stabilize the economy by establishing wage and price agreements to curb the slashing of prices and wages during the depression. To further support product prices, production quotas were established to deter the "dumping" of surplus inventories of products on the consumer market. Similarly, the Agricultural Adjustment Agency was created to curtail farm production in order to maintain higher farm prices (and prevent further bankruptcies in the farm sector).

Also established in 1933 was the Federal Deposit Insurance Corporation (signified by the FDIC window sticker at your local bank!). A primary responsibility of this entity was to restore public confidence in the banking system. The FDIC worked with participating banks to insure consumer bank deposits against bank insolvency. The federal government also collaborated with banks to address the millions of farms and homes threatened with foreclosure. For example, the federal government directly purchased from banks and refinanced (at a lower interest rate) the mortgages of needy farmers through passage of the Emergency Farm Mortgage Act and the Farm Relief Act, both enacted in 1933. A year later, the National Housing Act established the Federal Home Administration (FHA). Through this program the federal government insured home mortgages and home improvement loans, allowing banks to refinance the loans of needy families at lower interest rates.

Additional economic reforms included the establishment of the Tennessee Valley Authority (TVA) in 1933 and the Securities and Exchange Commission (SEC) in 1934. The goal of the TVA was to facilitate economic development in that region of the country. To this end, dams and generating plants were constructed, providing inexpensive electric power to the region. The TVA also developed flood-control projects, manufactured and sold fertilizer, and reforested large tracts of land. Regarding the SEC, many people felt that rampant speculation in the stock market played a significant role in causing the stock market crash and subsequent depression. Therefore, the SEC took on the responsibility of regulating speculation abuses by investors and stockbrokers.

Class Discussion: Presidents and Disabilities

Franklin D. Roosevelt is generally considered to be one of the three greatest presidents in American history, along with Lincoln and Washington. FDR also happened to have a disability, coping with infantile paralysis or "polio" throughout much of his adult life. Because the disease left his legs paralyzed, he could not walk without assistance.[17] Yet, during his campaign for president, FDR traveled 13,000 miles by train and made sixteen major speeches.[18] Throughout his presidency, people were amazed at his energy and optimism. He held office longer than any president in American history, leading the United States through two of its biggest crises in the twentieth century, the Great Depression and World War II. Could Roosevelt be elected president today? How would the press cover his disability? How would the voters react to a candidate who could not walk without assistance?

Roosevelt's first set of reforms, as previously stated, was an emergency stopgap measure. From November 1934 to November 1936, the Roosevelt administration implemented a second set of reforms meant to define an ongoing responsibility of the federal government, a responsibility for social welfare similar to that found in European nations.[19] The major piece of legislation passed during this period was the **Social Security Act of 1935.** This legislation constituted a package of social program consisting of both insurance and poor relief (later referred to as *public assistance* or *welfare*). With respect to insurance, the act contained both unemployment insurance and old-age pensions (known today as Social Security). Unemployment insurance was very unpopular with business leaders. To illustrate, as late as 1931, Henry Ford persisted in blaming mass unemployment on individual laziness. He claimed there was plenty of work for those who wanted it.[20] Yet, packaging unemployment insurance with more popular programs such as old-age pensions, Roosevelt was able to pass the legislation.

The Social Security Act also contained several federal poor relief programs. Meant to be a continuing federal responsibility, these programs included Old Age Assistance, Aid to the Blind, and Aid to Dependent Children (ADC).[21] ADC, as the name suggests, targeted relief to poor children in single-parent families. It was not until 1950 that the single parent became officially eligible for assistance also.

Note that prior to the New Deal, relief was a tool used by social workers to rehabilitate.[22] To get relief, a person had to accept rehabilitation services from a social worker (including a significant dose of moral instruction!). With the New Deal, poor relief became a right of American citizens meeting certain eligibility standards, including, of course, financial need. In other words, poor relief became, not a "means" to rehabilitation, but rather an "end in itself."

The Social Security Act promoted cooperation between the federal government and the states in providing poor relief through the use of **matching funding formulas.**[23] That is, for every dollar of state funding expended in the Old Age Assistance, Aid to the Blind, and Aid to Dependent Children programs, the federal government contributed a specified percentage of funding. Yet, the legislation allowed each state to determine eligibility standards and levels of benefits.

Also contained in the legislative package were a number of smaller-scale health and human service programs. These included child welfare and maternal health programs in Title V of the act and public health programs in Title VI of the legislation.

During this second round of reforms, the Roosevelt administration continued to confront massive unemployment and labor unrest. Numerous strikes took place throughout the country. To support the rights of union organizers, the Wagner Act was passed in 1936.[24] This legislation established the **National Labor Relations Board.** The board enforced the right of workers to start their own unions. For instance, specific procedures for starting unions were outlined, including voting procedures for choosing a collective bargaining agent.

The Roosevelt administration also implemented major federal initiatives during this "second New Deal," which were later terminated.[25] One was the **Works Progress Administration** (WPA), which replaced the Federal Emergency Relief Administration created at the start of the New Deal. About 85 percent of program participants were receiving poor relief. Program eligibility was limited to one member of each family. Because this was typically a male, the program was considered by some to be discriminatory. In any case, the WPA employed two million people a month building libraries, schools, hospitals, parks, and sidewalks.[26]

Eleanor Roosevelt was a strong advocate of a major program located within the WPA called the **National Youth Administration.**[27] A forerunner of modern student financial assistance, this program allowed high school and college students to finish their education by providing part-time public sector jobs. It also established rural camps where youth could learn trade skills.

The WPA also funded several projects that put people in the arts to work.[28] For example, the New Deal established the Federal Theater Project, which created jobs for actors and playwrights and entertainment for laborers. In addition, a Federal Writers Project and a Federal Art Project were funded. In so doing, writers were put to work preparing items such as tourist guides to American states and cities, whereas artists painted murals on the walls of public buildings.

After 1936, the Roosevelt administration met greater opposition to its reform agenda from Republicans and conservative Democrats. There were several reasons for this opposition.[29] First, the New Deal had not succeeded in ending the depression. The national economic troubles continued despite the broad array of reforms. Second, many political and business leaders felt uncomfortable with Roosevelt's continuing spending deficit. (To fund the New Deal and stimulate economic growth, the Roosevelt Administration spent more than the federal government was actually receiving in tax revenue.) Third was the fear of socialism in America. The New Deal with its massive public employment and national poor relief programs was a fundamental change in America's institutional structure, a change that threatened the ideology of the nation's conservative leaders. Adding to this fear was the growing power of labor unions across the country. Roosevelt, after all, had supported legislation (Wagner Act) to facilitate this development, despite the opposition of business leaders. All of these developments led to a growing resentment by conservative Democrats and Republicans of Roosevelt's administration, the so-called brain trust. Hence, the growing opposition to additional social reform.

Despite this opposition, the Roosevelt administration did manage to get the Wagner-Steagall Housing Act passed in 1937.[30] This act established the U.S. Housing Authority, which provided low-interest loans to local government for the development of public housing. Another late New Deal success was the Fair Labor Standards Act, passed in 1938. Building upon earlier Progressive Era policy proposals, particularly for women and children, this legislation established minimum wages and maximum work hours for male and female workers. However, to appease southern interests, the legislation did not cover farm labor.

The Role of Social Work in the New Deal

By the beginning of the Great Depression, social work in the United States had experienced much growth and maturation as a professional discipline. Responding to the criticism that social work was made up of kind-hearted people doing activities that almost anyone could do, the 1917 publication by Mary Richmond, *Social Diagnosis*, provided a body of knowledge for professionalization.[31] The book emphasized casework techniques that focused on persons in their environment. That is, although Richmond held the sociological perspective that individual problems (unemployment, etc.), were rooted in the social environment, her book adopted a medical model process of differential diagnosis of individual cases. Based on this careful collection of client information, treatment would then consist of some combination of individual and environmental change. (It should be noted, however, that Richmond was not a great enthusiast for *wholesale* social reform, preferring instead *retail* interventions.)

As the decade of the 1920s progressed, the social work profession increasingly reflected the conservative trend across the nation.[32] Times were good; jobs were plentiful. Once again, social problems such as poverty and unemployment were traced to the individual. Psychiatric social work, led in part by Smith College, became the rage within the profession. In the process, the psychoanalytic work of Sigmund Freud, which became popular nationally, provided social workers with needed theory and individual treatment methods. In the 1920s, as John Ehrenreich put it, individual need was not a matter for Saint Peter as much as it was for Saint Sigmund.

In any case, the emphasis on casework facilitated the professionalization of social work for numerous reasons.[33] Casework was much less threatening to the middle and upper classes than cause-related social work, better known as social reform. In fact, business and professional people were a ready clientele for psychoanalysis. To establish itself as a profession, social work needed the support of these middle- and upper-income groups. It needed their fees for service; it needed their sanction.

Thus the profession of social work with its growing emphasis on casework fit the social, economic, and political needs of the conservative and prosperous 1920s. By 1929, there were twenty-five graduate schools of social work.[34] Several professional organizations had been established, including the American Association of Social Workers in 1921. In addition, to further knowledge based in research, several professional journals were developed, including *The Compass,* which was later renamed, *Social Work.*

When Franklin Roosevelt took office, he made several social workers prominent figures in his administration. This is despite the fact that the profession as a whole was reluctant to return to a social reform (i.e., macro) emphasis.[35] Private nonprofit organizations remained the dominant provider of casework by social workers. Yet, during the New Deal, it was primarily public agencies that distributed relief funds to the needy. This is where the action and the jobs were to be found. And, as stated, social workers played major roles in policy development.

FDR's wife, Eleanor Roosevelt, was probably the most influential person in the White House. Although she did not hold a social work degree, Eleanor received on-the-job training working in New York settlement houses.[36] In fact, her approach to the role of First Lady reflected the settlement philosophy of research and reform. Her trips around the nation and the world collecting information for her husband are legendary. She attracted much press coverage and seemed to be everywhere. She was his eyes and ears, his data collector. He knew he could count on her to bring back detailed information concerning public sentiment and social need. All this research was a prerequisite for developing the social policy of the New Deal.

Harry Hopkins, a social worker with settlement house experience, was the next most influential person to the president. In fact, it was Eleanor who first observed Hopkins as a passionate, young social worker in New York and referred him to her husband.[37] After managing Roosevelt's relief program in New York, Hopkins was selected to head the Federal Emergency Relief Administration, and later its successor, the Works Progress Administration.[38]

A third prominent member of the Roosevelt administration with social work training and settlement house experience was Frances Perkins. Perkins was the first woman appointed to the president's cabinet in U.S. history, serving as Secretary, Department of Labor.[39] Early in her career, she worked at two Chicago settlement houses, Hull House and Chicago Commons.[40] In 1909, she attended the New York School of Philanthropy (which, as stated, became the Columbia University Graduate School of Social Work) to learn survey research methods. A year later, she received her Master's Degree in Political Science from Columbia University. Before becoming Labor Secretary, Perkins had headed the Roosevelt's New York State Industrial Board, a position in which she advocated for safer factory and labor standards.[41]

Other influential social workers in Roosevelt administration included Grace Abbott, Paul Kellogg, Adolph Berle, Henry Morgenthau, Jr., and Eduard Lindeman.[42] In addition to these prominent policy development roles, the New Deal created thousands of new "rank-and-file" jobs in social work. In fact, the Federal Emergency Relief Act required that every local public relief administrator hire at least one experienced social worker on his/her staff.[43] This requirement introduced social work ethics and methods into every county and township in America. During the 1930s, the number of employed social workers doubled from about 30,000 to over 60,000. This job growth created a major shift in social work practice from primarily private agency settings and clinical roles to public agencies and social advocacy. The New Deal also expanded the scope of social work from a predominantly urban profession to a nationwide profession practicing in rural areas as well.

Did You Know?

Harry Hopkins, a social worker, was so respected by President Franklin Roosevelt that before Hopkins's health started to deteriorate, some believed that Roosevelt was grooming him to be the next president of the United States.[44] During World War II, Roosevelt sent Hopkins to be his special representative in talks with both Winston Churchill and Joseph Stalin.

Successes and Failures of the New Deal

The New Deal had many shortcomings.[45] As stated earlier, it was World War II that did the most to solve unemployment during the Great Depression. And although the Social Security Act contained some relative small health programs, the New Deal as a whole established no major national health program. Furthermore, to appease southern politicians and get some reform legislation passed, Roosevelt did relatively little to help African Americans.[46] Many of these citizens were employed as domestic servants, migrant workers, and farm laborers. New Deal legislation concerning old-age pensions, unemployment insurance, and minimum wages did not cover workers in these occupations. Perhaps most regrettable from an ethical standpoint, the New Deal contained no antilynching legislation—even though the beating and lynching of black citizens was still a common occurrence in some parts of the nation. If America as a nation suffered during the Great Depression, African Americans and other minorities suffered worst of all.[47]

Eleanor Roosevelt was probably the most powerful political ally of African Americans during the Roosevelt administration. As historian Doris Kearns Goodwin has noted, Franklin Roosevelt thought in terms of what *could* be done politically, whereas Eleanor thought in terms of what *should* be done ethically.[48] While inspecting conditions in southern states for her husband, Eleanor discovered discrimination against African Americans in several New Deal programs. For instance, African Americans in southern work relief programs under the WPA received lower wages than their white counterparts. As a result, Eleanor made sure that black leaders received a hearing at the White House, resulting in a 1935 executive order from the president barring discrimination in WPA programs. In the context of the times, actions such as these showed African Americans that Franklin and Eleanor Roosevelt did care about them. More importantly, this advocacy gave young African Americans a glimpse of the potential power of the federal government regarding civil rights.

Whatever its shortcomings, the New Deal prevented many Americans, black and white, from starving to death during the Great Depression. While challenging the ideologies of the status quo in the United States, it reformed national institutional structures to meet the massive needs of millions of Americans in poverty. In doing this, the New Deal created a major federal health and human service system in addition to the services of local public and private agencies. The Social Security Board, set up to administer the Social Security Act, later became the United States Department of Health, Education, and Welfare.[49] And the Social Security Act became, and still is, the foundation of the American health and human service system.

Personal Profile: Mary McLeod Bethune

Mary McLeod Bethune, the daughter of former slaves, became head of the Division of African American Affairs within the National Youth Administration in 1936. She used this position to advocate for the needs of African Americans during the Great Depression, directing a more equitable share of New Deal funding to black education and employment.[50] Born in 1875 in Mayesville, South Carolina, Bethune received a scholarship to Scotia Seminary for Negro Girls in Concord, North Carolina. She later attended the Moody Bible Institute in Chicago from 1894 to 1895.[51] In 1904, she founded the Daytona Educational and Industrial School for Negro Girls in Daytona Beach, Florida, a school that later merged with the Cookman Institute of Jacksonville to become Bethune–Cookman College.

An educator, organizer, and policy advocate, Bethune became one of the leading civil rights activists of her era.[52] She led a group of African American women to vote after the 1920 ratification of the Nineteenth Amendment to the Constitution (giving women the right to vote). In her position in the National Youth Administration, she became the highest paid African American in the federal government and a leading member of the unofficial "Black Cabinet" of the Roosevelt administration. She later became the first African American woman to have a monument dedicated to her in Washington, DC.

Critical Analysis: Business, the Great Depression, and the New Deal

Given the primary role that the private for-profit market plays in American social welfare, the Great Depression represented the greatest failure of the business sector in American history. As a result of the massive economic collapse in the wake of the stock market crash in 1929, the federal government assumed a much larger role in promoting social welfare. This new partnership among U.S. institutional sectors was quickly developed, at times, over the opposition of business leaders. To illustrate, both the U.S. Chamber of Commerce and the National Association of Manufacturers considered the Social Security Act too radical.[53] Yet, there was much less opposition to the Social Security Act (with its employer contributions) than expected by the Roosevelt Administration. In fact, some prominent business leaders such as Gerard Swope of General Electric and Marion Folsom of Eastman Kodak publicly supported the legislation. At the same time, many social reformers attacked the Social Security Act and other New Deal legislation for being too moderate, too sexist, and too racist. Were they correct? Should the New Deal have replaced, rather than cautiously reformed, many U.S. institutions? Were Roosevelt and the New Deal too accommodating to the interests of conservative business and political leaders? Did America miss a fundamental opportunity for significant progress in terms of social and economic justice?

Social Policy in Postwar America

The Economic Context: Automobiles, Suburbs, and Corporate Social Responsibility

The late 1940s and the decade of the 1950s witnessed an increasingly strong U.S. economy. The victory of the United States and its allies in World War II left the United States economy positioned for world leadership. The economic infrastructures of Europe, Japan, and the Soviet Union had suffered tremendous destruction during the war, whereas the economy of the United States, boosted by war production, recovered from the Great Depression.

As the nation entered the 1950s, the U.S. economy, facilitated by federal government policies, boomed with the automobile and housing industries experiencing rapid growth. In fact, there was a large, pent-up demand for most products. General Motors was the world's largest, richest corporation and would soon pass the billion-dollar mark in gross revenues.[54] The Interstate Highway Act of 1956 provided billions of dollars for highway construction, thereby fueling the demand for automobiles by a growing population. Millions of Americans saw the opportunity to keep their urban industrial jobs while living in the suburbs. Once again, the federal government (working in partnership with the private banking industry) made possible low-interest home mortgages for these consumers, mortgages guaranteed by federal agencies such as the Veteran's Administration and the Federal Housing Authority. In addition, developer William J. Levitt began mass producing affordable homes for middle-class Americans.

While the economy grew, American businesses began to shift their priorities for charitable giving. Experiences of the Great Depression, New Deal, and World War II prompted American businesses to increasingly direct donations to community groups other than the traditional health and human services of the local community chests. This transition was facilitated by the 1953 ruling of the Supreme Court of New Jersey. The ruling legitimized corporate charitable giving, not only in the traditional terms of direct benefit to the corporation but also in terms of the broad social responsibilities of corporations to the nation.[55] Previous to this court ruling, corporate charitable gifts could be legally justified to stockholders only if the donation was a direct benefit to employees. For example, a donation by a railroad company to a local YMCA that provided housing for railroad workers was legal. The 1953 ruling interpreted "direct benefit" to mean a benefit to the free enterprise system and not solely to the corporation or its employees. Thus, a legal precedent was established for corporate giving to a wider range of causes, including educational, cultural, and artistic organizations.

At the same time, American corporations were becoming more aware of their responsibility to a wide range of community groups.[56] Throughout the 1930s, the business sector faced resentful, hostile public opinion as a result of the collapsed economy and widespread suffering. The subsequent New Deal legislation, as previously stated, was perceived by business as an enormous threat to the free market system. In addition to the unprecedented increase in the federal government's responsibility for national social welfare, the business sector feared future increases in government regulation. Thus, business was presented with the option of acknowledging its broader social welfare responsibilities on a voluntary basis or through increased government regulation.

As in the Progressive Era, business leaders responded to the threat of further regulation with a renewed emphasis on management professionalism and corporate social responsibility.[57] The idea of business management as the trustee for society at large was increasingly stressed in the business sector. Business management became more responsive to multiple groups in its environment: stockholders, employees, retirees, consumers, government, and local communities. For example, in 1954, General Electric became the first corporation to match employee and retiree contributions to charity with a corporate donation (i.e., matching gifts).[58] Furthermore, this broad range of stakeholders began efforts to hold corporations more accountable for their policies and social impact (eventually resulting in the consumer movement and ethical investing).

The Political Context: McCarthy and the Red Scare

Although the federal government worked with the business sector during the 1950s to build homes and highways, there was relatively little new social reform passed at the federal level.[59] Major New Deal programs such as Social Security survived the conservative political climate of the 1950s thanks to strong support by America's growing middle class. However, the administrations of Harry Truman (1945–1952) and Dwight Eisenhower (1953–1960) were relatively dormant with respect to major new social reform. The legislation that was passed included the 1946 National School Lunch Program, the 1946 National Mental Health Act (providing grants to states for mental health services), and the 1954 School Milk Program.[60]

One of the primary reasons for the lack of major new social reform during this period was the national concern about the growth of communism. As indicated earlier, some of the big government programs of the New Deal had been criticized for being communistic. American labor unions, to varying degrees, were influenced by Communist members. However, now the Soviet Union and China had emerged from World War II as military powers capable of rivaling the United States around the world. Events such as the postwar Soviet expansion in Eastern Europe alarmed a U.S. population that had recently witnessed the global aggression of Adolf Hitler.[61] At the same time, Communist Parties were gathering strength in countries such as France and Italy.[62] Consequently, the spread of communism became the number one voter concern.[63] Perhaps even more alarming to U.S. political leaders were government reports that the Soviet Union, in its quest for world domination, was secretly developing atomic weapons and sponsoring espionage activity in the United States.

President Truman responded to (and fueled) this Red Scare by setting up the Federal Employee Loyalty Program in 1947.[64] The program's goal was to eliminate subversive employees in the U.S. government. In the same year, the House Un-American Activities Committee (which included a young congressman named Richard Nixon) began a series of investigations of Communist infiltration of American labor unions, government, academia, and the motion picture industry. During these investigations, a senior editor from *Time* magazine, Whittaker Chambers, admitted to being a former member of the Communist Party and identified a former top U.S. State Department official and Secretary-General of the founding United Nations conference, Alger Hiss, as a communist doing espionage work for the Soviet Union.

The Red Scare became even more frightening in 1949 when President Truman announced that the Soviet Union had detonated an atomic bomb and when Mao Tse-tung declared communist sovereignty over the entire Chinese mainland. Then in 1950, Alger Hiss was found guilty of perjury in denying that he had committed espionage for the Soviet Union.[65] By the time Senator Joseph McCarthy later that year claimed to have list of communists working in the U.S. State Department on national policy, the Red Scare had become hysterical.

Implications for the Social Sector and Social Work

This sociopolitical environment generated much public support for a Cold War anticommunist foreign policy. Yet, it also turned public support against further social reform.[66] The writings of Karl Marx were banned from bookstores. Universities refused to invite controversial speakers. Radical militant unions were expelled by the Congress of Industrial Organizations (CIO). In the end, this anticommunist sentiment along with a strong economy resulted in relatively little interest in major social legislation by the Truman and Eisenhower administrations.

The conservative trend of the 1940s and 1950s was, again, reflected in the social work profession. That is, the focus of social work returned to professional status and to individual treatment (i.e., casework) rather than the social reform of the New Deal era.[67] In 1952, the Council on Social Work Education was established, providing a standard accrediting body, and three years later, several professional organizations were merged to form the National Association of Social Workers (NASW).

Furthermore, during the 1950s, a psychosocial orientation to casework evolved, merging techniques from competing schools of thought (diagnostic verses functional). Based in part on the writings of Heinz Hartman, Melanie Klein, Paul Federn, and Anna Freud, more attention began to be paid by therapists to ego functions. More attention was also given to use of the client–therapist relationship in the present (as opposed to the recovery of repressed unconscious information) and to issues of separation, through the use of termination in therapy. (See the writings of Margaret Mahler, Rene Spitz, and John Bowlby.) In addition, foreshadowing the age of "managed health care," caseworkers began examining techniques associated with brief therapy. Finally, Erik Erikson's 1950 publication, *Childhood and Society*, brought increased interest by social workers in psychosocial development across the lifespan. In summary, the emphasis of the 1950s in social work was casework. Then came the 1960s!

CONTENTSELECT

For more information on related social work topics, use the following search terms:

Civilian Conservation Corps
Civilian Works Administration
Fair Labor Standards Act
Federal Art Project
Federal Emergency Relief Admin.
Federal Theater Project
Federal Writers Project

Matching funding formulas
National Labor Relations Board
National Youth Administration
National Works Administration
The New Deal
Public Works Administration

Red Scare
Sit-down strike
Social Security Act of 1935
Wagner-Steagall Housing Act
Works Progress Administration

NOTES

1. Paul Johnson, *A History of the American People* (New York: HarperPerennial, 1999), p. 718.

2. Robert Caro, *The Years of Lyndon Johnson: The Path to Power* (New York: Vintage, 1983), pp. 502–504.

3. Bruce S. Jansson, *The Reluctant Welfare State: American Social Welfare Policies—Past, Present, and Future*, 4th ed. (Belmont, CA: Wadsworth/Thomson Learning, 2001), p. 167.

4. James T. Patterson, *America's Struggle Against Poverty: 1900–1994* (Cambridge, MA: Harvard University Press, 1995), p. 38.

5. Ibid.

6. Michael B. Katz, *In the Shadow of the Poorhouse*, 10th ed. (New York: BasicBooks, 1996), p. 214.

7. Patterson, p. 42.

8. Katz, p. 214.

9. Ibid., pp. 223–224.

10. Ibid., p. 224.

11. Paul F. Boller, Jr., *Presidential Campaigns* (New York: Oxford University Press, 1985), p. 239.

12. Katz, p. 214.

13. James Leiby, *A History of Social Welfare and Social Work in the United States* (New York: Columbia University Press, 1978), p. 104.

14. Edward D. Berkowitz, *America's Welfare State From Roosevelt to Reagan* (Baltimore: Johns Hopkins University Press, 1991), pp. 18–19; Richard Wade, "Expanding Resources: 1901–1945," Arthur M. Schlesinger, Jr., ed., *The Almanac of American History* (New York: Barnes & Noble, 1993), p. 470.

15. Jansson, pp. 179–184.

16. Ibid., pp. 184–188.

17. Frances Perkins, *The Roosevelt I Knew* (New York: The Viking Press, 1946), p. 37.

18. Boller, p. 234.

19. Jansson, pp. 194, 199.

20. Howard Zinn, *A People's History of the United States: 1492–Present* (New York: Harper-Perennial, 1995), p. 378.

21. Jansson, p. 203.

22. John H. Ehrenreich, *The Altruistic Imagination: A History of Social Work and Social Policy in the United States* (Ithaca, NY: Cornell University Press, 1985), p. 107.

23. Jansson, pp. 203, 205–207.

24. Ibid., p. 204.

25. Ibid., pp. 194, 207–208.

26. Doris Kearns Goodwin, *No Ordinary Time* (New York: Touchstone, 1995), p. 87.

27. Jansson, p. 208; Trattner, p. 283.

28. Goodwin, p. 87; Zinn, p. 394.

29. Jansson, p. 209.

30. Ibid., pp. 210–211.

31. Ehrenreich, pp. 64–65; Trattner, pp. 255–262.

32. Ibid.

33. Ehrenreich, pp. 72, 76.

34. Ibid., p. 78.

35. Ibid., p. 103.

36. Goodwin, pp. 96, 365, 381.

37. Ibid., p. 87.

38. Leiby, p. 224, Goodwin, p. 87.

39. George Martin, *Madam Secretary Frances Perkins* (Boston: Houghton Mifflin, 1976), pp. 3–4.

40. Ibid., pp. 60–63, 72–74.

41. Ibid., p. 205.

42. Ehrenreich, p. 104.

43. Walter I. Trattner, *From Poor Law to Welfare State: A History of Social Welfare in America*, 6th ed. (New York: The Free Press, 1999), pp. 285, 296–297.

44. Goodwin, pp. 106–107, 212, 257.

45. Zinn, pp. 393–394.

46. Goodwin, p. 163, Trattner, p. 282.

47. Trattner, p. 282.

48. Goodwin, pp. 162–163.

49. Trattner, p. 295.

50. Audrey Thomas McClusky and Elaine M. Smith, *Mary McLeod Bethune: Building a Better World* (Bloomington, IN: Indiana University Press, 1999), pp. xii, 4.

51. Sigerman, p. 20; McClusky and Smith, p. 5.

52. McClusky and Smith, pp. 3, 6, 8, 16.

53. Trattner, p. 291.

54. David Halberstam, *The Fifties* (New York: Villard, 1993), pp. 118, 132; Ehrenreich (1985), pp. 144–145.

55. Eleanor Brilliant, *The United Way: Dilemmas of Organized Charity* (New York: Columbia, 1990), p. 157; Barry D. Karl, *Corporate Philanthropy: Historical Background. In Corporate Philanthropy: Philosophy, Management, Trends, Future, Background* (Washington, DC: Council on Foundations, 1982), p. 132.

56. Frank E. Andrews, *Corporation Giving* (New York: Russell Sage, 1952), p. 17; Morrell Heald, *The Social Responsibilities of Business: Company and Community, 1900–1960* (New Brunswick, NJ: Transaction, 1988), p. 207.

57. Leiby, pp. 170–172; Heald (1988), p. 207.

58. Thomas J. Billitteri, "Donors Big and Small Propelled Philanthropy in the 20th Century," in *The Chronicle of Philanthropy*, January 13, 2000. Retrieved from http://philanthropy.com/free/articles/v12/i06/06002901.htm.

59. Jansson, p. 229.

60. Trattner, p. 312.

61. Christopher Matthews, *Kennedy & Nixon: The Rivalry That Shaped Postwar America* (New York: Touchstone, 1997), p. 48.

62. David McCullough, *Truman* (New York: Touchstone, 1993), p. 544.

63. Matthews, p. 37.

64. Ehrenreich (1985), p. 140; McCullough, p. 551.

65. Matthews, 1996, pp. 67–68.

66. Ehrenreich, pp. 122, 140–142.

67. Ibid., pp. 122, 136–137, 188.

8 Social Policy in the 1960s–1970s

Civil rights activist Martin Luther King delivers a speech.

The Economic Context

The Affluent Society

As the decade of the 1960s began, the United States had the "highest mass standard of living" in world history.[1] The strong American postwar economy of the late 1940s and 1950s continued into the 1960s. In fact, from 1940 to 1960, the U.S. gross national product increased fivefold.[2] There were several reasons for this economic growth. As previously discussed, the military spending during World War II finally pulled the economy out of the Great Depression. The temporary curtailment in production of many consumer products during the war resulted in a burst of consumer demand at war's end. Servicemen rushed home to take a job, buy a car, purchase a home in the suburbs, and start a family. This led to a baby boom and further consumer demand for products. During this period, growing U.S. corporations were well positioned to meet both domestic and foreign demand for products, given the crumbled economic infrastructure of foreign competitors such as Japan and Germany. Military spending during the Cold War rivalry with the Soviet Union added further to this economic expansion, creating a formidable military-industrial complex in the United States.[3]

Leading intellectuals began to deliberate on the nature of this society and the impact it was having on American citizens. In 1958, economist John Kenneth Galbraith published *The Affluent Society*, in which he described the growing power of American corporations, their success at producing material goods, their ability to create consumer demand through advertising, and the growing new class of highly educated business and professional people for whom work was no longer dirty and menial, but interesting and rewarding.[4] Galbraith argued that, in the old world, poverty was an all-pervasive fact of life, but that in the contemporary United States, social and economic policies should be based on the fact that "the ordinary individual has access to amenities—foods, entertainment, personal transportation, and plumbing—in which not even the rich rejoiced a century ago."[5]

Four years later, in 1962, social critic (and Socialist) Michael Harrington chose to emphasize *The Other America* and its *culture of poverty*.[6] This, he argued, was a land of between 40,000,000 and 50,000,000 relatively invisible poor people, the unskilled workers, the migrant farm workers, minorities, people for whom work was sporadic, demeaning, and demoralizing.

> To be sure, the other America is not impoverished in the same sense as those poor nations where millions cling to hunger as a defense against starvation. This country has escaped such extremes. That does not change the fact that tens of millions of Americans are, at this very moment, maimed in body and spirit, existing at levels beneath those necessary for human decency. If these people are not starving, they are hungry, and sometimes fat

with hunger, for that is what cheap foods do. They are without adequate housing and education and medical care.... But even more basic, this poverty twists and deforms the spirit. The American poor are pessimistic and defeated, and they are victimized by mental suffering to a degree unknown in Suburbia.[7]

Civil rights leader Martin Luther King, Jr., explaining the cause of the 1965 riots in the Watts section of Los Angeles, also focused on the poor in a land of plenty.

I believe what happened in Los Angeles was of grave national significance. What we witnessed in the Watts area was the beginning of a stirring of a deprived people in a society who had been by-passed by the progress of the previous decade. I would minimize the racial significance and point to the fact that these were the rumblings of discontent from the "have-nots" within the midst of an affluent society.[8]

In the early 1960s, poverty for a family of four was officially defined as living on an income of less than $3,000.[9] Populations at high risk of poverty in the 1960s included rural Americans, minorities, low-paid workers, and female-headed families. (The poverty status of older Americans improved considerably during the 1960s thanks to increases in Social Security benefits.) To illustrate, in 1966, the percentage of rural Americans in poverty was 19 percent, compared to 14 percent for urban Americans. In that same year, the percent of nonwhite Americans in poverty was 41 percent, in contrast to 12 percent of white Americans. Furthermore, 32 percent of poor families in 1967 contained a head of the household that worked full-time, and another 25 percent of poor "breadwinners" worked part-time. What is more, many poor female heads of households, because of child-rearing duties and lack of child care, could not work outside the home, leaving 11 million of the poor in 1963 in these families.

The Political Agenda

Kennedy and the New Frontier

Democrat John F. Kennedy won a close presidential election over the Republican candidate, Richard M. Nixon, in 1960. Kennedy, the first Catholic president in American history, won by 2/10 of 1 percent of the popular vote.[10] Much like the 2000 presidential election between George W. Bush and Albert Gore, the 1960 election was so close that there was talk of a recount in certain disputed states, but Nixon discouraged the effort, noting how impractical and disruptive a recount would be, and declaring, "No one steals the presidency of the United States."[11]

Did You Know?

John Kennedy was often criticized for his wealthy father's heavy financing of his political campaigns. Showing his sense of humor during public speeches, John (called Jack by relatives and friends) would pretend to have just received a wire from his father. Reading it to the audience, John would say: "Dear Jack, Don't buy a single vote more than is necessary—I'll be damned if I'm going to pay for a landslide [victory]."[12]

Although a Democrat and an activist relative to his predecessor, Dwight Eisenhower, Kennedy at first did not share the passion for social reform characteristic of traditional Roosevelt Democratic supporters. Given his father, Joseph P. Kennedy, Sr., was FDR's ambassador to England, Kennedy appeared more interested in foreign affairs than domestic policy.[13]

In any case, most of Kennedy's legislative agenda, called the New Frontier, was not approved by Congress during his lifetime. The reasons for this included his congressional inexperience and low status with older politicians in Congress.[14] In getting elected, Kennedy, to a significant extent, had circumvented the traditional political process and appealed directly to the American people through the media. His career in Congress (or any political position) had not been long or distinguished, typical qualifications for a serious presidential bid.

However, both John and his father were familiar with Hollywood and the modern media.[15] Most television viewers who watched the first 1960 debate between candidates Kennedy and Nixon thought that Kennedy with his movie star appearance had won, whereas radio listeners gave the edge to Nixon. As such, John Kennedy became the first made-for-television presidential candidate. But there was more than the television advantage. The Kennedy campaign adroitly used his photogenic qualities to appeal to the editors and readers of many popular magazines. During the campaign, the nation's newsstands were filled with positive articles on Kennedy and his wife and family.

And there was more to Kennedy than glamour. Setting a trend in modern American politics, the Kennedy family was the first to use private polling to ascertain local voter concerns during the campaign.[16] As a result,

Kennedy was able to directly address key issues of local communities as he traveled the nation in search of the presidency. These advantages in addition to the Kennedy family wealth got him elected, but congressional leaders, given the razor-thin victory, saw no significant mandate for Kennedy's legislative agenda.

Despite this disadvantage, the Kennedy administration did enjoy some legislative success.[17] The Manpower Development and Training Act of 1962 was the country's first major job training program. Also, the Kennedy administration increased federal funding to local welfare departments for casework, job training, and job placement through passage in 1962 of the Public Welfare Amendments to the Social Security Act (also known as the Social Service Amendments). Reflecting a stronger economy than in the 1930s, the focus on job training was more conservative than Franklin Roosevelt's emphasis on public employment during the Great Depression. It should also be noted that the Kennedy administration allowed states to include two-parent, unemployed families in their AFDC programs. The change was called Aid to Families with Dependent Children–Unemployed Parent, or simply, AFDC-UP.

During his campaign, Kennedy had visited the rural poverty areas of Appalachia. (A famous photo contrasts a handsome, well-polished Kennedy standing in front of a destitute Appalachian family on its front porch.)[18] Once elected, Kennedy created the Area Redevelopment Agency in 1961.[19] This agency provided support in the form of loans, subsidies, and public works to local businesses in poverty areas such as Appalachia.

The Kennedy family had also been sensitized to needs of people with mental illness, given that one of John's sisters had suffered with this problem. Consequently, the Community Mental Health Centers Act was passed in 1963.[20] This act provided federal funds to public or private nonprofit organizations for construction, and later staffing, of community mental health centers providing outpatient and prevention services.

Another Kennedy legislative success was the Juvenile Delinquency and Youth Offenses Control Act of 1961.[21] This program, although small and less well known, became a model for many of the Great Society programs. It sought to reduce juvenile delinquency by providing federal funding for local demonstration projects (such as Mobilization for Youth in New York) that created opportunities for youth education and training. These opportunities would be created through a comprehensive and rationally planned set of services to youth and their neighbors. These services might include individual, family, and group work as well as community organization.

Furthermore, in 1962, the Kennedy Administration passed tax credits for business investment and increased business depreciation allowances.[22]

These policy changes, along with an income tax cut passed in 1964, contributed to the continued economic growth of the 1960s.

Did You Know?

The night of his nomination for President, Kennedy decided to select Senator Lyndon Johnson from Texas as his vice presidential running mate. Some people close to Kennedy were shocked and angry with the selection. When confronted, Kennedy responded: "I'm 43 years old and I'm the healthiest candidate for president in the United States.... I'm not going to die in office. So the vice presidency doesn't mean anything."[23] Four years later in November of 1963, President Kennedy was assassinated in Dallas, Texas.

Although his legislative successes were few, Kennedy created a significant policy agenda before his death for his successor, Lyndon B. Johnson (LBJ).[24] This agenda included legislation dealing with civil rights, poverty, food stamps, health care, public school aid, and further tax reform. All of these were Kennedy initiatives in various stages of progress when he was assassinated in 1963.

Kennedy and Johnson, as a result, turned out to be a great team for the development of social programs. Kennedy created the agenda. He and his advisors were the intellectuals, the idea generators, the brains behind the legislative proposals.[25] In fact, Thomas "Tip" O'Neill, the long-time Speaker of the House, believed that one of Kennedy's greatest achievements as President was the talented people he brought to government.

Lyndon Johnson, who scoffed at intellectualism, subsequently pushed Kennedy's agenda through Congress. Johnson became the idea champion before Congress, the political muscle needed to pass legislation in the 1960s.[26] In contrast to Kennedy, Johnson had much congressional experience and knew how to get things done in Congress. He consulted many members of Congress during the legislative process. He gave credit to individual members of Congress for legislative successes. In short, Johnson was a better "politician" than was Kennedy in the traditional sense of negotiation and compromise. The result was the successful passage of much federal legislation during the Johnson administration.

Johnson and the Great Society

President Lyndon B. Johnson significantly expanded the federal partnership in American social welfare, a partnership of the federal government with private and other public institutions to promote social welfare. As discussed in earlier chapters, when traditional institutions in the for-profit and non-profit sectors failed during the Great Depression, the federal government under President Franklin Roosevelt was forced to create new institutional relationships in an attempt to solve the crisis. That is, Roosevelt was forced to establish a significant role for the federal government in maximizing social welfare throughout the country. The **Great Society,** as Johnson called his legislative agenda, greatly expanded this role.

The agenda of the Great Society consisted of numerous pieces of legislation. The first, and perhaps most important, was the **Civil Rights Act of 1964.** When Johnson took office, the Civil Rights Movement was already well underway through court action and the voluntary efforts of various groups in the nonprofit sector. In 1954, the Supreme Court had ruled that school segregation was unconstitutional.[27] Then in 1955, the refusal of an African American woman named Rosa Parks to give up her seat to a white rider on a Montgomery Alabama bus led to a boycott of all public buses in that city by African Americans. The Montgomery Improvement Association, headed by the Reverend Martin Luther King, Jr., organized the successful boycott, in which African Americans refused to spend their money on bus transportation until the busses were desegregated.

This civil rights victory led to further efforts to challenge segregation in southern states. African American college students began to use a sit-in strategy to desegregate lunch counters in stores across the South, refusing to leave their seats until served or jailed.[28] In 1961, eleven youth calling themselves Freedom Riders began a protest of segregated bus stations and other discriminatory interstate travel laws. Then, in 1963, the Southern Christian Leadership Conference, headed by King, and the Alabama Christian Movement for Human Rights led a campaign to protest segregation in Birmingham, Alabama, the largest industrial city in the South. King's coalition used a strategy of **nonviolent resistance,** employing peaceful mass marches, sit-ins, and business boycotts to achieve its objectives. His advocacy effort attracted media attention nationwide (indeed, worldwide), forcing the cooperation of the federal government in enforcing African American civil rights.

Jailed during the Birmingham campaign, King wrote a famous letter to a group of clergy that had publicly criticized King's coalition for moving too quickly for social change. Here is part of his letter written in response while in jail:

> We have waited for more than 340 years for our constitutional and God-given rights. Perhaps it is easy for those who have never felt the stinging darts of segregation to say, "Wait." But when you have seen vicious mobs lynch your mothers and fathers at will and drown your sister and brothers at whim...when you suddenly find your tongue twisted and your speech stammering as you seek to explain to your six-year-old daughter why she can't go to the public amusement park that has just been advertised on

television, and see tears welling up in her eyes when she is told that Fun-town is closed to colored children, and see ominous clouds of inferiority be-ginning to form in her little mental sky, and see her beginning to distort her personality by developing an unconscious bitterness toward white people; when you have to concoct an answer for a five-year-old son who is asking: "Daddy, why do white people treat colored people so mean?"... When your first name becomes "nigger"... when you are forever fighting a degenerating sense of "nobodiness"—then you will understand why we find it difficult to wait.[29]

King believed public pressure generated from the Birmingham demon-strations contributed greatly to the Johnson administration's passage of the Civil Rights Act of 1964.[30] The act promoted black voting rights by outlaw-ing poll taxes and literacy tests. It also called for desegregation of public fa-cilities and prohibited employment discrimination in organizations receiving federal money. To oversee the employment requirements, the Equal Employment Opportunity Commission was established. In addition, the U.S. Attorney General was given the right to file suits to desegregate schools. A weakness of the legislation was that enforcement was done on a case-by-case basis (i.e., individual law suits). This feature of the bill made it more difficult to enforce antidiscrimination.

To expedite legal action, the **Civil Rights Act of 1965** was passed.[31] This act gave the federal government the right to presume discrimination in any state (or its subdivisions) where less than 50 percent of minorities voted in the latest federal election. The act also presumed discrimination in any area using screening tests such as literacy tests. In these cases, federal au-thorities could directly administer elections. Within one week from the bill's signing, the federal Justice Department had filed suits to have poll taxes voided in Texas, Virginia, Mississippi, and Alabama.[32] In addition, voter screening tests were suspended in several states.

Did You Know?

The Reverend Martin Luther King credited the civil rights demonstrations in Selma, Alabama, with the passing of the 1965 Civil Rights Act. Indeed, Pres-ident Johnson encouraged King to go ahead with the march in an effort to build mass public support for the legislation.[33] They both hoped no one would get hurt, but Alabama state troopers used tear gas, clubs, and whips to stop the march. Television coverage of the graphic violence served to gen-erate support for the civil rights legislation, just as Johnson and King had hoped it would. The 1965 Civil Rights Act is a clear example of government and nonprofit voluntary groups working in partnership to produce social change.

A third major piece of legislation passed during the Johnson administration was Medicare (Title 18 of the Social Security Act).[34] Medicare made health care more affordable for older Americans. The mandatory part of the program, Part A, covered various hospital costs and was financed by a payroll tax on employers and employees. Another characteristic of the bill is that it required no means test (i.e., no income requirements for eligibility). Some of its weaker characteristics were its failure to cover many chronic or long-term conditions. Furthermore, it did not cover preventative and outreach services and contained few cost controls.

To assist the poor with health care, the Johnson administration passed Medicaid (Title 19 of the Social Security Act).[35] This legislation was funded through matching grants with states. States had to provide emergency care and certain other basic services. In addition, each state had to accept people receiving Aid to Families with Dependent Children. Beyond these requirements, it was left to each state to determine eligibility requirements and any additional services. The weaknesses of Medicaid were similar to those of Medicare. It did not promote outreach and preventative services and there were few cost controls in the legislation.

A fifth major piece of legislation passed as part of Johnson's Great Society was the Older Americans Act of 1965. Title 3 of this act authorized the creation of a national network of Area Agencies on Aging. These agencies coordinate and subsidize services such as homecare and nutrition programs for older Americans.

The Johnson administration also passed the Elementary and Secondary Education Act in 1965.[36] Johnson, a former public school teacher, had been sensitized to the needs of low-income schools while working in Texas. This act provided federal assistance to low-income public school districts. In so doing, the legislation allowed private schools to share books and supplies with public schools.

Other Great Society programs included the Work Incentive Program and the Food Stamp Program. The Work Incentive Program was part of the welfare amendment of 1967. This program funded training programs and child care for women on welfare.[37] It was one of the first punitive pieces of welfare reform in that clients could be cut off from AFDC if they refused job training or employment. Yet, the program allowed clients to keep part of their employment earnings without a reduction in benefits. Also, as stated, the Johnson administration passed the Food Stamp Act, which established a Food Stamp Program to assist the poor in purchasing food. This program was later expanded, standardized (in terms of eligibility), and made mandatory in all states during the Nixon administration.

The centerpiece of Johnson's Great Society legislative agenda, however, was the **War on Poverty.** This antipoverty legislation, officially entitled The Economic Opportunity Act of 1965, consisted of several programs including Job Corps and the Neighborhood Youth Corps.[38] Job corps provided urban school dropouts with alternative educational and training programs, and the Neighborhood Youth Corps provided part-time jobs to youth in local agencies.

The War on Poverty also offered a Work-Study Program that provided poor college students with campus jobs.[39] In addition, the Volunteers in Service to America program, better known as VISTA, was initiated. VISTA was a domestic version of the popular Peace Corps program. Instead of sending Americans to work in foreign countries for a stipend, VISTA sent them to do community organizing in poor U.S. neighborhoods. Furthermore, the War on Poverty included legal aid to the poor and the creation of medical clinics in poor neighborhoods.

The most controversial piece of the War on Poverty was the **Community Action Programs,** referred to as CAP agencies.[40] Housed in the Office of Economic Opportunity, these CAP agencies were given several objectives: to plan and coordinate local services for the needy, to fund and deliver certain services (such as the preschool program Head Start), and to advocate for the poor. Not only were the CAP agencies supposed to advocate for the poor, they were also instructed to encourage **maximum feasible participation** of the poor in their programs. Maximum feasible participation of the poor was viewed as a way to bridge social reform and individual change. More specifically, proponents reasoned that empowerment through participation in social change activities would lead to better mental health for the individual. To promote empowerment and maximum feasible participation of the poor, many of the CAP agencies employed paraprofessionals from their neighborhoods and client populations.

Although CAP programs such as Head Start have proven very successful over time, the CAP agencies suffered from several weaknesses.[41] Their objectives proved to be too broad, and at times, contradictory, therefore confusing the mission of the agencies. Were they a planning agency or an advocacy agency or a direct service agency? This ambiguity led to problems in implementing the programs at the local level. To illustrate, the Johnson administration wanted to reduce welfare dependency, whereas clients used Great Society legal aid services to challenge welfare denials. What is more, many CAP agencies suffered from poor management practices, including inefficiency, patronage, and corruption.

The CAP agencies were indicative of the weaknesses of the Great Society legislation in general. Johnson wanted to be a great president, even greater than his hero, Franklin D. Roosevelt. However, although many social programs were established under Johnson, his administration did not pay enough attention to adequate funding and proper implementation.[42] Fewer programs, better funded and implemented, may have been more effective in the long run for American social welfare. Instead, many Americans got the impression that the federal government was just "throwing money" at social problems. This perception, along with Johnson's prolonging of the Vietnam

War, turned popular opinion against him and undermined his Great Society programs. In the end, he decided not to run for reelection.

Yet, those close to Johnson maintain that his commitment to the poor and civil rights was genuine.[43] He accomplished in civil rights and national health care what Franklin Roosevelt and the New Deal did not. In so doing, millions of needy Americans have benefited from the right to vote, Medicare, Medicaid, legal aid, Head Start, student financial aid, and other Great Society programs.

Critical Analysis: Was the Johnson Presidency a Failure?

Some historians consider the presidency of Lyndon Johnson to be a failure, but is this a fair and accurate assessment? True, Johnson significantly expanded the United States' war in Vietnam, stating: "I am not going to be the President who saw Southeast Asia go the way China went [meaning communist]."[44] Yet, at least four presidents—Eisenhower, Kennedy, Johnson, and Nixon—can share some of the blame for the Vietnam War.[45] They all contributed to American involvement in the Vietnam War. In any case, haven't the Great Society programs helped millions of Americans at risk of racial discrimination and poverty? These programs weren't perfectly designed in hindsight, but weren't they critically needed? Does foreign policy failure outweigh domestic policy progress when evaluating a presidency?

Nixon and the Federal Social Welfare Partnership

Richard M. Nixon succeeded Lyndon Johnson as president of the United States in 1968. Although a Republican who was highly critical of Johnson's Great Society, Nixon continued expanding the federal partnership in social welfare.[46] Nixon's policy views on the Great Society reflected the anger and resentment of the middle class and many local community leaders with the concept of maximum feasible participation of the poor in local services. That is, the practical realities of empowering the poor to take more control of local community institutions and services threatened local community politicians and administrators, leaving a resentment that Nixon capitalized on politically.

Did You Know?

President Richard Nixon detested social workers! He felt that they coddled the undeserving poor. He also felt that many of the Great Society services were ineffective programs that served bureaucrats and social workers more than the country.[47]

At the same time, however, Nixon sought to build voter support for his presidency and the Republican Party by enacting more and better social legislation than the Democratic Party.[48] He did so by promoting legislation that helped the working poor and what America has historically viewed as the deserving poor—older Americans, people with disabilities, and children. Nixon pursued his strategy, to a considerable extent, by adding expansive amendments to Democratic policy proposals, by outbidding them on certain pieces of legislation that assisted the working and/or deserving poor. In short, he tried to beat the Democrats at their own game as he saw it. The result was the passage of a considerable amount of health and human service legislation during Nixon's presidency and a substantial addition to the federal government's responsibility for social welfare.

Legislation enacted by the Nixon Administration included the **Supplemental Security Income** program in 1972.[49] This legislation brought Old Age Assistance, Aid to the Blind, and Aid to the Disabled under the sole administration of the Social Security Administration of the federal government. Most of the cost for the program was assumed by the federal government. Supplemental Security Income, better known as SSI, provided assistance to people with mental and physical disabilities. This clientele included deinstitutionalized mental health patients. An important point to remember with SSI is that Nixon, the Great Society critic, greatly expanded the number of people receiving assistance in the various categorical services that comprise SSI.

Nixon also expanded the federal government's role in the Food Stamp Program by passing reforms to the program in 1970 and 1973.[50] He made funding and administrative oversight of the program a responsibility of the federal government. In doing this, Nixon established national eligibility standards for Food Stamps, which included the working poor. In addition, Nixon made participation in the Food Stamp Program mandatory for all states.

With respect to Social Security, during his first term, Nixon approved a 20 percent increase in Social Security benefits and indexed Social Security to inflation.[51] This meant that as the cost of living went up, benefits would also rise. Unfortunately, the legislation did not include a corresponding increase in the payroll tax to fund the benefit increase. This, along with double-digit inflation and an increase in retired people per worker, contributed to an eventual funding crisis in the Social Security Program.

Nixon also pioneered in the use of **revenue sharing** and **block grants**.[52] General revenue sharing provided federal funds to local government for general operating expenses, whereas special revenue sharing (including block grants) contributed federal funds to local government for broad categorical areas.

Examples of Nixon's special revenue sharing were the Comprehensive Employment and Training Act (CETA) and the Housing and Community

Development Act. CETA was a consolidation of job training programs, some of which included public service jobs. (Hence, CETA funds could only be used by local government for this purpose.) The 1974 Housing and Community Development Act contained the Community Development Block Grant Program. These federal grants could be used by local communities for neighborhood improvement.

Title XX of the Social Security Act, passed during the Nixon administration, was another block grant. This legislation contributed federal funds to states for a broad array of social services, including critically needed services such as child care and domestic violence shelters. (It should be noted here that many local private nonprofit health and human service providers ultimately received these funds through service contracts with state government—part of the federal, state, and local partnership in social welfare.)

Furthermore, Nixon was the first president to pass legislation that used the tax system to give resources to the poor. This was the earned income tax credit.[53] The credit was a payment to the working poor with dependent children of up to $400 based on a percentage of their earned income for the year.

Other legislation passed during the Nixon administration included the Rehabilitation Act (1973), the Education for All Handicapped Act (1975), the Health Maintenance Act (1973), the Family Planning Services and Population Act (1974), the Occupational Safety and Health Act (1970), the Juvenile Justice and Delinquency Act (1974), and the Child Abuse Prevention Act (1974).[54] The Rehabilitation Act led to major efforts to make buildings, public transportation, and jobs accessible to people with disabilities, whereas the Education for All Handicapped Act subsequently mainstreamed students with disabilities in public schools. A bill that would lead to significant changes in the U.S. health care system, the Health Maintenance Act provided funding for the development of health maintenance organizations. Another Nixon health bill, the Family Planning Services and Population Act, helped low-income women obtain family planning services. The Occupational Safety and Health Act provided federal oversight of safety standards in industry through the establishment of the Occupational Safety and Health Administration, better known as OSHA.

The final two pieces of legislation dealt with issues related to child welfare. In the early 1970s, there was a growing concern in America with child abuse. Part of this concern was the physical abuse of children guilty of minor delinquencies but institutionalized in adult facilities. Consequently, amendments to the Juvenile Justice and Delinquency Act in 1974 offered support to local juvenile diversion services for runaway and truant youth, whereas the Child Abuse Prevention Act provided funding to universities and demonstration projects for research on child abuse and neglect.

It should also be noted that Nixon took some positive steps on the issue of civil rights.[55] For example, he followed through on desegregation of southern schools. In addition, the Nixon Administration's Philadelphia Plan promoted affirmative action in the employment of women and minorities. Yet, Nixon's agenda in his second term became more conservative with respect to federal spending on programs that might benefit these groups. Public opinion polls showed that many white ethnic, blue-collar, and middle-class groups resented the militant tactics of activist groups and opposed further social spending. Thus, during his second term, Nixon attempted to focus more on the concerns of this "silent majority"—issues such as inflation, government spending, and, ironically, crime. Facing the possibility of impeachment because of his involvement in the cover-up of a burglary at the Democratic National Headquarters in Washington, DC, Nixon was forced to resign the presidency in 1974.[56]

Class Discussion: Politics, Social Workers, and Ethics

The burglary on June 17th, 1972 that led to the resignation of President Richard Nixon took place in the Watergate building in Washington, DC; hence, the scandal came to be known as "Watergate."[57] It took place during Nixon's campaign for reelection. One of the men arrested in the break-in of the Democratic National Headquarters, James McCord, was a security consultant for the Central Intelligence Agency (CIA) and security coordinator for the Committee to Re-Elect the President (meaning Nixon). As later revealed, Watergate was only part of a vast array of break-ins, wiretaps, and sabotage connected to Nixon.[58] Nixon's rationalization of the Watergate burglary was that this type of political behavior was not unique to him, except that he got caught. In fact, in his first congressional campaign, all of his pamphlets were stolen in a break-in at Republican Party Headquarters in California. The pamphlets, costing $3,000, had been purchased with money received from his wife's sale of a piece of land.[59] Was Nixon's conduct in political office pretty much standard or was it significantly different and unethical? Does gaining and maintaining public office in America often involve unethical behavior? In any case, what lessons and concerns should social workers involved in politics derive from the Nixon story?

Developments in the Social Sector

The Women's Movement

The Civil Rights Movement of the 1960s helped to rekindle the Women's Movement of the 1970s.[60] Women have often been empowered to organize around their own specific issues by prior involvement in other social movements. Women were very active in the Civil Rights Movement just as they were in the Abolition Movement, the Temperance Movement, and the Anti-pauper Movement.

But the Civil Rights Movement was not the only factor contributing to the growth in the Women's Movement.[61] Other factors included the publication of Betty Friedan's book *The Feminine Mystique*. This best seller discussed "the problem that had no name." This problem was the lack of identity of women in America. That is, American women at the time gained recognition only through the achievements of their husbands and children. For middle-class women in the 1950s and 1960s, working outside the home was not an option. Thus, the homemaker living in the dream home in the suburbs with all the latest labor-saving appliances was, in fact, suffering from depression.

Another influential book was Susan Brownmiller's *Against Our Will*, published in 1975. This book discussed the various ways that women throughout history have been the victims of domestic violence and rape. The prevention of violence against women, therefore, became a key issue for the Women's Movement.

Another issue underlying the Women's Movement was discrimination in the workplace. Those women who did work outside the home were paid a lower wage than men doing the same work—about 69 cents for every dollar the male was paid. Furthermore, the 1973 *Roe versus Wade* Supreme Court decision legalizing abortion and the fact that the Great Society had failed to adequately address women's issues served to galvanize women across America. These kinds of issues came up again and again in the growing number of women's groups and women's studies courses. The result was a major campaign to pass an Equal Rights Amendment to the Constitution. In the end, the amendment was not passed, but the campaign helped women to see their common interests, leading to successful efforts in the 1980s and 1990s for increased women's rights and services.

Personal Profiles: Fannie Lou Hamer and Shirley Chisholm

One of the most high profile civil rights activists of the 1960s was a woman named Fannie Lou Hamer. Born in 1917 in Montgomery County, Mississippi, Fannie dropped out of school at age 6 to help support her family by picking cotton.[62] Yet, during her civil rights career, she would receive honorary degrees from two colleges, including the prestigious Howard University.

In August of 1962, Hamer tried to register to vote, but was rejected when she failed to interpret a section of the Constitution correctly.[63] She finally passed the screening test in December of 1962. However, when she tried to vote in August of 1963, she was rejected again, because she had not paid a poll tax for two years. This occurred after she had been arrested in June of 1963 in Winona, Mississippi, while trying to integrate a segregated bus terminal with a busload of other African Americans. While in jail, she was severely beaten by two inmates on orders from police officers.

Showing incredible courage, Hamer continued her community organizing around voter registration and other social issues throughout her life. In September of 1965, she was asked to testify at a closed hearing of the House Elections Committee. During her testimony, Hamer stated that if "Negroes were allowed to vote freely, I could be sitting up here with you right now as a congresswoman."[64]

A second prominent female activist in the 1960s was Shirley Chisholm. Born in 1924 in Brooklyn, New York, to immigrants from Barbados and Guiana, Chisholm went on to earn a master's degree in Education from Columbia University.[65] She was elected to Congress in 1969 while emphasizing such social issues as job training, equal education, adequate housing, enforcement of antidiscrimination laws, child care, and an end to the Vietnam War. In 1971, Chisholm ran for president of the United States, becoming the first viable female candidate of color. After the campaign, Chisholm stated: "What I hope most, is that now there will be others who will feel themselves as capable of running for high political office as any wealthy, good-looking white male."[66]

Impact on Professional Social Work

By the 1960s, social workers were no longer leaders in developing social policy on a national level. As discussed previously, social work was more concerned with casework and professionalization in the 1950s. Therefore, with the possible exception of H.E.W. Secretary Wilbur Cohen and social workers involved in a few influential projects such as Mobilization for Youth, social work, as a profession, was not at the forefront of policymaking during the Great Society as it had been in the New Deal. According to John Ehrenreich, there were very few articles on civil rights in *Social Work* before 1963.[67] Those most influential in 1960s social policy, people such as Michael Harrington and the Reverend Martin Luther King, were not social workers.

In fact, the profession of social work came under attack.[68] The National Welfare Rights Organization, established in 1967, advocated for the rights of public welfare clients. The target of this advocacy was often social workers in administrative positions in the public welfare bureaucracy. In addition, social work students began to protest against schools of social work. Given key social issues such as civil rights and welfare rights during the 1960s, many students believed social work curriculums to be irrelevant. As a result, schools of social work started adding courses in community organization, social planning, as well as race, culture, and oppression. Furthermore, social work courses started to include more information on systems theory, prevention, and the causes of social problems.

During the 1960s, casework, itself, was attacked for either ignoring the poor or controlling the poor.[69] Those who criticized casework for ignoring the poor pointed to all of the caseworkers serving the middle class in family service agencies around the country. The poor, critics contended, did not benefit from these agencies. Those who claimed that casework was overly controlling of the poor based their claims on social control theory. They pointed to America's system of philanthropy, of services based on the wealthy giving to the poor, as another form of colonialism—philanthropic colonialism. In response, schools of social work began emphasizing client advocacy and radical casework.

Later, the women's movement also had an impact on professional social work. The theoretical base of casework (with its heavy Freudian emphasis) was criticized for being sexist.[70] Consequently, during the 1960s and early 1970s, social work once again began to reflect the sociopolitical environment at the time. This environment emphasized systemic causes of social problems and social action to remedy these problems.

CONTENTSELECT

For more information on related social work topics, use the following search terms:

Block grants
Business boycotts
Civil Rights Act of 1964
Civil Rights Act of 1965
Civil Rights Movement
Community Action Programs
Community Mental Health
  Centers Act

Culture of poverty
Great Society
Maximum feasible partici-
  pation
Nonviolent resistance
Revenue sharing
Sit-ins
Supplemental Security Income

Title XX
War On Poverty
Women's Movement

NOTES

1. Michael Harrington, *The Other America* (Baltimore, MD: Penguin, 1971), p. 1.

2. James Leiby, *A History of Social Welfare and Social Work in the United States* (New York: Columbia University Press, 1978), pp. 272–273.

3. John Kenneth Galbraith, *Economics and the Public Purpose* (New York: Mentor, 1975), p. 152.

4. John Kenneth Galbraith, *The Affluent Society*, 4th ed. (Boston: Houghton Mifflin, 1984), pp. 260–267.

5. Ibid., p. 2.

6. Harrington, pp. 1–2, 17.

7. Ibid., pp. 1–2.

8. Clayborne Carson, ed., *The Autobiography of Martin Luther King, Jr.* (New York: TimeWarner, 1998), pp. 291–292.

9. James T. Patterson, *America's Struggle Against Poverty: 1900–1994* (Cambridge, MA: Harvard University Press, 1995), pp. 158–159.

10. Paul F. Boller, Jr., *Presidential Campaigns* (New York: Oxford University Press, 1985), p. 300.

11. Ibid.

12. Ibid., p. 301.

13. David Halberstam, *The Best and the Brightest* (New York: Fawcett Crest, 1972), p. 126.

14. Christopher Matthews, *Kennedy & Nixon: The Rivalry that Shaped Postwar America* (New York: Touchstone, 1997), pp. 128–129.

15. Peter Collier and David Horowitz, *The Kennedys: An American Drama* (New York: Warner Books, 1985), p. 40.

16. Matthews, p. 129.

17. Bruce S. Jansson, *The Reluctant Welfare State: American Social Welfare Policies—Past, Present, and Future,* 4th ed. (Belmont, CA: Wadsworth/Thomson Learning, 2001), p. 244; Walter I. Trattner, *From Poor Law to Welfare State: A History of Social Welfare in America,* 6th ed. (New York: The Free Press, 1999), p. 320.

18. Philip B. Kunhardt, Jr., ed., *Life in Camelot: The Kennedy Years* (Boston: Little, Brown and Company, 1988), p. 110.

19. Jansson, p. 244.

20. Jansson, p. 244; Leiby, p. 308.

21. Leiby, p. 310.

22. Jansson, p. 244; Leiby, p. 302.

23. Collier and Horowitz, p. 303.

24. Jansson, p. 246.

25. Halberstam, p. 810; see Thomas P. O'Neill, Jr., and William Novak, *Man of the House: The Life and Political Memoirs of Speaker Tip O'Neill* (New York: Random House, 1987).

26. Ibid., p. 369; Jansson, p. 247.

27. John H. Ehrenreich, *The Altruistic Imagination: A History of Social Work and Social Policy in the United States* (Ithaca, NY: Cornell University Press, 1985), p. 156; Carson, p. 50.

28. Carson, pp. 137, 153, 170.

29. Ibid., p. 192.

30. Carson, p. 289; Jansson, p. 248.

31. Jansson, p. 248.

32. Joseph A. Califano, Jr., *The Triumph & Tragedy of Lyndon Johnson: The White House Years* (College Station: Texas A&M University Press, 2000), p. 58.

33. Ibid., pp. 55–56.

34. Jansson, p. 250.

35. Ibid., pp. 250–251.

36. Ibid., pp. 251–252.

37. Jansson, pp. 254–255; Trattner, pp. 330–331; Leiby, p. 325.

38. Leiby, pp. 314–315.

39. Leiby, pp. 314–315; Jansson, p. 252.

40. Ehrenreich, pp. 169–175.

41. Edward D. Berkowitz, *America's Welfare State: From Roosevelt to Reagan* (Baltimore: Johns Hopkins University Press, 1991), p. 118.

42. Halberstam, p. 788.

43. Califano, p. 341.

44. Halberstam, p. 364.

45. Ibid., pp. 180, 219, 805–806.

46. Trattner, pp. 349–351.

47. Trattner, p. 349; Jannson, p. 277.

48. Jansson, p. 277; Trattner, pp. 349–351.

49. Jansson, p. 279; Trattner, p. 348.

50. Jansson, pp. 281–282.

51. Jansson, p. 282; Trattner, p. 348.

52. Jansson, pp. 282–284.

53. Trattner, p. 350.

54. Jansson, pp. 285–286; Phyllis J. Day, *A New History of Social Welfare,* 2nd ed. (Boston: Allyn & Bacon, 1997), p. 355.

55. Ibid., pp. 284–285, 286–289.

56. David Halberstam, *The Powers That Be* (New York: Dell, 1979), pp. 190, 846–847.

57. Robert H. Ferrell, "Emerging as a World Power," Arthur M. Schlesinger, Jr., ed., *The Almanac of American History* (New York: Barnes & Noble, 1993), p. 593.

58. Halberstam, pp. 847, 858; Ferrell, p. 593.

59. Matthews, p. 36.

60. Howard Zinn, *A People's History of the United States: 1492–Present* (New York: HarperPerennial, 1995), p. 494.

61. Ibid., pp. 495–501.

62. Harriet Sigerman, *Biographical Supplement and Index,* ed. Nancy F. Cott, *The Young Oxford History of Women in the United States,* vol. 2 (New York: Oxford University Press, 1995), p. 73; Kay Mills, *This Little Light of Mine: The Life of Fannie Lou Hamer* (New York: Dutton/Penguin Books, 1993), pp. 12, 248–249.

63. Mills, pp. 36–37, 50–51, 57–58.

64. Ibid., p. 318.

65. Sigerman, p. 37; Reba Carruth and Vivian Jenkins Nelson, *Women Leaders in Contemporary U.S. Politics* "Shirley Chisholm: Woman of Complexity, Conscience, and Compassion," Frank P. LeVeness and Jane P. Sweeney, eds. (Boulder, CO: Reinner, 1987), pp. 11, 13, 16.

66. Sigerman, p. 37.

67. Ehrenreich, p. 190.

68. Ibid., pp. 195–197.

69. Ibid., pp. 201–203.

70. Ibid., pp. 204–205.

9 The Conservative Transition in American Social Policy

"What a delightful surprise. I always thought it just trickled down to the poor."

Liberal critics of Reagan's supply-side economics predicted that the poor would receive minimal benefit from tax cuts for the rich, derisively calling it "trickle-down economics."

The Economic Context

Rise of the Global Economy

Globalization, as defined in Chapter 1 of this book, is "the integration of markets, nation-states, and technology to a degree never witnessed before."[1] The technologies that make a global economy possible include computerization, digitization, satellite communications, fiber optics, and the Internet. These technologies, as previously stated, are allowing corporations to create a global market for their goods and services, a market that increasingly reaches across national borders, defense systems, and cultures.

Did You Know?

Although American corporations have been leaders in the application of Internet technology, the research that led to the development of the Internet was done in the government sector of the United States, not the business sector as one might expect.[2] Despite laissez-faire rhetoric about government staying out of the way, the Internet is a good example of the way the public sector contributes to the private sectors, both for-profit and nonprofit, in the United States. Ultimately, it is a partnership for social welfare.

The roots of the current global economy can be traced, in part, to the Great Depression and World War II.[3] Policy planners in the United States wanted to prevent another "Great Depression" from happening in the future. To this end, policy planners from an elite private nonprofit group called the Council on Foreign Affairs, collaborating with planners from the federal State Department, provided President Franklin Roosevelt with a policy proposal for creating a postwar global economy. More specifically, the group's recommendations called for the creation of an institutional framework for an open global economy. Combined with similar proposals from other sources such as the U.S. Department of Treasury, this policy planning was agreed to by the representatives of several western nations at an international meeting at Bretton Woods, New Hampshire, when World War II ended.[4] The global plan led to the establishment of the **International Monetary Fund** (IMF) and the **World Bank.** The IMF became responsible for facilitating world trade by maintaining stability and liquidity in national currencies around the globe. In addition, the World Bank was charged with the mission of promoting capital investments in developing countries.[5] As the Cold War developed, these global economic policy plans also became a means to counter the Soviet Union and the spread of communism around the world.[6]

During the 1980s, the policies of the Reagan administration facilitated a series of corporate acquisitions, mergers, and downsizing. It was said to be the largest corporate restructuring in U.S. history, with over 25,000 such deals during the Reagan presidency.[7] What looked to the average observer to be a corporate sector out of control in pursuit of profit, was really a substantial redesign of the American economic sector.[8] The objective was to position American corporations for success in the new global economy. Then in 1994, during the Clinton administration, Congress passed legislation that approved the establishment of the **World Trade Organization.**[9] This organization's purpose is to facilitate world trade, in large part, by serving as an arbitrator in trade disputes between various nations around the world. These policy decisions by the World Trade Organization are binding, enforceable through trade sanctions on uncooperative countries.

Thus the age of the **multinational,** the **transnational,** and the **global corporation** is on us for better or for worse.[10] The promise is an integrated free-market economic system, led by the United States, that will raise the standard of living of all nations, developed and developing. The threat is that American economic, political, and social values will extinguish, to a great extent, cultural diversity and self-determination around the world.

Class Discussion: September 11th and the Threat of Increased Terrorism

Samuel Huntington, author of the 1996 book *The Clash of Civilizations and the Remaking of World Order,* claims: "In this new world the most pervasive, important, and dangerous conflicts will…[be] between peoples belonging to different cultural entities…The predominant patterns of political and economic development differ from civilization to civilization."[11]

On September 11, 2001, Islamic terrorists hijacked four U.S. commercial airplanes, one of which crashed in Pennsylvania, one hit the Pentagon building in Washington, DC, and two toppled the World Trade Towers in New York City. Thousands of people were killed in the attack. To what extent is globalization a factor in the attack? In other words, to what extent does September 11 represent a clash of cultures? What policy changes should be made to address the threat of increased terrorism? With its emphasis on respect for diversity, self-determination, and empowerment, what role can the profession of social work play in these international developments?

The Political Context

Reagan and New Federalism

The Reagan administration accelerated a conservative trend in social policy that began in the second term of Richard Nixon and continued through the presidencies of Gerald Ford and Jimmy Carter. Nixon began proposing cuts in federal spending on numerous programs in his second term, whereas Ford and Carter passed very little health and human service legislation (although the Carter administration did enact legislation supporting adoption and foster care in 1980).[12] During the 1970s, the general public was increasingly concerned with a stagnate economy, high inflation rates in consumer prices, rising taxes, and the increasing deficit in the federal government budget. In addition, government regulation of the business sector had increased enormously during the 1960s and 1970s, reflecting public concern at the time for worker safety, product safety, and environmental quality.[13] By the early 1980s, the concern, particularly on the part of business leaders, was overregulation.

Republican Ronald Reagan defeated incumbent Democratic President Jimmy Carter in 1980. Reagan took office with an agenda that prioritized balancing the federal budget (through cuts in wasteful government spending), cutting individual and corporate taxes, reducing government regulations (particularly of business), and increasing military spending.[14] To achieve all of this agenda, Reagan sought to decrease the role of the federal government in the American partnership for social welfare, preferring to rely more on private for-profit and nonprofit institutions. In Reagan's view, poverty-related programs such as AFDC and Food Stamps should once again become primarily a responsibility of state and local government. Thus, Reagan's New Federalism was really a return to the old role of the U.S. federal government in advancing social welfare.[15]

The essence of Reagan's economic recovery plan, known as supply-side economics, was that tax cuts for the wealthy would be reinvested in business expansion. Business expansion would create more jobs and consumer goods. More jobs would create the income needed to buy those consumer goods. In short, increased production would create increased demand for the goods produced. This was the premise underlying the supply-side economics promise that supply would create its own demand.[16]

Liberal critics predicted that the poor and working class would only receive a minimal benefit from the tax cuts and derisively referred to this strategy as "trickle-down economics." Furthermore, Reagan's seemingly contradictory proposal to cut taxes, increase military spending, and balance the federal budget all at the same time became known, sarcastically, as **"Reaganomics."**[17] Even Vice President George H. W. Bush criticized Reagan's policies when he earlier campaigned against Reagan for president. Bush labeled Reagan's economic policies **"voodoo economics."**

To the general public, much of Reagan's political agenda reflected his conservative ideology. This was no doubt true. He believed that responsibility for many health and human services should be placed at the state and local level, much the way it was before the New Deal. He was also a product of the Red Scare and the Cold War and therefore increased military spending as a defense against communism. Yet reductions in government spending, business regulation, and taxes were also what business elites claimed were needed in a global economy. International investors in a global economy would be more willing to invest their money in countries with streamlined governments. As Thomas Friedman explains in his influential book on globalization, *The Lexus and the Olive Tree:*

> In the era of globalization it is the quality of the state [i.e., federal government] that matters. You need a smaller state, because you want the free market to allocate capital, not the slow, bloated government, but you need a better state, a smarter state and a faster state, with bureaucrats that can regulate a free market, without either choking it or letting it get out of control.... One of the most competitive...advantages that a country can have today is a lean, efficient, honest civil service.[18]

With his large victory over Jimmy Carter, Reagan believed that he had a mandate from the people for his political agenda. His administration moved fast during its first term to enact several pieces of legislation to meet this conservative mandate. Part of Reagan's strategy was to take numerous categorical programs and combine them into relatively few block grants, while at the same time cutting total federal funding for the programs. Thus, the Omnibus Budget Reconciliation Acts of 1981 and 1982 reduced or eliminated many "means-tested" programs (i.e., programs in which eligibility is based on a certain level of income).[19] AFDC, Food Stamps, SSI, unemployment insurance, and low-income housing were cut. Funding for Title XX social services, which was incorporated into the Social Services Block Grant, was capped. In addition, incentive payments in the Aid to Families with Dependent Children program were eliminated. The legislation confirmed the belief by liberals that much of what Reagan called government waste was, in fact, federal health and human services.

Class Discussion: Political Parties and Government Spending

A major campaign theme for Reagan was big government spending. As the Republican candidate for president, he promised to give the government less money, while letting each taxpayer keep more of their hard-earned income. Once elected, Reagan cut a total of $140 billion from social programs, including the elimination of free school lunches for over one million poor children.[20] At the same time, however, Reagan increased defense spending by $181 billion. Is it true, then, that only Democrats "spend" your tax dollars? Is it closer to the truth to say that both major political parties, Democrats and Republicans, spend tax dollars. The difference lies in their respective spending priorities—that is, the incremental differences in each party's spending on individual budget items.

A second major piece of legislation passed during Reagan's first term was the Economic Recovery Tax Act of 1981. This legislation resulted in massive cuts in personal income taxes, particularly for wealthy Americans, while virtually eliminating the corporate tax. Indeed, the legislation represented the largest package of business tax cuts in history.[21] To illustrate, while corporations contributed about a quarter of total government revenue in the 1950s, by 1983, they contributed only 6 percent of government revenue. What is more, one study showed that 128 out of 250 large, profitable U.S. corporations paid nothing in federal income taxes in at least one year from 1981 to 1983. (Even conservatives complained of AFDC as being Aid For Dependent Corporations.)

The Reagan administration also passed the Job Training and Partnership Act during its first term.[22] This program replaced the CETA job training program. Its distinction was the establishment of Private Industry Councils. These councils awarded contracts to job placement agencies, which received a fee for every person placed in private sector jobs. This emphasis on private, not public sector, employment reflected the more conservative nature of Reagan's approach to social welfare.

Reagan also supported reform in the Social Security and Medicare programs.[23] More specifically, to address the growing concern about the solvency of Social Security, Reagan taxed some social security benefits of wealthy Americans and returned the money to the Social Security fund. This reform also included a future delay in social security benefits until eligible citizens reached the age of 67. With respect to Medicare reform, the Reagan administration established national levels of payment for 467 specific diagnostic categories. The purpose of this payment cap was to help control rising health care costs.

Ironically, much of Reagan's second term was spent correcting the mistakes of his first term. For example, the Balanced Budget and Emergency Deficit Control Act (better known as Gramm-Rudman in the media) was enacted in 1985 and mandated across-the-board budget cuts if the federal budget did not meet specified reductions.[24] The act was needed to address the drastic increase in the federal budget deficit created by Reagan's combination of tax cuts and defense spending increases. Despite his rhetoric about "big government spending" and his campaign pledges to balance the federal budget, in eight years as president, Reagan never submitted a balanced budget to Congress. Even James Baker, a close adviser to President Reagan, later admitted that their administration had cut taxes more than they had intended. Whereas the Reagan campaign had pledged to cut taxes by $500 billion, once elected, the Reagan administration enacted a $750 billion tax reduction.[25]

What is more, the 1981 Reagan tax legislation had actually resulted in tax increases for the working poor.[26] By 1984, a family of four had to start paying taxes when its annual income reached $8,700, even though the U.S. government considered such a family "poor" until its income reached $10,600. Consequently, the Reagan administration passed another major tax reform bill, the Tax Reform Act of 1986.[27] This legislation removed 6 million low-wage earners from federal tax obligations. In addition, to further rectify the mistakes of the 1981 tax cuts, the 1986 tax reform increased corporate taxes and closed many "tax loopholes" through which corporations and individuals avoided paying federal taxes. While doing all of this, the legislation still benefited upper-income Americans as well. That is, the 1986 tax legislation reduced tax rates for wealthy Americans to rates comparable to middle-class families.

Congress did pass some legislation related to health and human services in Reagan's second term.[28] For instance, the Stewart B. McKinney Homeless Assistance Act was enacted in 1987. This legislation distributed funding for homeless shelters, the rehabilitation of single-room apartments, health care (including mental health care), job training, homeless children's education, and nutrition. In addition, the Reagan administration enacted the Family Support Act of 1988. This bill was a welfare-to-work program that contributed funding to AFDC mothers for education, training, and child care. Finally, although critics felt he moved too slowly, Reagan increased research and public health funds for AIDS during his second term.

Personal Profile: Ronald Reagan

Born in Tampico, Illinois, in 1911 to a father who was an alcoholic shoe salesman and a mother who was a frustrated actress, Reagan worked his way through obscure Eureka College in hopes of being an actor or sports announcer.[29] His mediocre grades gave no indication of a future president of the United States. Yet Ronald Reagan became a very effective public speaker, earning him the nickname of the "Great Communicator." He kept his message simple, while weaving into his speeches many anecdotes and self-deprecating humor. He acquired many of these skills in his jobs in radio, television, and movies. One of his heroes and role models was Franklin D. Roosevelt. In fact, during Roosevelt's first year as president, Reagan was beginning a job as a part-time sports announcer on radio in Davenport, Iowa. In contrast to the loud and flamboyant public speaking style of traditional politicians in town halls, Reagan mastered a more conversational style of public speaking, one more appropriate for radio and television. Thus, as president in an age of television, audiences loved him.[30] The last Gallup Poll taken during Reagan's presidency indicated a public approval rating higher than any president leaving office since Franklin D. Roosevelt.

The First President Bush: George H. W. Bush

Reagan's vice president, George H. W. Bush, defeated the Democratic governor of Massachusetts, Michael Dukakis, for president in 1988. During his campaign, Bush repeatedly told voters to "stay the course" of the previous eight years under Reagan. And when he became president, that is essentially what Bush did, proposing very little new health and human service legislation for several reasons.[31] He got elected with a campaign pledge of "no new taxes." At the same time, Bush inherited huge deficits in the federal budget from his predecessor, Ronald Reagan. Thus, Bush found it difficult to fund new federal programs. He blamed his inactivity regarding domestic social problems on the Democratically controlled Congress, claiming Congress was in a state of "gridlock." Yet, to some observers, Bush seemed disinterested in domestic social issues from the start of his term in office and more preoccupied with foreign policy and world leadership. The Persian Gulf War later made this perception a moot point.

In its single term in office, the Bush administration did enact legislation resulting in the Child Care and Development Block Grant, signing the legislation in 1990.[32] This federal grant provided funding to local child care providers for administration, staff training, and direct care. Also in 1990, the Bush administration passed a major civil rights act, the Americans with Disabilities Act. The legislation opposed discrimination against people with disabilities in several areas, including employment, education, housing, and public accommodations. The act required employers to make reasonable accommodations for people with disabilities, including accommodations such as building modifications and the provision of interpreters.

Clinton and Neoliberalism

The conservative shift of the Democratic Party beginning with the Carter administration became known in the late 1980s and early 1990s as neoliberalism.[33] In the late 1980s, a group of young, aspiring Democratic politicians, a group that had not grown up during the Great Depression and the New Deal, formed the Democratic Leadership Council. The council included Bill Clinton, who would serve as its chair before running for president, as well as Al Gore, Richard Gephardt, Paul Tsongas, and Bill Bradley. In 1989, the council issued a new political agenda for the Democratic Party, an agenda detailed in *The New Orleans Declaration: A Democratic Agenda for the 1990s.* This agenda de-emphasized the welfare state mentality of the New Deal and Great Society eras. Instead, it aimed for a more moderate mix of compassion and free market economics. With America poised for leadership in the global economy, this new Democratic agenda was more optimistic about the potential for corporate contributions to social welfare, and, therefore, more willing to support legislation favorable to the business sector. Not without controversy among traditional liberals, including many social workers, this new Democratic agenda included a continued withdrawal of the federal government in ensuring national social welfare, particularly with respect to the federal funding of health and human services.

In the presidential election of 1992, Arkansas Governor Bill Clinton defeated George H. W. Bush. Clinton's subsequent legislative successes reflected his neoliberal philosophy and the more conservative mood of voters around the country. One of the most important and immediate ways that Clinton could support the business sector in the global economy (by attracting international investors) was to cut the huge federal budget deficit. Consequently, Clinton signed the 1993 Omnibus Reconciliation Bill, which, in fact, began cutting the federal deficit through a combination of spending cuts and tax increases, including increases on wealthy Americans.[34] By 1999, Clinton succeeded in erasing the federal budget deficit.

The Clinton administration also supported the American business sector's global expansion efforts through enactment of two international trade agreements, the North American Free Trade Agreement, better known as NAFTA, in 1993 and the General Agreement on Tariffs and Trade (GATT) in 1994.[35] The basic purpose of NAFTA is to better integrate the economies of the United States, Mexico, and Canada by reducing barriers among the countries to the flow of goods, services, and jobs. It is the North American piece of the global economy. Similarly, but on a world level, GATT is also intended to open national markets and facilitate international trade. For this reason, the GATT agreement led to the establishment of the World Trade Organization on January 1, 1995.

Furthermore, the Clinton administration's major social reform was, again, legislation with perceived benefits for American corporations competing in a global economy. This was the Personal Responsibility and Work Opportunities Act, passed late in Clinton's first term.[36] Meant to satisfy antiwelfare sentiment and further reduce federal social welfare spending, the legislation had been a campaign promise of Clinton to "end welfare as we know it." In so doing, the act ended Aid to Families with Dependent Children as an entitlement and replaced the program with a block grant, called Temporary Assistance to Needy Families (TANF). Under this new legislation, no individual or family is entitled to welfare. Although the law gives states some flexibility in administering federal funds, as a general rule, individuals must participate in work activity within two years of receiving assistance and families are limited to a total of five years assistance in a lifetime. (More details on TANF will be provided in Part II of this book.)

Other important legislations passed during the Clinton administration included the 1993 Family and Medical Leave Act and the 1994 Crime Bill. The Family and Medical Leave Act requires public and private employers with fifty or more employees to offer family or medical leave for up to twelve weeks.[37] Legitimate reasons for leave under the act include the illness of an employee or family member or maternity-related reasons. Although employers are not required to provide paid leave, the employer is mandated to continue health benefits and offer the same or a comparable job when the employee returns to work. Responding to surveys showing crime to be the leading social problem in the minds of voters, the Crime Bill provided funding to increase the size of police forces, build new prisons, and deliver certain crime-related services (including domestic violence services).[38] Although Clinton failed in his attempt to enact new national health insurance legislation, it should be noted that he achieved a more incremental victory when he increased federal funding to states in 1997 for children's health insurance. In addition, legislation was passed in 1996 that prevented private insurance companies from discriminating against mental health coverage.[39]

Social Developments

America's Shrinking Middle Class

During the administrations of Ronald Reagan and George H. W. Bush, the income gap between the rich and the poor widened, while many people slid from the middle class into the ranks of the working poor. Kevin Phillips in his 1990 book *The Politics of Rich and Poor: Wealth and the American Electorate in the Reagan Aftermath* emphasizes the great wealth accumulation of upper-income Americans during the Reagan years.[40] According to Phillips, from 1980 to 1988, the number of millionaires in the United States roughly doubled. What is more, the number of billionaires went from five in 1981 to fifty-two in 1988 when Reagan left office. The transfer and concentration of income and wealth during this period was on a scale of the post–Civil War Industrial Revolution—the so-called Robber Baron era of the Vanderbilts, Morgans, and Rockefellers.

According to historian Howard Zinn, the wealthiest 1 percent of the U.S. population experienced an 87 percent increase in after-tax income during the 1980s, whereas the bottom 80 percent of the population saw little or no change in their after-tax income.[41] Pulitzer Prize–winning reporters Donald Bartlett and James Steele in their book *America: What Went Wrong?* provide further data.[42] Between 1980 and 1989, the average wage for families in the $0–$20,000 annual income category rose 1.4 percent. In contrast, during the same time span, the average salary of those earning over $1 million annually shot up almost 50 percent.

Part of the cause of this widening income gap was due to the previously described restructuring in the economic sector, the repositioning of American corporations for success in the global market place. This repositioning resulted in an increase in high-technology jobs. Concurrently, however, American corporations drastically reduced the number of manufacturing jobs in the United States. To illustrate, from 1981 to 1991, 1.8 million manufacturing jobs were lost in the United States.[43] Many of these losses were the result of corporate acquisitions, mergers, and downsizing (i.e., reductions in the number of employees). Many domestic jobs were moved to foreign countries where labor costs were lower. Consequently, millions of Americans lost their jobs, falling out of the middle class as they took lower-paying jobs, often in the service sector. With the passage of NAFTA, many critics predicted these trends would continue under the Clinton administration.

Case Study: Victims in a Post-Industrial Era

The transition to a global economy is like other epic events in American history. Some people win and some lose. As with Westward Expansion and the Industrial Revolution, some take advantage of changing institutional structures to become wealthy; other, more vulnerable groups cling to familiar institutional relations and fall victim to events.

Bartlett and Steele offer the cases of Larry Weikel and Belinda Schell, both former blue-collar workers at the Diamond Glass Company in Royersford, Pennsylvania.[44] For most of the twentieth century, Diamond Glass was a typical industrial era company offering solid middle-class wages and benefits to local community residents. The corporation expected hard work and loyalty from employees; employees expected to retire from the company.

During the 1980s, however, Diamond Glass took advantage of Reagan business tax policies (which allowed corporations to take a tax deduction for corporate debt) to borrow money and acquire other glass companies. Soon Diamond Glass, itself, was acquired by another glass company, which proceeded to downsize the number of employees at the company, while expecting more production from the remaining employees. At the same time, the new management refused to invest in new technology and modern equipment. The strategy of the new owners appeared to be to squeeze as much profit as possible out of the plant in the short term and then shut it down, perhaps building a modern plant in a low-wage foreign country.

In any case, all of the employees of the Diamond Glass plant lost their jobs, including Larry Weikel and Belinda Schell. In an interview, Weikel, who was forty-seven years old at the time he lost his job, described his predicament: "That's all I ever did in my life, work in a glass plant. I went to work there when I came out of the service and, you know, I really never learned anything because all I did was make bottles."[45]

Schell at the time of the layoff was thirty-three years of age, married with three children. Although she earned $10 an hour at Diamond Glass, she was forced to take a job as a nursing home aide, paying considerably less. Her husband also lost his manufacturing job and had to accept a lower-paying job. Like the Schells, millions of Americans—both blue-collar and eventually white-collar workers—were compelled to take lesser-paying jobs after becoming a casualty of corporate reengineering and the transition to a global economy.

Did You Know?

Part of the transition to a global economy involved the reengineering of American corporations. Michael Hammer and James Champy published a best-selling book on the subject in 1993. Essentially, reengineering the corporation involves the use of new computer and information technologies to redesign corporate work processes and employee structures. Of interest to social workers is the fact that a major characteristic of reengineering is combining several jobs into one, thereby lowering corporate personnel costs, but adding to the problems of unemployment and poverty in America.[46]

Promotion of Charitable Giving and Volunteerism

As the administrations of Reagan, Bush, and Clinton supported the devolution of federal responsibility for health and human services to the states, at the same time, each encouraged increases in **volunteerism** and **charitable giving** to address unmet social welfare needs. In fact, beginning in the 1960s and continuing through the 1970s and 1980s, the federal government took an active role in establishing several national volunteer programs. These included Volunteers in Service to America (VISTA), Foster Grandparents, and the Retired Senior Volunteer Program.[47] The Bush administration continued this policy emphasis with its **Thousand Points of Light** program as did the Clinton administration with **AmeriCorps.** In addition, Hillary Rodham Clinton, in her role as the First Lady, organized the first White House Conference on Philanthropy in October of 1999.

Given the healthy American economy, Americans did increase their charitable giving during the 1980s and 1990s.[48] Including donations from individuals, bequests, foundations, and corporations, total charitable giving as a percent of the GDP increased from about 1.8 percent in 1980 to about 2.1 percent in 1999. In terms of inflation-adjusted dollars, total charitable giving in the United States grew from just over $120 billion in 1988 to $190 billion in 1999.

Did You Know?

By his mid-forties, Bill Gates, the computer software pioneer, had already given more money to charity than did Andrew Carnegie and John D. Rockefeller, Sr., in their entire lifetimes.[49] Adjusted for inflation, the total value of Carnegie's philanthropy in the year 2000 was about $3 billion, while Rockefeller's was roughly $6 billion. At the time, Gates had given away $17 billion.

Corporate Strategic Philanthropy

With respect to corporate giving, a significant increase in the number of private nonprofit organizations during the 1960s and 1970s created increased competition for corporate philanthropy. Many of these nonprofits were social advocacy groups, reflecting the increased concern for social reform during the 1960s and early 1970s. Cutbacks in federal discretionary spending during the 1980s and 1990s further increased competition for corporate donations. Corporations were not prepared to process the ever-growing requests for support.[50] With limited contributions and budgets, and facing increased competition in the global economy, American corporations looked for a way to get "more bang for their charitable buck." One solution was **corporate strategic philanthropy.**[51] Strategic philanthropy is the integration of contributions management into the overall strategic planning of the corporation. That is, "to do well by doing good," corporations began to target charitable contributions to serve their business interests while also meeting the needs of recipient organizations. Corporations achieved this by directing their donations to stakeholders and social issues that were important to the success of the company. When a publishing company makes a donation to a literacy program, both the literacy program, and eventually, the company benefit. That is corporate strategic philanthropy.

Examples of major American corporations practicing strategic philanthropy in the 1990s were McGraw-Hill, Dupont, IBM, Exxon, Digital Equipment, and Enron.[52] McGraw-Hill, the publishing company, focused its donations on literacy. Dupont, IBM, and Exxon were among the leading corporate donors to Harvard University. In return for their charitable contributions, these companies, no doubt, expected to receive research and highly trained personnel to benefit the company. Furthermore, Digital Equipment Corporation, given increases in its foreign revenues, began targeting a greater percentage of its donations to international groups—a trend that may accelerate as American corporations become increasingly global.

What is more, in another illustration of strategic philanthropy, American corporations began establishing local **public–private partnerships** with public entities to address social problems of mutual concern. The most prominent efforts were the public–private partnerships in education.[53] These partnerships included adopt-a-school projects, work experience programs, mentor programs, and the Boston Compact, which guaranteed jobs in exchange for public school improvements. In an increasingly high-tech economy, such efforts addressed the growing concern of the business sector regarding quality public education in America. Partnerships such as these, as well as corporate philanthropy and corporate social responsibility in general, are expected to become ever more important in a global economy. Glenn Prickett, vice president for corporate partnerships at Conservation International, states:

> There is no hiding place anymore for bad corporate behavior in a world of globally interconnected activism.... Customers, regulators and shareholders everywhere can now reward or punish companies for what they do in faraway places. For those who behave well, they can open doors and for those who behave badly they can close them.[54]

And Charles O. Holliday, chairman of DuPont Corporation, warns:

> With the Internet and all, now it's like you have six billion neighbors that you have to satisfy.... You can get government approval for lots of things, but now it's a question of whether you can build wider [public] coalitions.[55]

Critical Analysis: Private Philanthropy versus Public Funding

The Reagan, Bush, and Clinton administrations, as a matter of social policy, encouraged increased volunteerism and charitable giving to offset cuts in federal discretionary spending on various programs. Philanthropy has been defined as "voluntary action for the public good."[56] Can voluntary action in the form of volunteering and charitable donations ever fully replace significant pieces of New Deal or Great Society programs? Does philanthropy have to be coerced through taxation? What is the proper mix of private and public funding in the U.S. social welfare partnership?

Developments in Social Work

Reflective of the conservative trend in American society during the late 1970s through the 1990s, the profession of social work returned to a casework emphasis, specifically, clinical social work (i.e., casework with a strong psychotherapy orientation).[57] Accordingly, the National Federation of Societies for Clinical Social Work was established in 1971. This period in social work history also witnessed a trend toward private practice. This was, in part, the result of the profession's successful lobbying for private insurance reimbursement as well as Medicare reimbursement. Schools of social work experienced healthy enrollments of students wanting concentrations in casework, whereas students focusing on macrolevel practice, including administration and community organization, decreased. In addition, the profession and its educational programs began to focus more on lifespan adjustments (particularly of the middle class), family therapy, and group work.

With the growth of managed health care in the 1990s, the broadness and flexibility of the social work profession allowed it to redefine its role in an increasingly cost-controlled health care system. Social workers began to emphasize existing roles and explore new roles in areas such as care management (including the appropriate use of services), community outreach and support, integrated care (ensuring continuity of service), ethical care (as advocates within and outside the health care system), brief psychotherapy, and prevention (including community organization roles in advocating for healthy community environments).[58]

Furthermore, as the 1990s came to a close, social workers could be found working for corporations in Employee Assistance Programs, community relations departments, and charitable contributions programs. It is likely that the knowledge, skills, and values of social workers in areas such as race, cultural, oppression, diversity, and self-determination will be even more attractive in the future to corporations doing business in nations around the world.

CONTENTSELECT

For more information on related social work topics, use the following search terms:

AmeriCorps

Charitable giving

Corporate strategic
   philanthropy

Global economy

International Monetary Fund

Neoliberalism

Public–private partnerships

Supply-side economics

Thousand Points of Light

Volunteerism

Welfare reform

World Bank

World Trade Organization

NOTES

1. Thomas L. Friedman, *The Lexus and the Olive Tree* (New York: Anchor Books, 2000), p. 9.

2. Friedman, p. 63.

3. David C. Korten, *When Corporations Rule the World* (West Hartford, Connecticut: Kumarian and San Francisco, C.A.: Berrett-Koehler, 1995), pp. 134–135.

4. Friedman, p. 59.

5. Korten, p. 136.

6. Friedman, p. xix.

7. Lou Cannon, *President Reagan: The Role of a Lifetime* (New York: Public Affairs, 2000), p. 8.

8. Friedman, p. 59.

9. Lori Wallach and Michelle Sforza, *Whose Trade Organization? Corporate Globalization and the Erosion of Democracy* (Washington, DC: Public Citizen, 1999), pp. 13, 18.

10. Neil Heilbroner and Lester Thurow, *Economics Explained: Everything You Need to Know About How the Economy Works and Where It's Going* (New York: Touchstone, 1994), pp. 246–248; see also Christopher Lasch, *The Revolt of the Elites and the Betrayal of Democracy* (New York: Norton, 1995) and Jeremy Rifkin, *The End of Work: The Decline of the Global Labor Force and the Dawn of the Post-Market Era* (New York: Tarcher/Putnam, 1996).

11. Samuel P. Huntington, *The Class of Civilizations and the Remaking of World Order* (New York: Touchstone, 1997) pp. 28–29.

12. Bruce S. Jansson, *The Reluctant Welfare State: American Social Welfare Policies—Past, Present, and Future,* 4th ed. (Belmont, CA: Wadsworth/Thomson Learning, 2001), pp. 291–293.

13. Lester Thurow, *The Zero-Sum Society: Distribution and the Possibilities for Economic Change* (New York: Penguin, 1981), p. 3; William C. Frederick, Keith Davis, and James E. Post, *Business and Society: Corporate Strategy, Public Policy, Ethics,* 6th ed. (New York: McGraw-Hill, 1988), pp. 166–168.

14. Deborah Hart Strober and Gerald S. Strober, *Reagan: The Man and His Presidency* (Boston, Houghton Mifflin Company, 1998), pp. 129–131; Cannon, p. 6.

15. Phyllis J. Day, *A New History of Social Welfare,* 3rd ed. (Boston: Allyn & Bacon, 2000), pp. 376–377.

16. Heilbroner and Thurow, p. 126.

17. Jeffrey H. Birnbaum and Alan S. Murray, *Showdown at Gucci Gulch: Lawmakers, Lobbyists, and the Unlikely Triumph of Tax Reform* (New York: Vintage, 1988), p. 25; Cannon, p. 223.

18. Friedman, p. 158.

19. Jansson, pp. 319–320; Day, p. 379.

20. Howard Zinn, *A People's History of the United States: 1492–Present* (New York: HarperPerennial, 1995), pp. 565–566.

21. Birnbaum and Murray, pp. 7, 11–12.

22. Jansson, p. 323.

23. Ibid., p. 322.

24. Jansson, p. 326; Birnbaum and Murray, p. 31.

25. Strober and Strober, pp. 130–131.

26. Birnbaum and Murray, pp. 54–55.

27. Jansson, p. 326.

28. Jansson, p. 326; Diana M. DiNitto, *Social Welfare: Politics and Public Policy,* 5th ed. (Boston: Allyn & Bacon, 2000), pp. 88–89.

29. Cannon, pp. 16, 172, 177.

30. Ibid., p. 84, xi.

31. Jansson, p. 328.

32. DiNitto, pp. 151–152, 370.

33. Howard Jacob Karger and David Stoesz, *American Social Welfare Policy: A Pluralist Approach,* 4th ed. (Boston: Allyn & Bacon, 2002), pp. 13–14.

34. Jansson, pp. 364, 404.

35. Korten, p. 80; Wallach and Sforza, p. 2.

36. Children's Defense Fund, *Summary of the New Welfare Legislation (Public Law 104-193).* Retrieved from the World Wide Web on August 27, 1997: www.childrensdefensefund.org/welfarelaw.html; George Stephanopoulos, *All Too Human: A Political Education* (Boston: Back Bay Books, 2000), p. 420.

37. Karger and Stoesz, pp. 82–83.

38. Jansson, pp. 368–369.

39. Ibid., p. 390.

40. Kevin Phillips, *The Politics of Rich and Poor: Wealth and the American Electorate in the Reagan Aftermath* (New York: HarperPerennial, 1991), p. 10.

41. Zinn, p. 569.

42. Donald L. Bartlett and James B. Steele, *America: What Went Wrong?* (Kansas City, Missouri: Andrews and McMeel, 1992), p. 7.

43. Ibid., p. xi.

44. Ibid., pp. 12–16.

45. Ibid., p. 15.

46. Michael Hammer and James Champy, *Reengineering the Corporation: A Manifesto for Business Revolution* (New York: HarperBusiness, 1994), p. 51.

47. Jerry D. Marx, "Motivational Characteristics Associated with Health and Human Service Volunteers," *Administration in Social Work,* 23, no. 1: 51 (1999).

48. Holly Hall and Nicole Lewis, "$190-Billion Bonanza for Charity," *Chronicle of Philanthropy,* 1 June 2000; Ann E. Kaplan, *Giving USA: The Annual Report on Philanthropy for the Year 1991*

(New York: AAFRC Trust for Philanthropy, 1992), p. 13.

49. Thomas J. Billitteri, "Who Gave the Most: Carnegie, Rockefeller, or Gates?" *Chronicle of Philanthropy*, 13 January 2000. Retrieved from the World Wide Web on July 19, 2000: http://philanthropy.com/premium/articles/v12/i06/06003201.htm.

50. Jerry D. Marx, "The Effect of Strategic Philanthropy on Corporate Support of Health and Human Services" (Ph.D. diss., Boston College, 1884), pp. 15–16.

51. Jerry D. Marx, "Corporate Strategic Philanthropy: Implications for Social Work," *Social Work* 43, No. 1: p. 35 (1998).

52. Jerry D. Marx, "Strategic Philanthropy: An Opportunity for Partnership Between Corporations and Health/Human Service Agencies," *Administration in Social Work* 20, No. 3: 58 (1996); Jerry D. Marx, "Corporate Philanthropy: What is the Strategy?" *Nonprofit and Voluntary Sector Quarterly* 28, No. 2: p. 187 (1999).

53. Marx (1996), pp. 58, 68–69.

54. Friedman, pp. 289–290.

55. Ibid., p. 290.

56. Robert L. Payton, *Philanthropy: Voluntary Action for the Public Good* (New York: Macmillan, 1988).

57. John H. Ehrenreich, *The Altruistic Imagination: A History of Social Work and Social Policy in the United States* (Ithaca, NY: Cornell University Press, 1985), pp. 207–208.

58. See the following journal articles: Kimberley Strom-Gottfried and Kevin Corcoran, "Confronting Ethical Dilemmas in Managed Care: Guidelines for Students and Faculty," *Journal of Social Work Education* 34, No. 1: pp. 109–119 (1998); Susan S. Manning, "The Social Worker as Moral Citizen: Ethics in Action," *Social Work* 42 No. 3: 223–230 (1997); Janet D. Perloff, "Medicaid Managed Care and Urban Poor People: Implications for Social Work," *Health and Social Work* 21, No. 3: pp. 189–195 (1996); Frederic G. Reamer, "Managing Ethics Under Managed Care," *Families in Society: The Journal of Contemporary Human Services:* pp. 96–100 (January/February 1997); Robert Sunley, Advocacy in the New World of Managed Care," *Families in Society: The Journal of Contemporary Human Services:* pp. 84–93 (January/February 1997).

PART TWO

Current Services and Issues in the American Social Welfare Partnership

10 Current Programs and Issues in Health and Human Services

"I would share my cookies, but I'm afraid I'll set up a cycle of dependency."

Critics claim that public assistance creates a cycle of dependency among the poor.

Social Insurance Programs

Social Security

American social welfare, thanks to Franklin D. Roosevelt and the **Social Security Act of 1935,** is furthered currently by two major categories of cash support programs: social insurances and public assistance.[1] Social insurances are based on the prior earnings and payroll contributions of an individual, whereas public assistance, typically referred to as *welfare,* is based on the financial need of an individual. The primary social insurance programs today in America are Old Age, Survivors, and Disability Insurance; unemployment insurance; and workers' compensation.

Let's begin with Old Age, Survivors, and Disability Insurance, commonly known as **Social Security.** Social Security, like other social insurances, is an example of a **universal program,** because American citizens are entitled to participate in the program as a social right.[2] In other words, program participation is not based on financial need.In 2001, a total of $432 billion was paid in Social Security benefits.[3] By the end of 2001, 45.9 million Americans were receiving these benefits. Funding for Social Security actually comes from a payroll tax, which is shared in an equal proportion by the employer and employee. A practice begun during the Nixon administration, Social Security benefits are adjusted when the cost of living increases.[4]

To receive Social Security, a person must contribute payroll taxes during his/her working years, earning credits toward future Social Security benefits.[5] Those individuals contributing payroll taxes for a minimum of ten years (i.e., forty quarters in social security eligibility terms) are covered permanently under the program. Individual benefit levels are determined by the level of covered earnings and the age of retirement. People born before 1938 can receive full Social Security retirement benefits at age 65, whereas this age gradually increases for others. For example, for those born in 1960 or later, the full retirement age is 67.

The disability insurance part of Social Security assists people of any age who meet certain eligibility criteria. More specifically, people can qualify if they have enough Social Security credits and show medical proof of a disability that will prevent them from substantial employment for a year or more. A person with a condition expected to result in death may also qualify.[6] When the individual turns 65 years of age, disability benefits automatically become old-age benefits. Finally, survivors insurance covers various categories of dependent children, parents, widowers, and widows. These categories of recipients receive benefits when a worker insured through Social Security dies.

A fundamental point to remember is that Social Security is a very effective antipoverty program. That is to say, most recipients are raised above the poverty line by social security.[7]

Unemployment Insurance

Unemployment insurance is a second major social insurance program. Like Social Security, unemployment insurance is an effective poverty prevention program, although it is a temporary aid.[8] That is, unemployment benefits normally last a maximum of twenty-six weeks. In the fiscal year 2001, a total of $28.13 billion was spent in the United States on unemployment insurance benefits. Although governed by federal standards, individual states determine eligibility for unemployment benefits, the amount and duration of the benefits, and the amount that employers must contribute. Except for three states, which require a minimal employee contribution, funding for unemployment insurance is derived solely from an employer payroll tax.

About 85 percent of the total American labor force is covered by unemployment insurance. Farmers, domestic workers, and self-employed workers are not eligible for unemployment benefits. In addition, few of the poor receive unemployment insurance. The poor can be excluded from benefits for several reasons. A poor individual may not qualify if that person worked less than two of four quarters in the qualifying year or if the person earned less than a minimum level of dollars. If the individual was terminated from a job for misconduct or quit voluntarily, he or she may be excluded. Furthermore, in most states, time spent in job training can prevent an individual from qualifying for unemployment benefits, because the individual is not immediately available and looking for work.

Workers' Compensation

The third major social insurance program in the United States is **workers' compensation.** In fact, it is the oldest major social insurance program in the nation, dating back to the Progressive Era at the beginning of the 1900s.[9] Spending by employers nationally on direct written premiums for workers' compensation totaled $31.7 billion in 2001.[10] Each state oversees its own workers' compensation program (with no federal standards). The program provides victims of work-related injuries with cash, medical care, and to a limited extent, rehabilitation services. It also compensates survivors if an injury is fatal. Like unemployment insurance, workers' compensation does not cover all workers. Farm and domestic workers are not covered in many states. For those wage and salary workers in the United States that are covered, state laws generally specify a payment rate of two-thirds of the injured worker's previous pay.

In contrast to injuries, coverage for occupational illnesses is a weak part of workers' compensation. Most states only pay benefits for illnesses that appear within "several" years after the worker leaves a company. In other words, the worker has a relatively short amount of time to prove his/her case.

Contributions of American Business to Retirement Planning

Employers, as previously stated, contribute to the current U.S. public Social Security system. However, many older Americans rely on both Social Security and private pension plans after they retire. To illustrate, in 1988, over half of wage and salaried workers over age 24 took part in a pension plan.[11] In that year, about three-quarters of workers in corporations employing over a thousand people were covered by such plans, whereas almost 80 percent of unionized workers participated in private pension plans. Many corporations (and other employers) offer **401(k) retirement plans** in which employees typically contribute a small percentage of their before-tax income to their 401(k) fund. These plans often include an employer contribution as well.[12] In addition, profit-sharing plans are frequently offered to employees in major American corporations. In 1984, there were close to a half-million profit-sharing programs in the American business sector.[13]

Another retirement-related corporate benefit is the employee stock ownership plan.[14] The number of these plans in the American business sector grew dramatically starting in the mid-1970s. By 2000, there were 11,500 such plans, covering 8.5 million employees. In an employee stock ownership plan, the employees invest some of their wages or salary in their company's stock and receive dividends regularly like other company investors. On retirement, the employee can either take the company stock from the fund or sell the shares back to the corporation.

The American government sector has played an important role in the development of these private plans. They are not just a good idea promoted by the business sector alone. Both the federal government and state governments have passed legislation to encourage business to offer these plans. For instance, between 1974 and 1985, Congress passed sixteen pieces of legislation encouraging the development of employee stock ownership plans, and thirteen states passed similar laws.[15]

The American government has also encouraged the use of another private retirement option, individual retirement accounts (**IRAs**). Tax legislation passed during the Clinton administration greatly increased opportunities for Americans to use IRAs.[16] The 1997 Tax Act, by increasing the income limits of those eligible to make tax deductible IRA contributions, will increase the number of individuals and couples using traditional IRAs. The law also created a new nondeductible IRA that accumulates income tax-free. In addition, the 1997 law facilitates the use of IRAs to pay for higher education expenses and first-time homes.

Critical Analysis: What about Enron and WorldCom?

In 2002, Americans were shocked by the news of several major cases of corporate accounting fraud.[17] Corporations such as Enron, a major energy company, and WorldCom, a long distance and data systems company, purposely misled investors and employees to appear more profitable than they actually were. When such companies file for bankruptcy, employees can lose all or most of their retirement savings. Can corporations be trusted as a major source of retirement savings? Are Enron and WorldCom exceptions in the corporate world or are they indicative of widespread corporate corruption? Are they clear examples of why some government regulation of the business sector is needed?

Current Issues in Social Insurance: The Viability of Social Security

The American Social Security system is considered by many observers to be seriously flawed. Some of the key issues include sustainability, the influence of the system on economic growth, and the equity of the system for various participants.[18] With respect to the sustainability issue, the U.S. Social Security system is a "pay-as-you-go" system, meaning that payroll taxes on today's workers and employers pay for the current Social Security benefits of former workers (i.e., retired workers). The sustainability of the system can become an issue when the ratio of retirees to workers becomes too large to finance.[19] In 1950, there were 0.14 retirees per worker in the United States. By 2020, with the aging of the "baby boomer" generation, there are projected to be 0.29 retirees per worker in the United States, and by 2040, 0.39 retirees per worker are expected. Thus, policymakers are concerned about the long-term financial viability of the currently structured Social Security system. As discussed earlier in this book, the Reagan administration raised the age for receiving Social Security retirement benefits to 67.[20] Policy alternatives considered in 2001 by President George W. Bush to address the sustainability of Social Security include raising payroll taxes, lowering Social Security benefits, tying future retirement benefits to inflation instead of wage growth, and privately-managed retirement savings accounts (also called private-investment accounts).[21]

The last option, the private-investment accounts, will establish personal retirement accounts, managed by private pension and investment companies, with part of the Social Security tax currently paid by workers.[22] Private-investment accounts will make America's Social Security system more of a public–private partnership than it is today. Proponents of this policy option state the potential for a higher rate of return on retirement savings, thereby addressing the sustainability issue. Opponents of this policy proposal warn of the market risks and relatively high administrative costs of private-investment accounts.[23]

Public Assistance Programs

The second major category of American cash support programs is called public assistance. **Public assistance programs** are **selective programs** in that benefits are based on individual need. Need is determined by a test of income, that is, a means test.[24] The three primary public assistance programs in the United States are Temporary Assistance to Needy Families, Supplemental Security Income, and General Assistance.

Temporary Assistance to Needy Families

The 1996 welfare reform enacted by the Clinton administration ended Aid to Families with Dependent Children (AFDC) as an entitlement and replaced the program with a block grant, called **Temporary Assistance to Needy Families (TANF)**.[25] In 2002, the federal government enacted close to $16.7 billion for TANF. To receive federal funds in the AFDC program, states had to provide matching funds. Under the 1996 legislation, states do not provide matching funds but they do need to meet a "maintenance of effort" requirement; that is, states must maintain spending equal to at least 75 percent of their fiscal year 1994 spending on AFDC and related services (80 percent if work participation rates are not met by the state). TANF gives states some flexibility in administering federal funds. For example, states can transfer up to 30 percent of their TANF block grant funding to either their Child Care Development Block Grant or their Social Services Block Grant, although starting in fiscal year 2003, TANF transfers to the Social Services Block Grant will be limited to 4.25 percent.

The fundamental difference between the new TANF and former AFDC programs is that under TANF, no individual or family is entitled to welfare.[26] As a general rule, individuals must participate in work activity within two years of receiving assistance and families are limited to a total of five years assistance in a lifetime. If a program participant refuses work requirements, states have the option to reduce or eliminate assistance to the family. This could include the loss of Medicaid. The exception to this provision is when participants refuse work because they cannot find or afford child care for a child under six years of age. Although the 1996 legislation did not guarantee that this needed child care would be provided to the participant, states are mandated to spend 70 percent or more of Child Care Entitlement funding, which is part of the Child Care and Development Fund, on families receiving TANF, transitioning from TANF, or at-risk of becoming TANF eligible. Child Care Entitlement was funded in fiscal year 2002 at $2.7 billion.

Another important feature of TANF, as originally designed, concerns minor parents.[27] Minors who are parents cannot receive TANF assistance unless they are living at home with their parents or in another adult-supervised setting. In addition, these minors must attend high school or an alternative educational or training program as soon as their child is 12 weeks old.

Supplemental Security Income

The **Supplemental Security Income (SSI)** program was established during the Nixon administration.[28] It was essentially a restructuring of the Social Security Act's public assistance programs for blind and older Americans. Aiming to assure a minimum monthly income, the program supplements the income of poor people who are aged 65 or older, blind, or disabled.[29] SSI recipients have grown from 4 million in 1974 to 6.4 million in January 2002. A total of $30.5 billion was spent by the federal government on SSI benefits in 2001. Contrary to the misconception that SSI is funded by Social Security trust funds, the program is funded out of general tax revenues.

People with disabilities are the largest group of SSI clients, representing 87 percent of total recipients in 2001. *Disability* is defined under SSI guidelines as a "physical or mental impairment that prevents substantial employment activity and has lasted or probably will last for at least a year or may result in death."[30] The Ticket to Work and Self-Sufficiency program, a new Bush administration program to help disabled SSI recipients with vocational rehabilitation and employment, is expected to be in operation nationwide by 2004.

General Assistance

The third major public assistance program in the United States is called **general assistance.**[31] It is a program for the needy who do not qualify for previously described federal assistance. Forty-one states and the District of Columbia offer general assistance, although in some states, only certain counties provide assistance. As its name suggests, the program provides general "safety net" help to the poor. Benefits include cash and/or in-kind payments. Similar to TANF, twenty-one states require "employable" adults to work or enter job training in order to maintain eligibility for general assistance benefits. Some states also impose time limits on all or certain categories of their general assistance caseload. These requirements reflect the increased tightening by many states of general assistance eligibility for adults considered employable during the 1990s.

Current Issues in Public Assistance: A Critical Analysis of Welfare Reform

There are many issues of concern to the social work profession regarding the Temporary Assistance to Needy Families (TANF) program.[32] The 1996 Personal Responsibility and Work Opportunity Act, which established TANF, contained no explicit requirement that poor families get cash assistance. That is, under this welfare reform legislation, states can opt to limit aid to vouchers or services. These features of the new approach to public assistance present a threat to the social work principle of self-determination, because they provide less flexibility to caseworkers and clients in the use of welfare assistance. The provisions of the law allowing states to reduce spending on welfare to 75 percent of fiscal year 1994 state spending and to transfer TANF funds to child care or social services block grants do give states some flexibility. However, there are potential negative ramifications to this aspect of the law as well. TANF funds spent on other services could result in less basic subsistence support to poor families. Such transfers of public assistance may "rob Peter to pay Paul."

Another issue concerning TANF involves the right of clients to appeal TANF decisions. The former federal law regarding public assistance was very specific in guaranteeing clients the right to appeal decisions against them. The 1996 legislation, however, is more general on this issue. States must submit their own plans, which may vary considerably in the protection of client rights.

A final issue regards the potential ramifications of the **charitable choice** clause of the 1996 welfare reform, a provision that encourages states to increase the involvement of religious organizations in federal programs such as TANF. Is this a significant step back in time to the colonial system of church-administered relief, a system that viewed immorality as a primary cause of poverty? Are today's church organizations willing and able to offer substantially increased services? Even if such organizations are funded under the charitable choice clause of the 1996 welfare reform, are these religious organizations the best qualified service providers? In other words, are faith-based partnerships between the public sector and the religious community in the best interests of TANF and other needy families?

Did You Know?

Welfare reform got its major push from city and state governments.[33] These levels of the public sector began experiencing severe budget crises during the 1970s and 1980s. A primary example was New York City. New York experienced a fiscal crisis in 1975. Public assistance, among other things, was blamed for the city's fiscal problems, precipitating a movement to reform city welfare. During the 1980s, other cities followed New York's example. At the same time, state governments around the country began asking for waivers of federal regulations concerning public assistance. As a result, many features of TANF, including time limits and teen parent restrictions, had already been implemented at the state level when the 1996 federal legislation was enacted.

Health Services

Medicare and Medicaid

The federal government supports a number of health services for the poor, including services for war veterans, Native Americans, women, and children.[34] It also supports a national network of community health centers, meant to supplement the services of private physicians, particularly in low-income communities. Medicare and Medicaid, however, are the two major public health care programs in the United States. Established during the Johnson administration and the Great Society, both programs are **in-kind services,** meaning no cash support is given directly to the individual.[35]

Medicare covers most hospital and medical costs for people aged 65 and over as well as for those on Social Security disability.[36] Medicare is provided without regard to the individual's income. Social Security recipients, railroad retirees, federal and state government employees, in addition to some people with kidney disease or a permanent disability, are eligible for Medicare.

Medicare is the second largest domestic program, second only to the Social Security program. In fiscal year 2002, Medicare's budget totaled $212.3 billion. The program is funded by a payroll tax paid by employers and employees.

There are two parts to the Medicare program: Part A and Part B. Part A is basic hospital insurance. It assists in covering the costs of hospitalization (including inpatient and outpatient services in rural critical access hospitals), skilled nursing facilities, hospice care, and some home health services. Part B is an optional supplementary medical insurance. It helps in covering the costs of physician services, outpatient hospital care, physical and occupational therapy, and some home health care. Those who choose Part B pay a premium, which was $54 per month in 2002. Unfortunately, as of August 2002, a key issue in the Medicare program continues to be its inadequate coverage of prescription drugs, particularly for older Americans.

The second major public health program, **Medicaid,** helps to finance health care for the poor.[37] In 2002, the federal government's budget for Medicaid was $36.8 billion. Although there is a federal contribution, the states also pay a share of Medicaid's costs. Federal regulations specify mandatory Medicaid eligible groups and the basic health services that must be offered under Medicaid. Services are primarily administered by individual states, including decisions regarding the duration of services and optional services. About 45 percent of Medicaid recipients in fiscal year 1998 also received cash assistance, either TANF or SSI. Most recipients of Medicaid are children, representing 51 percent of recipients in fiscal year 1998. However, most Medicaid dollars go to people who are blind or have other disabilities. In fiscal year 1998, this group accounted for 39 percent of total Medicaid spending.

Medicaid, historically, has been a **vendor system.** That is, payments are made directly to the service provider. In fiscal year 1998, fee-for-service payments constituted 79 percent of total Medicaid spending. Yet, by 2000, most Medicaid enrollees (57 percent) were actually enrolled in Medicaid managed care, reflecting a growing trend in the United States.

Private Insurance and the Managed Care System

Millions of Americans, of course, obtain private health insurance through their employer. To better control the rising costs of health care, employers in the United States have increasingly utilized managed care. Although forms of managed care have existed on the West Coast and in the Northeast since the 1930s and 1940s, respectively, **health maintenance organizations (HMOs)** were introduced nationally in the 1970s.[38] Health care consumers under managed care select a **primary care physician** from a network of health care providers. Unless they are experiencing an emergency, those needing medical attention usually see their primary care physician first. If needed, the primary care physician will then make a referral for more specialized services. Thus, the primary care physician serves as a gatekeeper in managing health care services and costs.[39]

In most managed care models, health care is provided to a defined number of enrollees in the health care plan.[40] Under capitation-based plans, all revenue for participating service providers is earned upfront through a contractual agreement between the employer and managed care organization. The HMO or other managed care entity, therefore, receives a fixed dollar amount per enrollee per month. Consequently, the services of physicians and hospitals participating in the managed care system become cost centers that need to be managed to stay within the contracted budget. The aim is to create an incentive to keep people well (i.e., prevention) and to serve clients in the most cost-effective manner when they do need health care.

Current Issues in Managed Care

The fundamental problem with managed health care is the conflict between the goals of high quality and low costs.[41] More specifically, managed care becomes a problem for health care consumers when minimizing costs takes priority over patient needs and quality health care. Since the emergence of managed care, many issues related to this fundamental problem have come to the attention of consumers, social workers, and policymakers.[42] The downgrading of personnel qualifications to save money was an immediate concern. In addition, patients were faced with predetermined service cut-off dates. Women giving birth, for example, were given hospital stay limits based on cost considerations. Patients also perceived policies regarding the use of specialists to be arbitrary and not necessarily based on patient need.

A more recent issue is the effect that managed care might have on urban community service systems, including public hospitals and public health clinics frequently used by Medicaid patients.[43] The number of states implementing mandatory managed care plans for Medicaid recipients is growing. To illustrate, from 1993 to 1994, Medicaid managed care enrollment in the United States jumped from 4.8 million to 7.8 million. That represented an increase of 63 percent. And as previously stated, by 2000, most Medicaid recipients (57 percent) were enrolled in Medicaid managed care. Underlying this trend is the assumption that competition for managed care contracts will increase the supply of health care providers in low-income communities. However, without adequate capitation payments, this may never happen.

Furthermore, managed care companies may leave out certain community-based organizations that serve the poor from their service provider networks. These community organizations often are in poor financial condition, have outdated management information systems, and use decaying facilities and equipment. In short, they are relatively costly to a managed care organization. More fundamentally, traditional community-based health and human services adhere to value systems that conflict with cost-centered systems. These organizations historically have provided service with an emphasis on individual need in contrast to other criteria such as ability-to-pay or profit. In any case, they are inexperienced in competing for clients in a managed care system. For these traditional service providers, the emergence of managed care may result in significant losses of revenue and ability to serve uninsured clients.

Added to all of this is the prospect of state government contracting with managed care organizations to administer SSI and TANF programs.[44] Hence, this type of partnership between business and government appears to be gaining momentum. Yet, it is a trend with many key issues to be addressed by policy planners, social workers, and other health and human service providers.

Food and Shelter Programs

Food Stamps

The federal government provides food to poor Americans through a variety of programs. Public, private nonprofit, and private for-profit organizations all cooperate in the provision of these programs. For example, child nutrition programs (including the school lunch program) reach out to poor children in schools, childcare centers, and summer camps. The largest federal food program, representing about two out of every three federal dollars in the food and nutrition category, is the **food stamp program**.[45] In fiscal year 1998, Congress appropriated $25.1 billion for the food stamp program, whereas the average monthly allotment of food stamps per person in that year was $71. And as of October 2001, the maximum monthly allotment for a family of four was $452. These benefits are adjusted yearly in accordance with changes in food prices generally. Food stamp households, however, are expected to contribute about 30 percent of their resources to food costs. Although states administer their food stamp programs, the federal government pays for the direct costs of food stamps and a portion of state administrative expenses.

Participants in the food stamp program receive a monthly allotment of stamps through an electronic benefit transfer system. Using a plastic debit card, food stamp recipients can purchase food at most retail stores. Alcohol, tobacco products, and hot ready-to-eat foods cannot be purchased. In recent years, consistent with the push for welfare reform in general, work requirements have been attached to food stamps. The 1996 welfare reform legislation passed by the Clinton administration limits able-bodied recipients between the ages of 18 and 50 (without children) to three months of food stamps in a three-year period unless the person is working or engaged in a workfare program (other than job search) for twenty or more hours per week.[46]

Public Housing and Section 8 Housing Assistance

The federal government assists many middle- and upper-income families with housing through its tax policies and loan programs. Our national government also collaborates with local public and private entities to provide housing assistance to low-income individuals and families. Most of this support is provided through the Department of Housing and Urban Development in two major programs: the public housing program and the Section 8 program. In fiscal year 2002, a total of $30.8 billion was enacted for HUD programs.[47]

The public housing program, dating back to the New Deal era, provides federal subsidies for construction costs on housing units built by local public housing authorities.[48] These local housing authorities subsequently own and operate the units. As part of the program, the federal government offers rent subsidies to cover the difference between the operating cost of individual housing units and 30 percent of the tenant's adjusted household income.

During the Reagan, Bush, and Clinton administrations, federal funding for public housing was cut drastically. One reason for this diminishing support is the tendency of public housing projects to concentrate multiproblem families into low-income neighborhoods. Increasingly, this approach has witnessed a high incidence of crime and vandalism, resulting in relatively high operating costs for local public housing authorities and high social costs for victimized families. These problems, along with rising construction costs, compelled policymakers to look for alternative low-income housing proposals.

The Section 8 program (referring to Section 8 of the Housing and Community Development Act) emerged in the 1980s as the major alternative to public housing.[49] It subsequently became the largest federal housing assistance program for the poor. To illustrate, in 1996, the U.S. federal government spent $15.8 billion on Section 8 assistance, whereas the public housing program received $4.5 billion. Section 8, now called the Housing Choice

Voucher Program, is essentially a rent supplement program. Tenants typically pay 30 percent of their (adjusted) income on rent; the federal government pays the difference between the tenant contribution and the market rate for the apartment. In contrast to public housing, tenants have a choice of using their subsidy in publicly or privately owned housing where available in their community. (The 1990 Housing Act, passed by the George H. W. Bush administration, sought to increase the supply of low-income rental housing through block grants to state and local government.)

More recently, major cities such as Chicago, Boston, and Atlanta have begun destroying their old high-rise public housing units and moving tenants into new low-rise public housing units or private housing. In either case, the aim is to better integrate poor tenants with other socioeconomic groups around the city. Furthermore, some states and cities are now establishing housing trust funds to assist in creating more affordable housing units. In 2002, there were an estimated 275 housing trust funds nationwide, generating $750 million for low-income housing.

Contributions of Business and the Voluntary Sector to Housing

The federal government encourages business investment in low-income housing through the low-income rental housing tax credit.[50] The tax credit was established as part of the Reagan administration's Tax Reform Act of 1986. Between 1990 and 1994, this tax incentive added about a quarter million low-income housing units to the housing supply. Developers qualify for the tax credit if they set aside specified percentages of their rental units for low-income tenants.

Habitat for Humanity International is probably the most well-known voluntary housing development program. Between 1976 and 2000, this non-profit nondenominational Christian organization, using donated material and voluntary labor, produced about 30,000 affordable houses in the United States.[51] The program refers to recipients of the houses as partners because the partner family helps build their house. On completion, Habitat for Humanity sells the home to the partner at no profit, while ensuring the partner a no-interest mortgage. The average sales price for a Habitat home built in the United States in 2000 was about $46,600. Although Habitat for Humanity by itself is not capable of solving the shelter problem in America, it is a valuable part of the collaborative effort to address the problem.

Current Shelter Issues: The Homeless

Despite various public and private efforts to provide decent low-income housing and temporary shelter, including the 1987 Stewart B. McKinney Homeless Assistance Act, the National Coalition for the Homeless believes that the number of homeless people in American continues to grow.[52] Estimates of homelessness vary, in part, because the definition of what constitutes homelessness varies. The National Coalition for the Homeless uses a broad definition, claiming that people who live in unstable housing arrangements and lack a permanent place to stay are, in fact, experiencing homelessness. Although the National Law Center on Homelessness and Poverty estimates that as many as 2 million people experience homelessness during a given year in the United States, the National Coalition for the Homeless, because of the difficulty in counting the homeless, chooses to cite the shortage of available services for the homeless. According to the coalition, in 1998, 26 percent of requests for emergency shelter in thirty U.S. cities went unmet due to a lack of resources. What is more, another study showed that in fifty cities around the United States, the individual city's official estimated number of homeless typically exceeded that city's available number of shelter and transitional housing spaces. Rural areas of the United States generally have even fewer resources for the homeless. Thus, in a nation that has never adequately housed all its people, homelessness continues to be a serious policy issue.

Other Publicly Funded Programs in American Social Welfare

A wide range of other publicly funded programs contributes to American social welfare. Many of the services are funded by government through vehicles such as the **Social Services Block Grant** but delivered by private organizations. Hence, they are part of an interdependent network of public and private efforts to further social welfare. These services include child welfare programs such as child abuse and neglect prevention, foster care, adoption, shelter, and outreach services.[53] Other programs benefiting children include publicly funded health insurance (State Children's Health Insurance Program), child care, education, and family planning services.[54] Head Start (the preschool program) and student loan programs are part of the education category. In addition, the U.S. government supports employment and training programs for those seeking employment.[55]

Other Voluntary Services in the Nonprofit Sector

The United Way System

One of the major voluntary efforts in the advancement of American social welfare is the **United Way,** formerly known as the Community Chest, and for a time, the United Fund. Over one hundred years old, the United Way is primarily a partnership in community problem-solving among private organizations—private for-profit and private nonprofit organizations.[56] For the most part, businesses raise the funds for services, whereas nonprofit organizations deliver the services.

The United Way network, itself, is composed of a national umbrella organization called United Way of America and about 1,400 local United Way organizations, each independently incorporated as private nonprofit entities serving their respective communities. Each local United Way organizes an annual fund-raising campaign among business and professional groups in its community. Subsequently, the local United Way, with direction from donors and volunteers, allocates the donated funds to a variety of nonprofit health and human services in the community. In the 2000/2001 fiscal year, United Way campaigns around the nation raised a total of $3.91 billion for health and human services.

Perhaps the most important partner in the United Way system is the business community. Without the support of community business leaders, United Way would be much less effective in its fund-raising role, and, therefore, much less valuable to community health and human service providers. Business leaders help organize and conduct the individual United Way fund-raising campaigns in each community. Through the use of payroll deduction, businesses enable their employees to make annual donations to their local United Way in an efficient and financially "pain-free" manner. As a result, employees of local business typically comprise the largest source of United Way donations.

With these donations, each United Way funds a broad range of health and human services. Many of these services also receive public funding; some do not. In any case, the mix of health and human services funded by each United Way varies from community to community. To illustrate the diversity of services funded at any one United Way, however, consider the list of agencies affiliated with the United Way of Massachusetts Bay in 2001.[57] This list included the American Cancer Society-New England Division, the American Red Cross of Massachusetts Bay, the Asian Task Force Against Domestic Violence, the Boys and Girls Club of Lynn, the Boston Area Rape Crisis Center, Catholic Charities, Combined Jewish Philanthropies, Community Legal Services & Counseling Center, the Disability Law Center, the Dorchester Bay Economic Development Corporation, the Salvation Army, the Chinese Progressive Association, the Massachusetts Coalition for the Homeless, The Home for Little Wanderers, the Hispanic Office of Planning & Evaluation (HOPE), the John F. Kennedy Family Service Center, and YWCA Boston.

This diversity in services and service populations is not unique to the United Way of Massachusetts Bay. As a second illustration, let us examine the Mile High United Way in Denver, Colorado. Its agency list in 2001 included the Jefferson Center for Mental Health, the Jewish Family Service of Colorado, the Asian Pacific Development Center, the Latin American

Research and Service Agency, the Lutheran Family Services of Colorado, the Mi Casa Resource Center for Women, the Colorado AIDS Project, the Colorado Coalition Against Domestic Violence, the Mile High Council on Alcoholism and Drug Abuse, Senior Support Services, and the Northeast Denver Housing Center. As indicated by the preceding illustrations, a strength of the United Way is the community empowerment that comes from volunteers organizing resources to meet specific and diverse community needs.

Current Issues in the United Way System

United Way continues to be the major federated fund-raising campaign in the United States. Over the years, the American business community has viewed United Way as an alternative to higher taxes and bigger government in promoting social welfare. Business and professional leaders value the community needs assessment, community organizing, and community problem-solving roles that their local United Way organizations perform.

That said, United Way has its share of critics.[58] Recent issues include the United Way tradition of funding a relatively exclusive set of member nonprofit agencies. At times, organizations not affiliated with United Way have felt left out and hampered in their fund-raising efforts. More radical critics have contended that United Way is too conservative, funding primarily status quo services, not offensive to the business community. Still others point out the virtual monopoly that United Way enjoyed for years in its access to corporate employee fund-raising campaigns and payroll deduction. In the 1970s and 1980s, competing federated campaigns began to emerge as an alternative to United Way. These competing federations included Children's Charities of America, The Combined Federal Campaign (focused on federal employees), Earth Share (involving agencies such as the National Audubon Society and the African Wildlife Foundation), and The National Black United Federation. Yet, the vast majority of federated campaign giving still goes to United Way.

More recently, especially with an incident of administrative corruption at United Way of America in the early 1990s, United Way has faced the issue of increased donor accountability.[59] Donors to United Way desire more control in determining which health and human services receive their gift. Furthermore, donors want to know if their donations to United Way actually make a difference in addressing various social problems.

United Way, as it has throughout its history, continues to change in an effort to address emerging issues.[60] The diversity in the agencies affiliated with the United Way of Massachusetts Bay, for example, indicates an effort by some local United Way organizations to be more inclusive in their funding. In addition, United Way has instituted a donor choice option by which donors can indicate specific health and human service recipients of their gift. Furthermore, United Way, serving as an accountability mechanism for donors, has begun a push for better program evaluation (i.e., program outcome measurements) among its affiliated service providers.

The Child Welfare League of America: A Public–Private Partnership in Child Welfare

The Child Welfare League of America (CWLA), founded in 1920, is a voluntary association of over 1,100 public and private nonprofit organizations that serve at-risk children and their families.[61] The organization traces its roots to the 1909 White House Conference on the Care of Dependent Children, which recommended the creation of the Children's Bureau and other child welfare organizations. Member organizations are involved with services such as child abuse and neglect prevention, foster care, adoption, residential group care, child care, and various youth development programs, among other services.

The CWLA offers many services to its members, including legislative advocacy, practice consultation, conferences, training sessions, child welfare publications, and financial support for accreditation. According to 2001 agency information, the CWLA has a budget of about $16 million. It raises its funding from public and private sources, including member dues, foundation grants, publication sales, investment income, consultation fees, as well as corporate and individual donations. The CWLA is truly a cooperative effort in the advancement of American child welfare.

Personal Profile: Marian Wright Edelman

One of the outstanding contemporary social advocates is Marian Wright Edelman.[62] After graduating from Spelman College and Yale Law School, she became the first African American woman admitted to the Mississippi Bar. In Mississippi during the 1960s, she headed the NAACP Legal Defense and Educational Fund. Later, in 1968, she moved to Washington, DC, to serve as counsel for the Poor People's March, which Martin Luther King was organizing before his assassination.

Edelman in 1973 founded the **Children's Defense Fund,** a private nonprofit organization that has become one of the strongest children's advocates in the nation. Based in Washington, DC, the Children's Defense Fund regularly documents the needs of America's children, focusing particularly on the needs of children from poor families, children of color, and children with disabilities. Its legislative advocacy emphasizes preventative investments in child welfare. As president of the Children's Defense Fund, Edelman continues to serve as a policy leader and national voice for millions of vulnerable children in America. In 2000, in recognition for her social advocacy, she was awarded the Presidential Medal of Freedom, the country's highest civilian award.

The Challenge for Professional Social Work

There are many other social problems, issues, and services not mentioned in this chapter. Due to limited space, I do not attempt to cover them all here. The aim of the chapter is to provide the reader with an understanding of some of the major programs and issues in American social welfare, especially those involving health and human services. This is because the fundamental challenge for current social workers is to make important contributions to the development of policies and programs that will better address major social problems and issues in the United States. But how can social workers meet this challenge? The answer to this question is the subject of the next section of this book.

C O N T E N T S E L E C T

For more information on related social work topics, use the following search terms:

Capitation-based plans
Charitable choice
Children's Defense Fund
Food Stamp program
401(k) retirement plans
General assistance
Habitat for Humanity International
Health maintenance organizations HMO

In-kind services
Medicaid
Medicare
Primary care physician
Public assistance programs
Selective programs
Social Security
Social Security Act 1935
Social Services Block Grant

Supplemental Security Income (SSI)
Temporary Assistance to Needy Families
Unemployment insurance
United Way
Universal program
Workers' compensation

N O T E S

1. Bruce S. Jansson, *The Reluctant Welfare State: American Social Welfare Policies—Past, Present, and Future,* 4th ed. (Belmont, CA: Wadsworth/Thomson Learning, 2001), pp. 194, 199; Sar A. Levitan, Garth L. Mangum, and Stephen L. Mangum, *Programs in Aid of the Poor* (Baltimore: Johns Hopkins University Press, 1998), p. 58.

2. Neil Gilbert, Harry Specht, and Paul Terrell, *Dimensions of Social Policy,* 3rd ed. (Englewood Cliffs, NJ: Prentice Hall, 1993), pp. 71–72.

3. Social Security Administration, "2002 OASDI Trustees Report: Overview." Retrieved from the World Wide Web on August 18, 2002: www.ssa.gov/OACT/TR/TR02/II_highlights. html.; Levitan et al., pp. 58–63.

4. Jansson, p. 282.

5. Levitan et al., p. 61; Social Security Administration, "A Snapshot." Retrieved from the World Wide Web on August 16, 2002: www.ssa.gov/pubs/10006.html.

6. Levitan et al., p. 61; Linda P. Anderson, Paul A. Sundet, and Irma Harrington, *The Social Welfare System in the United States: A Social Worker's Guide to Public Benefits Programs* (Boston: Allyn & Bacon, 2000), p. 27; Social Security Administration, "A Snapshot," 2002.

7. Levitan et al., pp. 63–64.

8. Levitan et al., pp. 93–95; U.S. Department of Labor Employment and Training Administration, "Unemployment Insurance Fact Sheet." Retrieved from the World Wide Web on August 19, 2002: http://workforcesecurity.doleta.gov/unemploy/uifactsheet.asp; Mike Miller, U.S. De-

partment of Labor Employment and Training Administration, Office of Workforce Security, personal communication, August 20, 2002.

9. Theda Skocpol, *Protecting Soldiers and Mothers: The Political Origins of Social Policy in the United States* (Cambridge, MA: Harvard University), pp. 290–293.

10. Frank Kimball, Maine State Department of Professional and Financial Regulation, Bureau of Insurance, personal communication, August 21, 2002; Levitan et al., pp. 96–98.

11. Levitan et al., p. 68.

12. Amanda Paulson, "The 401(K): Who's Contributing What?" *Christian Science Monitor* 93, No. 229: p. 14 (22 October 2001).

13. William C. Frederick, Keith Davis, and James E. Post, *Business and Society: Corporate Strategy, Public Policy, Ethics,* 6th ed. (New York: McGraw-Hill, 1988), p. 301.

14. James E. Post, Anne T. Lawrence, and James Weber, *Business and Society: Corporate Strategy, Public Policy, Ethics,* 10th ed. (New York: McGraw-Hill, 2002), p. 343.

15. Frederick et al., p. 256.

16. Deloitte and Touche, "Promises Kept: The 1997 Tax Law," *Tax News & Views,* 2000. Retrieved from the World Wide Web on November 27, 2001: www.dtonline.com/promises/chap3.htm.

17. Fred Kaplan, "Bush Takes on 'Corporate Abusers,'" *Boston Globe,* 10 July 2002, p. A1; Associated Press, "WorldCom Offers Not to Sell Assets: Seeks to Delay Creditors' suit," *Boston Globe,* 18 July 2002, p. E4.

18. Estelle James, "Reforming Social Security in the U.S.: An International Perspective," *Business Economics:* p. 34 (January 2001).

19. Thomas I. Palley, "The Economics of Social Security: An Old Keynesian Perspective," *Journal of Post Keynesian Economics* 21, No. 1: p. 94 (1998).

20. Jansson, pp. 322.

21. Jane Bryant Quinn, "Star Wars and Social Security," *Newsweek,* 3 September 2001, p. 37; Leigh Strope, "Social Security Panel Shifts Purpose," *Boston Globe,* 7 November 2001, p. A9.

22. James, pp. 33, 36, 38.

23. Quinn, p. 37; Palley, p. 104.

24. Gilbert et al., 1993, pp. 71–72.

25. Children's Defense Fund, "Summary of the New Welfare Legislation." Retrieved from the World Wide Web on August 27, 1997: www.childrensdefensefund.org/welarelaw.html; U.S. Department of Health and Human Services,

the Administration for Children and Families, "ACF Overview: Discretionary Spending." Retrieved from the World Wide Web on August 18, 2002: www.acf.dhhs.gov/programs/olab/budget/Press03.htm; U.S. Department of Health and Human Services, the Administration for Children and Families, Office of Family Assistance, personal communication, August 22, 2002.

26. Children's Defense Fund, 1997; U.S. Department of Health and Human Services, the Administration for Children and Families, "ACF Overview: Discretionary Spending," 2002.

27. Children's Defense Fund, 1997; U.S. Department of Health and Human Services, the Administration for Children and Families, Office of Family Assistance, personal communication, 2002.

28. Jansson, p. 279; Walter I. Trattner, *From Poor Law to Welfare State: A History of Social Welfare in America,* 6th ed. (New York: The Free Press, 1999), p. 348; Social Security Administration, "A Snapshot," 2002.

29. Levitan et al., pp. 85–87; Social Security Administration, "A Snapshot," 2002; Social Security Administration, "Executive Summary." Retrieved from the World Wide Web on August 18, 2002: www.ssa.gov/OACT/SSIR/SSI02/exec_sum.html.

30. Levitan et al., p. 87; Social Security Administration, "Executive Summary," 2002.

31. Levitan et al., p. 88; Urban Institute, "State General Assistance Programs 1998." Retrieved from the World Wide Web on August 18, 2002: http://newfederalism.urban.org/html/ga_programs/ga_full.html; Steven G. Anderson, Anthony P. Halter, and Brian M. Gryzlak, "Changing Safety Net of Last Resort: Downsizing General Assistance for Employable Adults," *Social Work* 47, No. 3: pp. 249–258 (2002).

32. Children's Defense Fund, 1997; Ram A. Cnaan, and Stephanie C. Boddie, " Charitable Choice and Faith-Based Welfare: A Call for Social Work," *Social Work* 47, No. 3: pp. 224–235 (2002).

33. Michael B. Katz, *In the Shadow of the Poorhouse,* 10th ed. (New York: BasicBooks, 1996), pp. 290–292, 310.

34. Levitan et al., pp. 109–118.

35. Jansson, pp. 250–251.

36. Levitan et al., pp. 110–111; U.S. Government, "Medicare: What is Medicare?" Retrieved from the World Wide Web on August 16, 2002: www.medicare.gov/Basics/WhatIs.asp; U.S. Department of Health and Human Services, "HHS

Fact Sheet: HHS Programs and Initiatives for an Aging America." Retrieved from the World Wide Web on August 16, 2002: www.hhs.gov/news/press/2002pres/aging.html.

37. Levitan et al., pp. 111–112; U.S. Department of Health and Human Services, "HHS Fact Sheet: HHS Programs and Initiatives for an Aging America," 2002; Centers for Medicare & Medicaid Services, "Medicaid Eligibility." Retrieved from the World Wide Web on August 20, 2002: www.cms.hhs.gov/medicaid/eligibility/criteria.asp; The Kaiser Family Foundation, "Medicaid Enrollees by Cash Assistance Status." Retrieved from the World Wide Web on August 23, 2002: www.statehealthfacts.kff.org; The Kaiser Family Foundation, "Distribution of State Medicaid Enrollees by Enrollment Group, FFY 1998." Retrieved from the World Wide Web on August 23, 2002: www.statehealthfacts.kff.org; The Kaiser Family Foundation, "Distribution of Medicaid Spending by Enrollment Group, FFY 1998." Retrieved from the World Wide Web on August 23, 2002: www.statehealthfacts.kff.org; The Kaiser Family Foundation, "Distribution of Medicaid Spending by Service, FFY 1998." Retrieved from the World Wide Web on August 23, 2002: www.statehealthfacts.kff.org; The Kaiser Family Foundation, "Medicaid Managed Care Enrollees as a Percent of State Medicaid Enrollees, 2000." Retrieved from the World Wide Web on August 23, 2002: www.statehealthfacts.kff.org.

38. Tim Davidson, Jeanette R. Davidson, and Sharon M. Keigher, "Managed Care: Satisfaction Guaranteed…Not! *Health & Social Work* 24, No. 3: p. 164 (1999).

39. Jane Kolodinsky, "Consumer Satisfaction with a Managed Health Care Plan," *Journal of Consumer Affairs* 99, No. 33: p. 223 (1999).

40. Janet D. Perloff, "Medicaid Managed Care and Urban Poor People: Implications for Social Work," *Health & Social Work* 21, No. 3: pp. 189–190 (1996).

41. Cynthia J. Rocha and Liz England Kalbaka, "A Comparison Study of Access to Health Care Under a Medicaid Managed Care Program," *Health & Social Work* 24, No. 3: p. 170 (1999).

42. Robert Sunley, "Advocacy in the New World of Managed Care," *Families in Society:* pp. 88–90 (January/February 1997).

43. Rocha and Kalbaka, pp. 169–172; Perloff, pp. 191–192; The Kaiser Family Foundation, "Medicaid Managed Care Enrollees as a Percent of State Medicaid Enrollees, 2000," 2002.

44. Davidson, Davidson, and Keigher, p. 164.

45. Levitan, pp. 131–133; U.S. Department of Agriculture, "About FSP—Introduction." Retrieved from the World Wide Web on August 16, 2002: www.fns.usda.gov/fsp/MENU/ABOUT/ABOUT.HTM; U.S. Department of Agriculture, "Fact Sheet on Food Stamp Resources, Income, and Benefits." Retrieved from the World Wide Web on August 16, 2002: www.fns.usda.gov/fsp/MENU/APPS/BENEFITS/fsResBenEli.htm; U.S. Department of Agriculture, "Food and Nutrition Service Programs." Retrieved from the World Wide Web on August 26, 2002: www.fns.usda.gov/fns/MENU/PROGRAMS.htm.

46. Children's Defense Fund, 1997; U.S. Department of Agriculture, "About FSP—Introduction," 2002.

47. Department of Housing and Urban Development, Office of Budget, personal communication, August 20, 2002.

48. Jansson, pp. 210–211; Levitan, pp. 122–124.

49. Levitan, pp. 125–127; David Thigpen, "The Long Way Home," *Time*, 5 August 2002, p. 42; Bret Ladine, "Housing Trust Funds Gaining Momentum," *Boston Globe*, 19 August 2002, pp. A1, A4. Retrieved from the World Wide Web on August 19, 2002: www.boston.com/daily globe2/231/nation/Housing_trust_funds_gaining_momentumP.shtml; Department of Housing and Urban Development, "Housing Choice Vouchers Fact Sheet." Retrieved from the World Wide Web on August 19, 2002: www.hud.gov/offices/pih/programs/hcv/about/fact_sheet.cfm.

50. Levitan et al., p. 126.

51. Habitat for Humanity International, "A Brief Introduction to Habitat for Humanity International." Retrieved from the World Wide Web on November 14, 2001: www.habitat.org/how/tour/1.html; Habitat for Humanity International, "Habitat for Humanity Fact Sheet." Retrieved from the World Wide Web on November 14, 2001: www.habitat.org/how/factsheet.html.

52. National Coalition for the Homeless, "How Many People Experience Homelessness? NCH Fact Sheet #2." Retrieved from the World Wide Web on November 15, 2001: www.national-homeless.org.

53. Levitan, pp. 171–172.

54. Ibid., pp. 154–156, 161–170, 150–151.

55. Ibid., pp. 176–177, 137.

56. Eleanor Brilliant, *Dilemmas of Organized Charity* (New York: Columbia University, 1990), p. 19; United Way of America, "Basic Facts about United Way." Retrieved from the World Wide Web on November 21, 2001: http://national. unitedway.org/bfact.cfm.

57. United Way of Massachusetts Bay, "Community Links—United Way Affiliated Agencies." Retrieved from the World Wide Web on November 21, 2001: www.uwmb.org/aboutus/agencies.htm.; Mile High United Way, "Our Family of Agencies." Retrieved from the World Wide Web on November 27, 2001: www. unitedwaydenver.org/home/html/agency.html.

58. Marjorie Cotton, "Yes, I Would Like a Choice Where My Contribution Goes!" *Fund Raising Management:* pp. 36–37, 48 (December 1991); W. Olcott, "United Way Growth Stagnant," *Fund Raising Management:* p. 15 (June 1994); Jerry D. Marx, "Federated Fundraising,"

The International Encyclopedia of Public Policy and Administration, vol. 2 (Boulder, CO: Westview Press, 1997), pp. 877–881; Jerry D. Marx, " Corporate Philanthropy and United Way: Challenges for the Year 2000," *Nonprofit Management & Leadership*, 8, No. 1: p. 20 (1997).

59. Ibid.

60. Marx, *Nonprofit Management & Leadership*, p. 20; Olcott, p. 15; United Way of America, 2001.

61. Child Welfare League of America, "More about CWLA." Retrieved from the World Wide Web on November 18, 2001: www.cwla.org/whowhat/more.htm

62. Children's Defense Fund, "Marian Wright Edelman's Public Life." Retrieved from the World Wide Web on April 25, 2001: www.childrensdefense.org/marian.htm; Children's Defense Fund, "About Us." Retrieved from the World Wide Web on November 18, 2001: www.childrensdefensefund.org/aboutus.htm

PART THREE

What Can Be Done: A Process for Social Policy Development

11 A Conceptual Framework for Policy Development

President John F. Kennedy deliberates with policy advisors in October 1962.

Theoretical and Conceptual Definitions

Theoretical and Conceptual Approaches to Policy Analysis

Policy analysis as a subject can be examined from the perspective of several theoretical and conceptual models.[1] The institutional model examines policy as a product of institutions. That is, policies are developed within the context of a society's institutions. In a course on public policy, that context is the public sector (i.e., governmental organizations). In a course on business and society, that context is the modern American corporation, whereas a non-profit management course would focus on the structure of a voluntary organization. In any case, the institutional approach emphasizes a description of the characteristics of policy-making organizations.

The **systems theory** offers a second model by which to approach policy analysis. Figure 1.1 is an example of a societal model based on the systems theory.[2] In the more specific case of public policy, government is viewed as a system that receives inputs from its environment in the form of constituent demands and support. Government's output is public policy.

A third model through which to view policy analysis is the **group theory model.** This model sees politics as a struggle among competing groups to influence policy.[3] The context of this struggle could be a government, business, or nonprofit organization. From this perspective, policy is the state of equilibrium reached in this struggle among various groups. In developing and passing individual policy proposals, policymakers seek to organize support from a majority of the most powerful groups with a stake in the policy issue.

A fourth policy analysis model is based on **elite theory.** Those who choose to analyze policy analysis from this perspective may agree that policy is an outcome of competing groups, but for the most part, policy primarily reflects the interests of one group—society's elite.[4] The elite theory maintains that society is divided into a tiny elite with power and the masses with relatively little power. It is the elite who define the ideology and values used to construct society's major institutions. Thomas Jefferson was an elite. John Adams was an elite. It is the elite who write a nation's legislation. It is the elite who actually make the decision to pass or not pass a legislative proposal. Consequently, according to this model, the elite influence public policy more than the masses do.

Although the approach in this part of the text contains elements of the four previous models, the process model will be the fundamental model employed here. More specifically, this text examines policy analysis as a developmental process with underlying theory and methodology.[5] Consistent with the values of the social work profession, this process will emphasize political advocacy in the pursuit of social and economic justice.

Definitions of Policy Analysis as a Developmental Process

Jacob Ukeles offers one definition of **policy analysis** as a developmental process. According to Ukeles, policy analysis is

> The systematic investigation of alternative policy options and the assembly and integration of the evidence for and against each option. It involves a problem-solving approach, the collection and interpretation of information, and some attempt to predict the consequences of alternative courses of action.[6]

Duncan MacRae provides a similar definition in much fewer words. MacRae states that policy analysis is "the choice of the best policy among a set of alternatives with the aid of reason and evidence."[7]

Patton and Sawicki examine policy analysis as a process also. In so doing, they detail two fundamental types of policy analysis.[8] One type is **descriptive policy analysis.** This type includes both **retrospective policy analysis** and **evaluative policy analysis.** Retrospective analysis refers to the description and interpretation of past events in policy development. It attempts to answer the question: What happened? Evaluative policy analysis often takes the form of program evaluation. That is, policies many times produce programs to achieve their goals. If the programs are implemented and conducted successfully, the policy is a success. Therefore, evaluative policy analysis seeks to answer the question: Did the program achieve its goals?

The second fundamental type of policy analysis is **prospective policy analysis.** This type can also be broken down into two more specific categories of policy analysis: **predictive policy analysis** and **prescriptive policy analysis.** Predictive analysis requires the projection of future outcomes resulting from implementing individual alternatives. In other words, it requires a forecasting of possible outcomes for each policy option. Taking predictive analysis one step further, prescriptive analysis includes specific recommendations for the decision-maker, given projected outcomes for each policy alternative. Note, however, that all these types of policy analysis are often integrated to various degrees when doing policy analysis.

Policy Analysis versus Policy Research

Majchrzak makes a distinction between **policy analysis** and **policy research.** She defines policy research as

> the process of conducting research on, or analysis of, a fundamental social problem in order to provide policymakers with pragmatic, action-oriented recommendations for alleviating the problem. In other words, policy research

begins with a social problem, continues through a process whereby alternative policy actions for addressing the problem are developed, then these alternatives are communicated to policymakers.[9]

This text does not attempt to distinguish between policy research and policy analysis. Instead, the premise here is that effective policy analysis requires, at the very least, an understanding of basic research methods. Edward Quade supports this argument when he defines policy analysis as

> a form of applied research carried out to acquire a deeper understanding of sociotechnical issues and to bring about better solutions. Attempting to bring modern science and technology to bear on society's problems, policy analysis searches for feasible courses of action, generating information and marshaling evidence of the benefits and other consequences that would follow their adoption and implementation, in order to help the policy-maker choose the most advantageous action.[10]

Policy versus Planning

A further distinction needs to be made here between the terms policy and planning.[11] A policy, as stated in the first chapter of this text, involves an intervention that uses sanctions of some kind. For example, these may be regulatory sanctions such as licensing, certification, zoning, or fines. A plan, particularly in health and human services, involves an intervention that may use sanctions or may provide programming. A plan may also provide both sanctions and programs or neither one of them. In other words, planning is the broader concept, the more general term. As such, social workers may find themselves doing policy planning or program planning. Typically, these are two different assignments in any agency. Policy plans often call for the development of programs. Program plans, in turn, often call for the development of specific services. Thus, an outline of concepts from the most general to the most specific might look as follows:

*I. Planning
  A. Policy planning
    1. Program planning
      a. Service details (i.e., treatment methods, activities, etc.)

Given the use in this text of a process model for policy analysis, I will use the terms **policy planning** and **policy development** frequently and interchangeably. Each term suggests policy analysis as a process and is therefore appropriate for my purposes.

Rational Policy Development

When examining policy analysis as a process, in theory, there are two fundamental approaches: the **rational policy development** approach and the **incremental policy development** approach.[12] Different authors describe the
rational approach to policy development in slightly different terms. My version of rational policy planning is outlined in the following steps:

1. Define the problem.
2. Clarify values.
3. Establish a goal.
4. List objectives.
5. Choose a criterion.
6. Outline alternative courses of action.
7. Predict outcomes for each alternative.
8. Select a course of action.

Now let us discuss each step at a time using health care as a simple illustration. In rational policy planning, a thorough definition of the problem
is a must. A social problem can be defined simply as an unmet need of some
group of people. Notice that this definition of a social problem is consistent
with the definition provided in the first chapter of a "social policy." To review, a social policy can be defined as a collective course of action, set by policymakers, involving the use of sanctions, to address the needs of some
group of people. Although social problems can be defined in various ways,[13]
defining social problems in terms of unmet needs may be less stigmatizing
to people involved in the problem. (It is also more consistent with the
strengths perspective in social work.) In any case, in terms of American
health care, a problem of concern today is the fact that millions of American
families are without health insurance. To illustrate, in 1999, 16.1 percent of
Americans under age 65 had no health insurance, which represents 38.5 million people.[14] Without health insurance, people in America have difficulty
finding and paying for quality health care. Thus, health insurance coverage
is clearly an unmet need in the United States.

That said, there may be some people who feel that 38.5 million Americans without health insurance is not a problem. Based on their personal
values and beliefs, they may feel that these uninsured people could obtain
health insurance if they really tried to get a job. In other words, it is their
choice not to obtain health insurance. Yet, there are others who feel that 38.5
million cannot be to blame for their lack of health insurance, and that there is
a problem in the U.S. health care system.

The clarification of values is the second step in rational policy planning. Put simply, a value is a desired principle. Statistics do not become

problems unless a principle generally desired in America is violated. One such value is that the sick should be cared for. If one adheres to this value, then 38.5 million Americans without health insurance is a problem. If enough voters adhere to this value, then 38.5 million Americans without health insurance become a priority for national policymakers (i.e., members of Congress).

Given a clearly defined problem and a clear statement of related values, tasks done perhaps by a social worker in the role of a policy analyst, rational policy planning requires the setting of a goal. A **goal** is an action-oriented phrase, meant to direct and motivate someone or some group regarding an identified issue. In short, we have a problem; let's do something about it! The rational analyst tries to maximize progress toward goal achievement. For the sake of illustration, let's say that our goal in relation to the 38.5 million uninsured Americans is to establish universal health insurance in America.

But how will we know when we have achieved this goal? To answer this question requires a fourth step in the rational policy planning process. **Objectives** need to be established. Each goal should have one or more related objectives. Objectives can be distinguished from goals in two ways. Objectives are (1) time-limited and (2) measurable. In this case, our objective could be to have 99 percent of the U.S. population covered with health insurance by the year 2010. That is to say, policymakers can claim the goal of universal health insurance has been met if, in fact, 99 percent (or more) of the U.S. population has health insurance by 2010.

After goals and objectives are established, a policy analyst will want to explore alternative courses of action for achieving these goals and objectives. But first, a criterion needs to be selected. A **criterion** is information that allows the policy analyst to evaluate policy alternatives.[15] Without going into a detailed discussion of various criteria, let us choose one for our purposes: cost effectiveness. Virtually every policy proposal must consider its inherent costs. Given several alternative policy proposals, each claiming to cover 99 percent of the American population by 2010, we will select the policy alternative that is least costly to the American public.

Now the rational policy analyst is ready to identify alternative courses of action to achieve the policy goal. Rational policy planning is sometimes referred to as rational-comprehensive[16] planning because, in this step, all possible courses of action need to be identified. The rational policy analyst wants to examine all options before a decision is made. To continue with our illustration, let us say that the policy analyst identifies three policy proposals that will extend universal health insurance to all Americans (i.e., each proposal covers at least 99 percent of the U.S. population by the year 2010). We will call them policy options A, B, and C.

In the seventh step of the rational planning sequence, the policy analyst then predicts the outcomes of each policy alternative (A, B, and C) in relation to the established criterion. Because we chose cost-effectiveness as our criterion in step five, the rational policy analyst will use existing data to predict the total cost of each of the three policy proposals. The analyst, perhaps employed on the staff of a Congressional member, would provide the policymaker with this information.

In the eighth and last step in the rational policy planning sequence, the policymaker will then decide which of the three competing health insurance proposals to support. In rational policy planning, the best alternative is the one that maximizes goal attainment in relation to the established criterion.[17] Therefore, the rational policymaker will select the universal health insurance proposal (or bill) that has the lowest projected cost to the American public.

A Critical Analysis of Rational Policy Development

There are many critics of the rational approach to policy planning.[18] These critics say that rational policy planning is impractical due to several weaknesses. Weaknesses include the fact that policy decision-makers do not have an agreed-on set of values. Many values are conflicting. Take health care policy for example. One value related to health care policy would be high quality. A second value would be low cost. Yet, these values are conflicting, and it is hard to compare or weigh one value versus another. It is more difficult to measure quality in health care than it is to measure the cost of health care. Be that as it may, does one unit of quality equal one unit of cost when measuring values in health care policy? Obviously this is difficult to determine.

A second weakness in rational policy planning is its requirement that policymakers examine all possible policy alternatives. This is a weakness because large investments in existing programs and policies prevent decision-makers from considering all alternatives. An illustration would be the opposition of the American Medical Association over the years to various Medicare proposals.[19] In addition, collecting information on all alternatives is too costly and too time-consuming. The result is that all pertinent information is not always available to policymakers. Consequently, decisions are often made on the best information available at the time.

Rational policy planning's attempt to predict the outcome of each alternative course of action is a third weakness in the approach. This is because the full consequences of each alternative cannot be predicted or calculated with great certainty in the real world. It is very difficult to predict or calculate full benefits and costs of any one policy option during the planning process. This uncertainty about the consequences of various policy alternatives makes policymakers stay close to previous policies and programs when considering future policy alternatives.

A final weakness in the rational policy planning approach is its requirement that the final policy selection be based on a maximization of goal achievement in relation to established objectives and criteria. In the real world, policymakers typically are not motivated to maximize goal achievement. Instead, they try to satisfy constituent demands for progress on a given social problem or issue. At times, any progress on an issue by policymakers is considered a success by policymakers and voters alike.

Case Example: The Cuban Missile Crisis

Although it has its weaknesses, rational policy planning can be very useful. The Cuban Missile Crisis provides an illustration of the utility of rational policy planning.[20] The year was 1963 and the Kennedy administration had just discovered that the Soviet Union was in the process of installing missiles in Cuba, a tiny island nation just south of the state of Florida. In terms of rational policy planning, the Soviet missiles were a problem for the United States. The reason this was a problem was that it violated a fundamental value of the United States, which is national security. The immediate policy goal then was to remove the Soviet missiles from Cuba. As the Kennedy administration considered alternative courses of action to remove these missiles, the primary criterion was the effectiveness of each of these alternatives in preventing nuclear war while maintaining the balance of power between the Soviet Union and the United States. That said, Kennedy's advisors believed there were six alternative actions available to the United States. As they considered each alternative, they tried to predict possible outcomes for each option.

The first option was to do nothing. Doing nothing is always an alternative in policy planning. Doing nothing, however, would result in a shift in power between the Soviet Union and the United States. In other words, the predicted result of doing nothing would have been Soviet military supremacy over the United States. A second policy option was to put diplomatic pressure on Khrushchev, the leader of the Soviet Union. This option would involve meeting and negotiating with Khrushchev either overtly or covertly. The Kennedy administration ultimately rejected this option, because it believed that Khrushchev would want concessions from the United States. It was predicted that military concessions would disrupt the balance of power in favor of the Soviet Union. This was an unacceptable outcome.

A third policy option was to put diplomatic pressure on Fidel Castro, the leader of Cuba. In so doing, U.S. leaders would demand that Castro oppose the Soviet missile installation. Yet, there was a drawback to this policy option also. Castro had relatively little power vis-à-vis the Soviet Union. That is to say, the Soviets controlled the missiles. It was a Soviet decision that was needed to remove the missiles.

As a fourth option, Kennedy advisors also considered a land invasion of Cuba; however, a possible outcome of this course of action might have been a Soviet counterinvasion of Berlin, Germany. Therefore, this option was rejected. A fifth option, which would later be used in the Persian Gulf War, and again, in the Afghanistan War after the terrorist attack of September 11, 2001, was a surgical air strike. But there were predicted problems with this option also. Some Americans might consider a surgical air strike of Cuba to be a Pearl Harbor in reverse. After all, we would be attacking a country, Cuba, that had not declared war on the United States. Also, Kennedy advisors predicted that if any Soviet personnel were killed, the Soviet Union would surely invade Berlin, Germany, or even Turkey. In any case, there was always the possibility that a surgical air strike might miss some of the missiles in Cuba. Thus, this option was rejected.

The sixth and final course of action considered was a naval blockade of Cuba. The purpose of the blockade was to block Soviet ships from delivering any more missiles to Cuba. Some of the possible outcomes of this policy option included the fact that a blockade might allow the Soviets to complete installation of missiles already in Cuba. Also, Soviet ships sailing for Cuba might not stop at the U.S. blockade, requiring a U.S. naval attack on the intruding Soviet ships. In addition, a U.S. naval blockade of Cuba would be a violation of the Freedom of Seas Act.

In the end, however, the naval blockade option was selected because of its projected advantages. Remember, the criterion on this policy decision was the effectiveness of each alternative in preventing nuclear war between the United States and the Soviet Union while maintaining the balance of power between the two countries. A naval conflict in the Caribbean Sea was the most favorable confrontation for the United States. What is more, the blockade allowed the United States to use the threat of subsequent nonnuclear steps, such as a land invasion of Cuba, to stop the Soviets.

Another predicted advantage of the naval blockade was that it represented a middle course of action between inaction by the United States and an attack on the Soviet Union by the United States. By not directly starting a conventional war with the Soviet Union, the naval blockade prevented Khrushchev from having to decide between a humiliating defeat in a conventional war on the one hand and a nuclear war with the United States on the other. For all of these reasons, the naval blockade was the option selected and the results were as predicted. The Soviet Union not wanting to risk a conventional war in America's backyard or a nuclear war stopped further installation of missiles in Cuba. People all over the world, fearing nuclear war and holding their breath, exhaled together at the good news. A fundamental point of this case example, however, is that the rational policy planning approach can be, in fact, useful.

Incremental Policy Development

A second fundamental approach to policy development is called incremental policy planning.[21] The steps in the incremental approach to policy planning are as follows:

1. Define the problem.
2. Establish a goal.
3. Outline a limited number of alternative courses of action.
4. Predict outcomes for each alternative based on past experience.
5. Select an agreeable course of action.

First, the incremental policy analyst defines a problem as in the rational policy planning approach. Second, the analyst specifies a policy goal, but without trying to prioritize all related values. In the third step, a relatively few policy alternatives are outlined. In other words, the incremental policy analyst does not try to list all conceivable policy options related to the problem and policy goal. In the fourth step, the analyst predicts a limited number of consequences for each policy alternative. In contrast to the rational policy analyst who would use all possible sources of information, the incremental policy analyst makes predictions based on past experience with the subject matter. In other words, past policy experiences are used to predict future policy outcomes. In the fifth and final step, the incremental policy analyst, this time perhaps a social worker employed with a national advocacy organization, provides this information to policy decision-makers, who ultimately select the policy alternative that is agreeable to the majority of decision-makers. In short, the best policy option is the one that is agreeable to the majority of policymakers and, therefore, passable.

Note that decision-makers may agree on a policy option for different reasons. Universal health insurance can be used as an example once again. Liberals might support universal health insurance because it extends coverage to the poor, whereas conservatives might support universal health insurance because they feel it has the potential to lower business costs. In this case, the policymakers would agree on the same policy alternative but for different reasons.

Note also that each policy alternative may have a different combination of values inherent in the policy.[22] Let us take the low taxes versus high quality conflict again, this time in the context of education policy. The incremental policy approach maintains that the decision-maker makes incremental comparisons among policy alternatives. Policy option number one might offer the highest quality education as well as the highest cost and taxes. Policy option number two might offer the lowest cost in terms of taxes, but also the lowest quality education. Similarly, policy number three might offer moderate quality education as well as a moderate tax increase. In any case, each policy alternative contains a combination of values that are marginally different from those found in the other alternatives. Therefore, the incremental policymaker chooses among values and policy alternatives at the same time.

Another important distinction is that incremental policymakers, to a limited extent, may engage in successive "means–ends" comparisons.[23]

(This assumes they see any distinction at all between means and ends!) They ask not only whether a given solution fits a problem but also ask whether a given problem fits existing solutions. The War on Drugs during the first Bush administration is a classic example.[24] With the Soviet Union dissolving, suddenly the American military was left with no major communist threat to fight. (Communist China has been much less aggressive than the former Soviet Union in spreading the communist system worldwide.) Hence, the American military, at least temporarily, represented a solution without a problem. Therefore, Washington policymakers decided to use the military to cut off the supply of drugs entering the United States from foreign countries, particularly from Central America. In so doing, the American military became a solution to the problem of American drug abuse.

To summarize, the incremental approach to policy planning maintains that policy is developed through a succession of incremental comparisons, comparisons among alternative policy options and comparisons between existing policy and future policy alternatives.[25] Furthermore, policymaking is a process of successive approximations to some desired objective, and what is desired often changes over time.[26] For this reason policy is not made once and for all, it is made and remade.[27] (Witness the 1996 welfare reform.) Some say, in fact, that policy is not made at all, it just accumulates over time.[28] Incremental policy planning seems to work best with short-term remedial policy action. The outcomes of the incremental approach are often small variations on the status quo. In short, existing policies and programs are considered as a base. Attention is focused on modifications of these existing policies and programs.

Although incremental policy planning does not seem to be hampered by the rigid requirements of the rational approach, it does have its weaknesses.[29] Incremental policy planning, by definition, favors the status quo. Decisions are likely to reflect the interest of the most powerful groups in society. And, because it favors the status quo, incremental policy planning is apt to neglect fundamental policy innovation. What is more, the incremental approach with its "baby steps" is more subject to policy drift. That is, incremental policy planning may result in policy action without a long-term vision of what is best for society and is more likely to stray from the original intent of policy developers.

Case Example: Medicare

Let us now look at the history of Medicare as an example of the incremental approach to policy planning.[30] Bills to establish national health insurance were introduced regularly in Congress between 1935 and 1951. Each time, however, the bills failed to receive a Congressional hearing. In 1951, a strategy was developed during the Truman administration to limit national health insurance coverage to Social Security recipients. This strategy produced the initial Medicare proposal in 1952. In 1958, the Committee on Ways and Means began Congressional hearings on the Medicare proposal. A year later in 1959 this committee rejected the first serious Medicare Bill called the Forand bill. This bill would have covered all Social Security recipients. Coverage included hospitalization, nursing homes, and in-hospital surgical procedures. A more conservative alternative to the Forand bill was introduced in 1960. This was the Kerr-Mills bill. Although benefits were subject to few limits, this Medicare bill limited benefits to older Americans in severe financial need. This legislation was, in fact, passed in 1960. However, the Kennedy administration introduced its own Medicare proposal, the King-Anderson bill in 1961. Like the Forand bill, it covered all Social Security recipients, but benefits were limited to hospital and nursing home costs. Surgical expenses were not covered in the Kennedy proposal as they had been in the Forand bill. The King-Anderson bill died in committee with no vote taken on the proposal. Later, in 1964, a Medicare bill similar to the King–Anderson bill was also defeated. Finally, in 1965, thirty years after public debate on national health insurance began, Medicare as we know it today was passed during the Johnson administration.

Notice the incremental characteristics of Medicare's legislative history. When it became clear that national health care for all Americans could not be passed, policymakers took a smaller step, proposing to cover only older Americans. The various alternative Medicare bills that were introduced over the years varied from one another in incremental ways regarding people covered and benefits received. The final Medicare legislation that was passed during the Johnson administration was not what anyone planned at first. Yet, the bill did satisfy enough decision-makers to get passed. An incremental policymaker would claim, therefore, that it was the best Medicare proposal at the time.

The Strengths Perspective in Policy Development

Rosemary Kennedy Chapin in a 1995 article in *Social Work* claims that policy planning from a strengths perspective would proceed as follows:[31]

1. Identify basic needs and barriers to meeting those needs.
2. Negotiate with client groups (regarding Step 1).
3. Identify ways that barriers are currently overcome.
4. Identify opportunities and resources required.
5. Formulate policy.
6. Negotiate consensus on policy goals.
7. Design programs.
8. Implement programs.
9. Evaluate program outcomes.

First, the policy analyst should identify the basic needs of a client group and the barriers this group faces in meeting those needs. A second step, closely related to the first step, is to include that client group in a negotiation regarding these needs and barriers. In other words, client populations should be included in identifying their basic needs and barriers to meeting those needs.

A third step in the policy planning process is the identification of ways barriers are currently overcome by clients and programs that serve them. This step also includes clients, perhaps sharing stories of ways that they have overcome barriers to need fulfillment. This third step then leads to a fourth step, which is the identification of opportunities and resources required for people to meet their basic needs.

According to Chapin, only after these first four steps have been completed is the policy analyst ready to formulate a policy proposal as a fifth step. In developing this policy proposal, policy goals will be established through a negotiated consensus with relevant stakeholders including policymakers and client groups. Once policy goals are established as a sixth step, then the seventh step is to design programming to achieve these policy goals. The eight and ninth steps, respectively, are to implement these programs, and then finally, evaluate the outcome of the implemented programs. This ninth and final step involves clients in the evaluation of the program.

Class Discussion: The Strengths Perspective and Ethics

Does the strengths perspective offer a third fundamental approach to policy planning? Chapin claims that the strengths perspective can be useful in providing new tools for conceptualizing social needs and problems.[32] She also says that the use of the strengths perspective may help in developing a more inclusive approach to policy planning. Furthermore, it may expand the range of policy options by identifying the ways that clients already overcome barriers to need fulfillment. But does the strengths perspective provide a third distinct model for policy development? I will let the student decide.

In any case, even if the strengths perspective is viewed only as a different perspective by which to utilize rational or incremental policy planning, it does have an ethical value to professional social workers. I agree that using a strengths perspective in policy planning can result in a more inclusive approach to policy development. When client populations are viewed as having strengths, they are more likely to be included in policy planning. A more active involvement in policy development for those impacted by these policies can be empowering. In addition, any time a strengths perspective is used in policy planning, there is a greater possibility that negative labeling of clients will be avoided and individual dignity respected.

CONTENTSELECT

For more information on related social work topics, use the following search terms:

Descriptive policy
Elite theory
Evaluative policy analysis
Group theory model
Incremental policy
  development

Policy analysis
Policy development
Policy planning
Policy research
Predictive policy analysis
Prescriptive policy analysis

Prospective policy analysis
Rational policy development
Retrospective policy analysis
Strengths perspective
Systems theory

NOTES

1. Thomas Dye, *Understanding Public Policy* (Englewood Cliffs, NJ: Prentice Hall, 1981), pp. 11–31; also see Stephen J. Wayne, G. Calvin Mackenzie, David M. O'Brien, and Richard L. Cole, *The Politics of American Government: Foundations, Participation, and Institutions* (New York: St. Martin's, 1995), Chapters 12–15; James E. Post, Anne T. Lawrence, and James Weber, *Business and Society: Corporate Strategy, Public Policy, Ethics*, 10th ed. (New York: McGraw-Hill, 2002); Peter Drucker, *Managing the Non-Profit Organization* (New York: HarperCollins, 1990).

2. Demetrius Iatridis, *Social Policy: Institutional Context of Social Development and Human Services* (Pacific Grove, CA: Brooks/Cole, 1994), p. 21.

3. David B. Truman, *The Governmental Process: Political Interests and Public Opinion* (New York: Knopf, 1951), pp. 3–8; Thomas Dye and Harmon Zeigler, *The Irony of Democracy: An Uncommon Introduction to American Politics* (Belmont, CA: Wadsworth, 1971), pp. 196–197.

4. Dye and Zeigler, p. 10.

5. Ann Majchrzak, *Methods for Policy Research* (Newbury Park, CA: Sage, 1984); Robert R. Mayer, *Policy and Program Planning: A Developmental Perspective* (Englewood Cliffs, NJ: Prentice-Hall, 1985).

6. Jacob B. Ukeles, "Policy Analysis: Myth or Realty?" *Public Administration Review* 37, No. 3: p. 223 (May/June, 1977), as quoted in Patton and Sawicki, *Basic Methods of Policy Analysis and Planning*, 2nd ed. (Englewood Cliffs, NJ: Prentice Hall, 1993), p. 22.

7. Duncan MacRae, Jr., "Concepts and Methods of Policy Analysis," *Society* 16, No. 6: p. 17

(September/October 1979), as quoted in Patton and Sawicki, p. 22.

8. Patton and Sawicki, pp. 23–25.

9. Majchrzak, p. 12.

10. Edward S. Quade, *Analysis for Public Decisions* (New York: Elsevier Scientific, 1982), p. 5, as quoted in Patton and Sawicki, p. 23.

11. Mayer, pp. 21.

12. Charles Lindblom, "Disjointed Incrementalism: The Science of 'Muddling Through'," in Neil Gilbert and Harry Specht, eds., *Planning for Social Welfare, Issues, Models and Tasks* (Englewood Cliffs, NJ: Prentice Hall, 1977), pp. 98–112.

13. See Jonathan Bradshaw, "The Concept of Social Need," in Gilbert and Specht, pp. 290–296.

14. National Center for Health Statistics, "Health Insurance Coverage." Retrieved from the World Wide Web on February 8, 2002: www.cdc.gov/nchs/fastats/hinsure.htm.

15. Kurt Finsterbusch and Annabelle Bender Motz, *Social Research for Policy Decisions* (Belmont, CA: Wadsworth, 1980), p. 24.

16. Lindblom, p. 101.

17. Lindblom, p. 98; Finsterbusch and Motz, p. 24.

18. Finsterbusch and Motz, pp. 24–31; Lindblom, pp. 98–112; Amitai Etzioni, "Mixed-Scanning: A 'Third' Approach to Decision-Making," in Gilbert and Specht, pp. 87–89.

19. Theodore R. Marmor, "Enacting Medicare: The Politics of Medicare," in R. B. Hudson, ed., *The Aging in Politics* (Springfield, IL: C. C. Thomas, 1981), pp. 105–133.

20. Graham T. Allison, "Conceptual Models and the Cuban Missile Crisis," *The American*

Political Science Review, LXIII, No. 3: pp. 689–696 (1969).

21. Lindblom, p. 98.

22. Ibid., pp. 99, 103.

23. Ibid., p. 101.

24. Bruce S. Jansson, *The Reluctant Welfare State: American Social Welfare Policies—Past, Present, and Future,* 4th ed. (Belmont, CA: Wadsworth/Thomson Learning, 2001), pp. 328–330; Lou Cannon, *President Reagan: The Role of a Lifetime* (New York: Public Affairs, 2000), p. 291; Paul Johnson, *A History of the American People* (New York: HarperPerennial, 1999), p. 934.

25. Lindblom, p. 101.

26. Ibid., p. 108.

27. Ibid.

28. John W. Kingdon, *Agendas, Alternatives, and Public Policies* (New York: HarperCollins, 1984), p. 18.

29. Etzioni, pp. 90–92; Mayer, pp. 43–46.

30. Marmor, pp. 105–133.

31. Rosemary Kennedy Chapin, "Social Policy Development: The Strengths Perspective," *Social Work,* 40, No. 4: pp. 506–513 (1995).

32. Ibid., p. 506.

12 Preparing for Policy Development

President Ronald Reagan confers with policy advisors in July 1982.

Feasibility Study

Problem Definition

Now that we have a conceptual framework in place, let us look at a specific process for developing policy. The major stages of the process are primarily based on those recommended by the policy author Ann Majchrzak.[1] I refer to the first stage in this process as **feasibility study.** In this stage, we want to answer the following questions: Can the policy analysis be done? Is there sufficient support for the analysis? And is it likely that its final recommendations will be passed, or at least given serious consideration, by policymakers? To answer these questions, though, information needs to be gathered by the social work policy analyst.

First, the social problem needs to be defined. This will require both qualitative and quantitative information.[2] Quantitative information is information appropriate for statistical analysis; it depends on numbers. Qualitative information, in contrast, is information not readily translated into numbers. It is more nonnumerical; it is more narrative than quantitative data. Qualitative information is often produced from direct observation of some phenomenon in its natural setting. An example would be a reporter covering a women's rights march for a newspaper or magazine. The reporter directly observes the event, perhaps interviewing participants in the march. Once enough information is collected, the reporter writes up an account of the event for publication in a subsequent issue of the newspaper or magazine. In any case, a well-defined problem typically uses both quantitative and qualitative information to provide a thorough description of the problem. (One can often get an indication of how well a problem has been defined just by scanning the narrative to see if there is a sprinkling of numbers or statistics throughout that section of the study.)

Another way to examine social problems in a feasibility study is to consider their **life cycles.**[3] At birth one sees much investigative activity by government and other interested institutions. During childhood, the problem starts to warrant research grants and the development of task forces to address the problem. During its adult stage, one sees the development of programs to alleviate or solve the social problem. In the older years of a social problem, one often sees funding and interest starting to dry up. The fifth stage of the problem life cycle would, in fact, be its death. The problem may have been solved or perhaps it is considered unsolvable. Perhaps society has begun to blame the victims of the problem. Whatever the reason, the condition does not receive public attention any longer unless it experiences some sort of resuscitation or rebirth in subsequent years. The fundamental point to remember here is that a social worker considering a policy analysis on a given problem needs to understand where the problem is in its life cycle. The possibility for passing new social policy and developing new social programs will be greater if the social problem is in its adulthood stage.

Be that as it may, gathering information on the social problem gives the policy analyst a sense of the availability of information on the topic. This is important in testing the feasibility of doing policy analysis on any given social problem. If there is a scarcity of existing information on the social problem, the policy analyst will have to spend more time and money collecting data. This may involve original research by the policy analyst in contrast to using existing research. In the feasibility stage of policy development, the analyst has to decide whether sufficient time and money is, in fact, available. (Of course, in the real world, the policy analyst often does not have a choice in the social problem that is selected for analysis. In other words, the social problem is selected beforehand. For instance, perhaps the social problem is of interest to a particular funding source, which has provided money for the analysis.)

Key Issues

A second step in the feasibility stage of policy development is to identify the **key issues** that are involved in the selected social problem.[4] That is, social problems tend to be multidimensional. They are complex phenomena resistant to solutions. Otherwise, society would have solved them years ago. In gathering information about the social problem in the feasibility stage, the policy analyst needs to break down the social policy into its various dimensions. During this step, the policy analyst should, in fact, prioritize a key aspect of the problem on which to focus during the policy analysis.

For example, the social problem of inadequate childcare services in America involves several key issues (Figure 12.1). These issues include affordability, quality of care, teacher compensation, home versus center care, hours of service, and location of childcare. Perhaps the policy analyst works for the governor of a poor state where affording existing childcare services is a prevalent concern. In this instance, the policy analyst may prioritize affordability as the key issue in his or her policy analysis.

More fundamentally, consider the problem of poverty in America. This social problem contains many key issues such as unemployment, low wages, globalization, the feminization of poverty, child poverty, access to health care, and welfare reform (Figure 12.2). In this case, the policy analyst may work in a state where many traditional industrial jobs have been moved to lower-wage foreign countries, creating a relatively high unemployment rate. Thus, the influence of globalization on the state economy is a key issue.

Not prioritizing a key issue on which to focus presents several potential dangers. Given the multidimensions of many social problems, trying to cover all aspects of the problem may lead to overruns on costs for the policy study. In addition to costs, time becomes a factor in any extended policy analysis. Decision-makers increasingly want timely information on specific

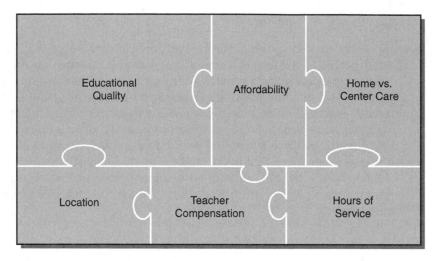

FIGURE 12.1   Key Issues in Child Care

issues.[5] A comprehensive analysis of all aspects of a social problem, therefore, is often impractical and undesired.

A second danger in not prioritizing a key issue early in policy analysis is that the analysis may become overly complex and unwieldy. At this point, the policy analyst is in danger of "paralysis by analysis." (Students often refer to this as *information overload.*) In addition, the final policy analysis, if not targeted to a specific issue, may become scattered and confusing to

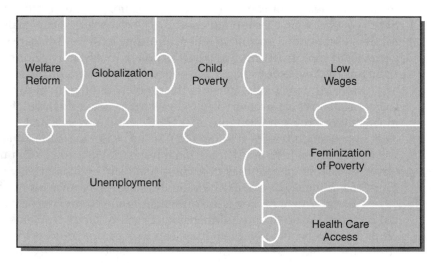

FIGURE 12.2   Key Issues in American Poverty

decision-makers. Remember that policymakers often have little time to analyze an issue and make a decision on policy. Therefore, the policy analyst's job is to present an analysis that facilitates precise and timely decision making on policy matters. In any case, identifying all of the key issues that comprise a social problem will enable the policy analyst to gain a thorough understanding of the social problem before proceeding in the feasibility stage of policy development.

Legislative History

A third step in a feasibility study for policy development is to analyze the **legislative history** of the selected key issue.[6] There are a number of sources of such information. Writings by political scientists, sociologists, social workers, and historians in various professional journals are one such source. Government web sites are a second source. For instance, the Library of Congress maintains a web site called "Thomas," as in Thomas Jefferson.[7] This web site contains much information on current and past legislation. The policy analyst can search for specific legislation on a policy issue by typing key words as in other Internet-based searches. The web site also includes the Congressional Record, which contains the text of bills and other documents. Congressional Records provide information on any action taken on a given day on a specific bill as well as a record of remarks made by various participants in the policy-making process. Furthermore, the Thomas web site includes committee reports, historical documents, and an outline of the law-making process in the federal government.

Another source of legislative history, particularly for current legislation, is state government.[8] Individual states maintain a legislative web site accessible to policy analysts and other interested parties. Similar to the federal government's web site, state web sites include a list of recent bills introduced in their respective state senates and houses. These state web sites also include some legislative history of individual bills. This information includes the names of sponsors of the bill, relevant committees, the last hearing date for the bill, and the outcome of recent hearings on the bill. Legislative information on specific bills typically includes both the summary of the bill as well as the full text of the bill.

Professional organizations, such as the National Association of Social Workers (NASW), are an additional source of legislative information.[9] The NASW maintains a web site that includes an advocacy link for social workers concerned with policy issues. This advocacy link includes an outline of the key issues on which the NASW will focus in the current congressional session. It also includes more in-depth position papers by NASW on each key issue. The NASW's individual position papers, like most position papers, describe the key issue and what legislative action the organization would support regarding the issue. In addition to its legislative agenda for

the current congressional session and a list of position papers on various key issues, NASW also provides information on the status of key issues before Congress as well as links to the text of pertinent bills before Congress. For example,
the NASW provides a direct link to the Thomas legislative web site where the
policy planner can obtain the full text of specific bills before Congress.

Legislative histories are important during the feasibility stage of policy
development because they provide information on the success of previous
policy proposals, on populations affected by the legislation, and on the committees involved with the legislation. All this information can be used in
subsequent steps in the policy development process, including the organizing of support for a specific legislative proposal (partnerships, again!).

Past Research

Another step in the feasibility stage is to review **past research** on the selected
policy issue.[10] Research findings are important in that they can assist in identifying the most significant factors related to the key issue. Given that the
aim of social workers involved in policy development is to better address
identified social problems and issues, future policy and program proposals
must consider significant factors related to the key issue. In this way, social
workers can ensure that new social policies are based in scientific research.
Relevant research can be obtained through various professional journals as
well as through the reports of pertinent research centers around the country.

Major Stakeholders

A fifth step in the feasibility stage is to identify major stakeholders involved
with the selected policy issue.[11] A **stakeholder** by definition is any individual or group that can affect or be affected by the proposed legislation. Obviously, many stakeholders will be affected by a new social policy; therefore, it
is important to identify the most influential stakeholders in relation to the
key policy issue. Some stakeholders have more power than others, and some
stakeholders have more interest than others in the identified issue. Some
stakeholder groups, including social work clientele, may be more affected by
a specific policy proposal than other stakeholder groups may be. Given these
considerations, it is important during the feasibility stage to identify ten to
fifteen major stakeholders. In addition to populations whose needs will be
addressed by the new legislation, major stakeholders typically include congressional or state legislative leaders, the chairpersons on pertinent committees and subcommittees, government agencies, and often, taxpayers.

At this point, it is also often helpful to obtain organizational charts of
decision-making bodies involved with the selected policy issue.[12] In addition, an outline of the policy-making process should be done. For example,
on the national level, the policy analyst needs to determine which congressional committees will hear a bill on the selected issue, which subcommittees

might be involved with the bill, who are the chairpersons of these committees and subcommittees, and so forth.

Identifying major stakeholders will enable the policy analyst to understand which influential groups and individuals will be involved if the policy analysis is, in fact, undertaken. In so doing, the policy analyst should ascertain whether each major stakeholder agrees that the issue is important and should be dealt with in the near future. Strong agreement among major stakeholders on these questions will increase the probability that a future policy proposal will gain acceptance and that sufficient resources will be available to implement the policy.

Agenda Building, Process Streams, and Windows of Opportunity

Agenda Building

Policy researcher John Kingdon offers additional conceptual tools for evaluating the feasibility of a policy analysis.[13] He begins by distinguishing between government agendas and decision agendas in policy making. Government agendas contain problems (and I would include "solutions") that have been introduced in the policy-making arena at some point in time. In other words, these problems and/or solutions have been "floated" in the policy-making arena to gauge how important or attractive they may be to decision-makers. They now are beginning to receive serious attention by policymakers. However, no action has been taken on either an individual problem or individual solution by policymakers. An illustration would be the many years that the sponsors of the first national health insurance bills spent attempting to get hearings before Congress. Medicare was a solution that was well known to policymakers, yet really did not get close to passage until the late 1950s and early 1960s.[14]

In contrast to the government agenda, the decision agenda contains problems and solutions ready, or close to ready, for action by policymakers.[15] The decision agenda, therefore, contains specific bills nearing a vote by policymakers during a given legislative session. To use national health insurance as an illustration again, the Forand bill was introduced and rejected in 1959, the Kerrs-Mills bill introduced and passed in 1960, and the Medicare bill introduced and passed in 1965 as part of the Great Society legislation.[16] All are examples of legislation that made it to the decision agenda.

Process Streams

Next, Kingdon discusses his concept of **process streams.**[17] There are three types. First, there is the **problem stream.** The problem stream consists of the many conditions generally problematic in society. These are unmet needs of various groups. Also, threats and dangers to specific groups would be considered problematic. More specific examples include problems such as crime, inadequate health care, racism, and unemployment. The problem stream contains the social problems of interest in the government policy agenda.

The challenge for social workers involved in policy advocacy is to get the problem of interest to them from the general government agenda to the more immediate decision agenda. A policy analyst in the feasibility stage needs to consider the various techniques for accomplishing this and estimate just how difficult it will be. Techniques for moving a specific problem from the government agenda to the decision agenda include using the media to educate the public about the problem. In this way pressure may be put on elected officials to take action on the social problem. A second technique is to organize a coalition of people who are concerned about the problem. An example might be the organizing of a coalition of childcare professionals and advocates to bring attention to the problem of inadequate childcare in a given state. Similarly, organizing demonstrations, rallies and/or marches concerning the problem is a third technique. An example is the 1987 demonstration in Washington, DC, during the first Bush administration for increased federal funding to address the AIDS epidemic.[18]

Another way to move a problem onto the decision agenda of policymakers is to support a political candidate for office who will champion the cause. At various times, people running for office will identify themselves with an issue such as education and, as a result, commit themselves to taking action on a given problem if elected to office.

In addition, the policy analyst might present the problem as a crisis that will get worse if no action is taken. An example is the AIDS epidemic in the early 1980s. And finally, framing the problem in a way that lends itself to available solutions may encourage policymakers to take action. As discussed previously, the Bush administration's use of an available military to fight a war on drugs during the 1980s is an illustration.[19]

Although Kingdon calls his second type of process stream the policy stream, for my purposes, I refer to it as the **solution stream**.[20] Solution streams contain the various policy mechanisms (such as sanctions), administrative strategies, program designs, and treatment methodologies currently in use. If they are not in use, they are at least known to academics, and possibly, to practitioners and policymakers. Solution streams, therefore, include those potential problem-solving initiatives currently receiving attention by policymakers as part of the general government policy agenda.

Again, the challenge is to get a preferred solution coupled with an identified problem on the decision agenda of policymakers during a given legislative session. The policy analyst considering the feasibility of a given policy project needs to forecast the various techniques for doing this. First of all, the policy analyst could present his/her preferred solution as the most

feasible solution to an existing social problem. It may be most feasible technically (in terms of current research), financially, ideologically, and/or admin-
istratively. To provide a general illustration, the second Bush administration,
which took office in 2001, advocated increased federal funding of "faith-
based" organizations (meaning religious organizations) to address a variety
of social problems.[21] Given his religious convictions, Bush clearly took office
with this as a preferred solution to many human service problems.

A second technique is to present a preferred solution as one of few options for addressing a specific social problem. During my year as a community organizer, I once witnessed a town meeting in which neighborhood
planners presented three options to community residents to address a local
problem, only one of which was expected to be attractive to neighborhood
residents. Although the ethics involved in this sort of democracy are questionable, the neighborhood planners obtained their preferred solution to the
problem.

Another technique is to run for office with the desired solution as a
major part of one's campaign. An example of this technique is the campaign
of millionaire and fiscal conservative Steve Forbes for president in 1996, presenting the flat tax as the solution to an unfair and overly complicated U.S.
tax system.[22]

The third and final type of process stream presented by Kingdon is the
political stream.[23] This is really just another term for describing the sociopolitical environment in which policy is developed. In any case, the political
stream is made up of various types of institutions, organizations, and events.
For Congress and state legislatures, the political stream consists of public
opinion, constituent support, campaign donors, advocacy groups, lobbyists,
the media, and powerful political leaders (committee chairs, etc.). For other
types of public organizations, such as the Department of Health and Human
Services at the national level, political streams consist of things such as legislative guidelines, administrative regulations, taxpayer views, client feedback,
and the views of elected officials. For private nonprofit organizations, political streams contain items such as funding opportunities and guidelines, professional ethics, court rulings (such as the rulings on the tax-exempt status of
nonprofit organizations), advocacy groups, client demands, and community
support. Finally, for business organizations, political streams include government regulations, lobbyists, tax rates, and campaign contributions.

Policy Windows of Opportunity

To conclude his discussion, Kingdon argues that there are **windows of opportunity** for passing new policy.[24] These windows of opportunity occur
when problems, solutions, and political streams converge at some point in
time. The challenge for a policy analyst considering the feasibility of a specific policy study is to estimate the likelihood of such a convergence in the

near future. To illustrate using the history of Medicare once again, the problem was inadequate health care coverage for U.S. residents. The solution presented, at least for older Americans, was Medicare. However, no major legislation was passed until the problem stream and the solution stream converged with the political stream that included a supportive president, Lyndon Johnson, and a supportive chair of the House Ways and Means Committee, Wilbur Mills (although this support was at first reluctant).[25]

Class Discussion: Incrementalism versus Rationalism

Is John Kingdon's concept of policy windows of opportunity an illustration of incremental or rational policy planning? Provide examples to support your argument.

Feasibility and Partnership in Policy Development

Throughout the feasibility stage of policy development, the concept of partnership should be used. Given the importance of social change and social justice in social work, social workers involved in policy development want to pass legislation that better addresses some aspect of a social problem. The preceding history of American social welfare shows that those who are successful in promoting social change are also those who have organized successful partnerships among like-minded groups. Therefore, the social worker as policy analyst should examine each step in their feasibility study in terms of the potential for partnership with other groups.

For example, in defining the social problem and key issue on which to focus, the policy analyst should ask: Which groups define the social problem in a comparable way? Which groups agree with the policy analyst in identifying key aspects of the social problem? These are potential allies in organizing coalitions and/or associations to better address the issue.

In terms of examining the legislative history of the key issue, what committees and departments were involved in passing prior legislation related to the issue? Who were some of the important individuals on these committees and in these departments? Are these people still working in the same positions? If they are, these are potential supporters in the policy analyst's attempt to develop and pass new social policy. What client populations were affected by prior legislation? Do these client populations have advocacy groups? If so, these advocacy groups are potential supporters in passing new social policy.

With respect to examining past research on the policy issue, which organizations were involved in conducting the research? How was the research applied and which groups benefited from the research? These are potential allies in developing future policy. And as previously discussed in identifying major stakeholders, which stakeholders are most likely to be involved in addressing the social issue? Which of these stakeholders have the most interest in the identified policy issue? Which have the most power and influence in the policy-making process? Which will be affected most by new social policy that better addresses the social issue?

And finally, using John Kingdon's notion of coupling problems and solutions, which groups are the biggest proponents of solutions of interest to the policy analyst.[26] This is not to say that the policy analyst necessarily has a solution already picked out to address the social issue; however, based on their prior experience, several potential solutions may be of interest to the policy analyst and their employer. Therefore, other proponents of certain programming and treatment methodologies are potential partners in developing future social policy to address the social issue. It is my hypothesis that the greater the number of influential partners identified during the feasibility stage by the policy analyst, the greater the likelihood of developing and passing new social policy, and, therefore, the more feasible the policy analysis.

Once the policy analyst has collected the preceding information, a fundamental question can be answered: Is the policy analysis feasible? In other words, is there sufficient support for the policy analysis and will policymakers give serious consideration, and, better yet, take decisive action regarding the policy recommendation?

Note that social work students considering a policy analysis will have slightly different considerations in the feasibility stage. These considerations will include their career interests, the quantity of information available on the subject matter, the accessibility of that information to the student, as well as the other courses and responsibilities with which the student is dealing. Whatever the circumstances, at this point, the policy analyst or student should be able to decide whether to continue with the policy analysis.

CONTENTSELECT

For more information on related social work topics, use the following search terms:

Feasibility studies	Problem definition	Stakeholder
Key issues	Problem stream	Windows of opportunity
Legislative history	Process streams	
Life cycles	Qualitative and quantitative	
Past research	information	
Political stream	Solution stream	

NOTES

1. Ann Majchrzak, *Methods for Policy Research* (Newbury Park, CA: Sage, 1984).

2. Allen Rubin and Earl Babbie, *Research Methods for Social Work,* 2nd ed. (Pacific Grove, CA: Brooks/Cole, 1993), p. 30.

3. Nancy M. Henley, "Women as a Social Problem: Conceptual and Practical Issues in Defining Social Problems," in Edward Seidman and Julian Rappaport, eds., *Redefining Social Problems* (New York: Plenum Press, 1986), pp. 65–79.

4. Majchrzak, p. 34.

5. Carl V. Patton and David S. Sawicki, *Basic Methods of Policy Analysis and Planning,* 2nd ed. (Englewood Cliffs, NJ: Prentice Hall, 1993), p. 2.

6. Majchrzak, p. 34.

7. See http://thomas.loc.gov.

8. For example, see www.state.nh.us.

9. See www.socialworkers.org/advocacy/default.htm.

10. Majchrzak, p. 35.

11. Ibid., p. 36.

12. Ibid., pp. 35–36.

13. John W. Kingdon, *Agendas, Alternatives, and Public Policies* (New York: HarperCollins, 1984), pp. 3–4, 21, 123, 187.

14. Theodore R. Marmor, "Enacting Medicare: The Politics of Medicare," in R. B. Hudson, ed., *The Aging in Politics* (Springfield, IL: C. C. Thomas, 1981), pp. 105–133.

15. Kingdon, p. 149.

16. Marmor, pp. 105–133.

17. Kingdon, pp. 20–21.

18. Bruce S. Jansson, *The Reluctant Welfare State: American Social Welfare Policies–Past, Present, and Future,* 4th ed. (Belmont, CA: Wadsworth/Thomson Learning, 2001), pp. 334–335.

19. Jansson, pp. 328–330; Lou Cannon, *President Reagan: The Role of a Lifetime* (New York: Public Affairs, 2000), p. 291; Paul Johnson, *A History of the American People* (New York: HarperPerennial, 1999), p. 934.

20. Kingdon, pp. 181–182.

21. MSNBC, "Bush to Unveil Faith-Based Legislation." Retrieved from the World Wide Web on February 7, 2002: www.msnbc.com/news/701500.asp; Mary Leonard, "Lawyer to Head Faith-Based Effort." Retrieved from the World Wide Web on February 2, 2002: www.boston.com/dailyglobe2/033/nation/Lawyer_to_head_faith_based_effortP.shtml.

22. Jansson, p. 385.

23. Kingdon, p. 152.

24. Ibid., pp. 174, 187.

25. Marmor, pp. 105–133.

26. Kingdon, p. 181.

13 Thoroughly Understanding the Social Problem

"Why do you think you cross the road?"

Social workers employ various approaches to problem definition.

Problem Definition

Various Approaches to Problem Definition

Once the social worker in the role of policy analyst has decided to carry out a specific policy analysis, the next stage in policy development is to thoroughly define the problem.[1] That is, the social work policy analyst wants to expand on the definition of the social problem and key issue, which was completed during the feasibility stage. This is because the policy analyst needs to have a thorough grasp of the social problem and key issue before researching possible solutions to the problem. In doing so, it may be helpful to think about different approaches to problem definition.[2]

One approach to problem definition is the **functional approach.**[3] This approach claims that a social problem is any condition that upsets the smooth functioning of society. An obvious example is the problem of terrorism in America, particularly after the September 11, 2001, airplane crashes into the World Trade Towers in New York City and the Pentagon in Washington, DC[4] Street crime is another example. Both can make people fearful of going about their normal daily routines.

A second way to define a problem is the **normative approach.**[5] The normative method stresses that a social problem is any condition that deviates from accepted societal norms. An illustration of such a condition would be the child sexual abuse scandal in the Catholic Church, a problem that began to receive widespread public attention in 2002.[6] The sexual abuse of children violates society's norms, and the fact that Catholic priests have carried out the abuse makes the whole problem even more shocking to average Americans.

A third approach to problem definition is the **objective approach,** which maintains that a social problem is recognized when the quantitative indicators of a problem become indisputably large over time.[7] For instance, about a quarter of the total American labor force was unemployed at the height of the Great Depression.[8] Any reasonable observer could not dispute that the country was in economic crisis and that something drastic had to be done. Thus, Roosevelt was able to push through his New Deal.

The **subjective approach** to defining social problems is a fourth method that should be considered by policy developers.[9] In this approach the quantitative evidence has been available for a considerable amount of time; it is the public's perception of the data that changes. To illustrate, domestic violence was once considered a personal matter, a private issue that was no one's business. Today, in contrast, domestic violence is considered a social problem that requires public attention.[10]

The policy analyst may also want to look at the selected problem and key issue in terms of **value conflict.**[11] This approach to problem definition argues that social problems are created when groups have conflicting values.

A good example is the pro-life versus pro-choice debate around abortion in America. Given the passion associated with the values of both groups, it is not a problem likely to be solved in the near future.

A sixth and final approach to problem definition is the **claims-making approach.** This approach uses the social construction theory to argue that problem definition is, in fact, "the activities of individuals or groups making assertions of grievances and claims with respect to some putative condition."[12] In other words, social problems are human constructions. Therefore, it is the process of constructing social problems that is the focus in the claims-making approach. Problem definition becomes an outcome of negotiation among competing groups.

Case Example: The Civil Rights Movement of the 1960s

To illustrate, consider the evolution of African American segregation from a (supposedly) natural condition to an intolerable social injustice.[13] One of Martin Luther King's organizing strategies in the Civil Rights Movement of the 1960s was to make the segregation of African Americans problematic for Southern business and political leaders. To this end, King and other civil rights organizers persuaded the African American community of Montgomery, Alabama, to stop riding city busses until laws regarding segregated bus seating were abolished. In a second civil rights campaign, King and others organized a boycott of businesses in Birmingham, Alabama. The boycotts continued in each case until negotiation between civil rights leaders and southern segregationists resulted in an end to racial segregation.

A rigorous examination of the social problem and key issue may benefit from the distinct insights derived from each of these approaches to problem definition. And while each perspective can provide a unique contribution to problem definition, the six approaches are not necessarily mutually exclusive. There is overlap among them. The value conflict approach, for instance, is inherent in the claims-making approach. All use the objective approach to some extent.

Furthermore, various approaches to problem definition may be useful in organizing partnerships among special interest groups to pass and implement the proposed legislation. That is, social workers employed in policy development may solicit the support of individual stakeholder groups through selection of one or more of the six approaches to problem definition. Some groups are motivated by statistical information that quantifies the problem and its key aspects. The policy analyst, therefore, may want to emphasize the objective approach in this case. Other potential supporters are more motivated by their values concerning the problem. They do not need statistics; they just know what they believe to be important in the matter. For these groups, an approach such as the value conflict approach to problem definition may be more effective. In short, the way a social problem is defined can assist in generating support for policy proposals.

Modeling and Problem Definition

Types of Models

In completing a thorough definition of the social problem and key issue, it is also helpful to develop a model of the problem and/or issue.[14] A **model** by definition is a "simplified representation of some aspect of the real world."[15] In this case, the model can depict the general social problem, including the more specific key issue, or it can focus strictly on the key issue itself. The social work policy analyst can obtain information for constructing the model from the earlier feasibility stage of policy development. The analyst may also want to do a further review of the literature at this point to provide additional information. In any case, social workers involved in policy development should have a basic understanding of different types of models.[16] Models are a useful tool in policy analysis.

One type of model is simply a **physical model.**[17] Physical models tend to be three-dimensional in form. Examples of a physical model include a model car or airplane that one might have built as a child or even a favorite doll from childhood. A miniature scale model of a new building planned for your local university is another example.

A second type of model is a **diagrammatic model.**[18] This type of model provides the essential features of a subject, but is generally two-dimensional in form. Samples of diagrammatical models are road maps or blueprints for a house. Flow charts are also an example of a diagrammatic model. A flow chart diagrams how something passes from one state or condition to another. An example is the flow chart on how a bill becomes law provided in Chapter 1. Other familiar types of diagrammatic models include charts and graphs such as the bar charts and histograms provided by social science statistics packages. Also, social workers educated in casework will be relieved to know that genograms and ecomaps are examples of diagrammatic models.[19]

A third category of models is the **conceptual model.**[20] Conceptual models, in part, are used to make predictions about human or organizational behavior. Conceptual models familiar to social workers include Sigmund Freud's psychodynamic model as well as Erik Erikson's life span model.[21]

Descriptive/predictive models are a fourth category of models.[22] In policy development, these models may be used to describe policy alternatives and predict outcomes for proposed policy alternatives. For instance the equation of a line where various values for variable x are used to predict corresponding values for variable y given the linear equation, $y = mx + b$. (In this equation, m is the slope of the line, b is the point at which the line crosses the y axis). This equation of a line serves as the basis for linear regression analysis, a statistical procedure used in social policy and the social sciences in general.[23]

A fifth type of model is the **prescriptive model**.[24] Not only does the prescriptive model describe options and predict outcomes for the policy planner, it also provides a rule for choosing among alternatives. For instance, the cost–benefit analysis framework is a prescriptive model.[25] In choosing among several policy options, the fundamental rule of cost–benefit analysis is to choose the option with the greatest net benefit to society. Therefore, the policy alternative is prescribed by the model itself.

Deterministic models are also useful in policy development.[26] Deterministic models are models in which the outcomes are assumed to be certain. Examples of deterministic models include cohort models used to predict population growth. This type of model is useful when trying to predict the number of people to be served in a given year in a given geographic region, such as a state, or in a specific institution, such as a city school system. The outcome of such models is assumed to be certain because the population under study tends to be relatively stable and easy to predict.

A final type of model is the **probabilistic model**.[27] Probabilistic models are models in which outcomes are assigned a probability. The probability of each outcome is estimated by the policy analyst. To illustrate, a simple random sample is based on a probability model. That is, all members of the population have an equal chance of being selected in the sample.[28] Simple random sampling is the most basic sampling method assumed in policy analysis that employs social science research methods.

In summary, there are several reasons to use models in policy development.[29] First, they help to describe, predict, and prescribe policy options. Second, models are a simplification of reality, thus making reality easier to examine. Third, models force the policy analyst to focus only on the most important elements of a problem or key issue. In so doing, they help to eliminate nonessential aspects of the problem or issue. Fourth, models help to prevent the omission of important factors in a social problem or key issue. Finally, models assist in communicating information about social problems and issues to decision-makers. This communication benefit of modeling is particularly important given the limited time policy analysts have to educate decision-makers and the general public. It is also important given the preference today for visual information sources. If the policy analyst finds it very difficult to model the selected problem or key issue, it may indicate that the analyst does not understand the problem or issue well enough yet. If so, a further review of relevant literature may be needed.

A final note regarding modeling, particularly for students and beginning policy analysts, is to be sure to model the problem and not the solution to the problem. My experience in the classroom shows that students often have a favorite solution in mind when beginning their policy analysis and problem definition. This solution may be a familiar program design or treatment methodology. However, potential solutions should be set aside until the problem and key issue are thoroughly defined and understood. This patience, in the end, will increase the likelihood of an unbiased, thoroughly researched policy recommendation.

Illustration: A Model of the Feminization of Poverty

If we select as our social problem for analysis, poverty in America, then one key issue would be the feminization of poverty in America. Women in America are more likely than men to live in poverty regardless of age or race.[30] The social work policy analyst may use information collected on the topic in their prior feasibility study to identify factors associated with women in poverty. For the sake of discussion, I will use research on the topic published by Starrels and Bould in 1994. Based on this information, a simple diagrammatic model of one scenario leading to female poverty might look like that shown in Figure 13.1.[31]

Causation in Social Policy and Social Science

As the reader looks at this model of women in poverty, it is important to be precise about the way in which the various components of the model are described. May variables such as divorce and women working part-time be described as causal factors? In answering this question, the policy analyst needs to remember the three basic criteria for determining **causation** in social research.[32] First, the independent variable must occur before the dependent variable to establish causation. In other words, the cause must occur before the effect. In this illustration, the dependent variable is women in poverty, whereas the other variables are independent variables. Second, the independent and dependent variables must be empirically related. For instance, based on the policy analyst's observation, as an independent variable increases so does the dependent variable, or as the case may be, as an independent variable increases, the dependent variable decreases. In any case, the two variables tend to occur together. Third, the observed relationship between the independent and dependent variable is not the result of the influence of some third variable that causes them both. If all three criteria hold true, then one can state with certainty that the independent variable causes the dependent variable.

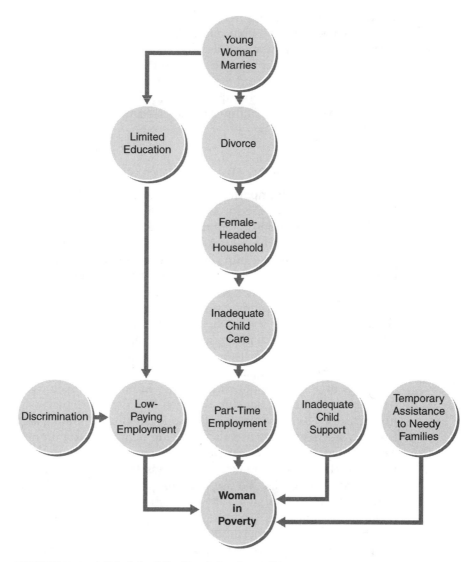

FIGURE 13.1   A Model of the Feminization of Poverty

Source: Based on research by Marjorie E. Starrels and Sally Bould, "The Feminization of Poverty in the United States," *Journal of Family Issues* 15(4), pp. 590–607 (December 1994).

However, when trying to predict human behavior, social scientists typically speak in terms of probabilistic causation.[33] This is because of the difficulty in social science of determining whether all three criteria have been met. A social work policy analyst, therefore, may describe an independent variable as a causal factor in regards to a dependent variable if the presence of the independent variable makes the dependent variable more likely to occur. Social researchers also use the term *contributing factor,* meaning that the independent variable contributes to the causation of a dependent variable. Other frequently used terms include *associated factor* or *related factor.* In any case, the precise term used to describe components of one's model should be based on the findings of past research on the social problem and/or key issue.

Values, Assumptions, and Model Development

Not only is research important in constructing a model for the social problem and/or key issue, the social work policy analyst must also consider the values and assumptions inherent in the model.[34] The reader will remember that we earlier defined a value as a principle or quality considered desirable by some individual or group. There are several values inherent in the preceding model of the feminization of poverty. First, no one should live in poverty. Children, in particular, should not grow up in poverty. Women should not be punished for assuming responsibility for child rearing. Absent fathers should play a greater role in the financial support of their children. And finally, women should be paid equal pay for equal work in relation to men in the job place. These are just a few of the values that make poverty in America a problem and the feminization of poverty a key issue in that problem.

Identifying assumptions is another important consideration in model development. If a relationship between two factors depicted in a model is not supported by research, then the policy analyst is making an assumption. Social workers working in policy development want to minimize the use of assumptions in defining problems and issues. That is not to say that all policy analysts do not make assumptions from time to time, but the best among them minimize the use of assumptions and identify those assumptions that are, in fact, made. My hypothesis in this discussion is that the fewer the assumptions used in defining social problems and issues, the more effective the resulting social policy and programs. One assumption made in the preceding model of the feminization of poverty is that women would be more likely to work full time if they did not have childcare responsibilities. In the absence of research that supports this statement, the statement must be considered an assumption inherent in the model.

Once the policy analyst is satisfied that he/she has thoroughly defined the social problem and the specific key issue, he or she is then ready to answer the fundamental policy analysis question. That is, is there a more effective policy or program for addressing the key policy issue than currently exists? Methods for answering this question are the topic of the next two chapters. First however, additional illustrations of problem/key issue modeling are presented.

Illustration: A Model of Factors Influencing Late Prenatal Care

In research published in 1999, Perloff and Jaffee examined individual and neighborhood factors associated with late entry into prenatal care.[35] The study involved 220,694 pregnant New York City residents. If inadequate health care in the United States is a recognized social problem, then inadequate prenatal care can be considered a key aspect of that problem. Quality, timely prenatal care is very important for the health of both mother and baby. Figure 13.2 shows the most significant factors identified in the study.

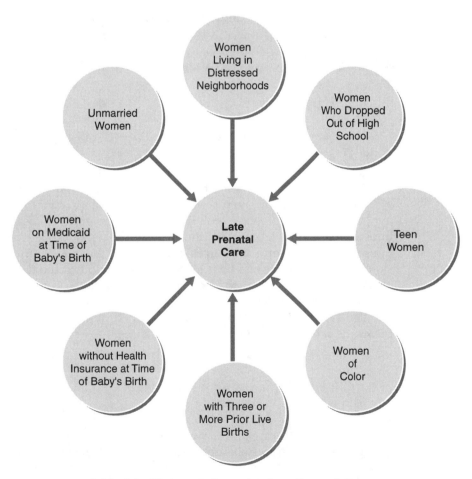

FIGURE 13.2   A Model of Factors Influencing Late Prenatal Care

Source: Based on research by Janet D. Perloff and Kim D. Jaffee, "Late Entry into Prenatal Care: The Neighborhood Context," *Social Work* 44(2): 116–128 (March 1999).

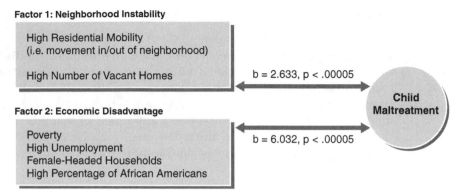

Factor 1: Neighborhood Instability

High Residential Mobility
(i.e. movement in/out of neighborhood)

High Number of Vacant Homes

b = 2.633, p < .00005

**Child
Maltreatment**

Factor 2: Economic Disadvantage

Poverty
High Unemployment
Female-Headed Households
High Percentage of African Americans

b = 6.032, p < .00005

FIGURE 13.3   A Model of Child Maltreatment

Note: b = unstandardized regression coefficient; p = level of significance

Source: Based on research by Joy Swanson Ernst, "Community-Level Factors and Child Maltreatment in a Suburban Country," *Social Work Research* 25(3): 133–142 (September 2001).

Illustration: A Model of Child Maltreatment

Joy Swanson Ernst did a study published in 2001 on the influence of neighborhood factors on child maltreatment.[36] Child maltreatment in the research was defined as physical abuse, neglect, or sexual abuse. The aim of the study was to examine whether some families are at greater risk of abusing or neglecting their children given certain neighborhood characteristics concerning poverty, population mobility, the prevalence of female-headed households, and racial composition. These characteristics were indicators of the social and economic resources of families in the neighborhood. Regression analysis of eleven neighborhood variables hypothesized to contribute to child maltreatment produced two significant factors—economic disadvantage and neighborhood instability—as shown in Figure 13.3. Note that more detailed statistical information can be provided in the model depending on the needs of policymakers and other audiences.

CONTENTSELECT

For more information on related social work topics, use the following search terms:

Causation
Claims-making approach
Conceptual models
Descriptive/predictive
    models
Deterministic models

Diagrammatic models
Functional approach
Model
Normative approach
Objective approach
Physical models

Prescriptive models
Probabilistic models
Problem definition
Subjective approach
Value conflict

NOTES

1. Ann Majchrzak, *Methods for Policy Research* (Newbury Park, CA: Sage, 1984), p. 43.

2. Nancy M. Henley, "Women as a Social Problem: Conceptual and Practical Issues in Defining Social Problems," in Edward Seidman and Julian Rappaport, eds., *Redefining Social Problems* (New York: Plenum Press, 1986), pp. 65–79.

3. Ibid., p. 70.

4. Anne E. Kornblut, "US hunt of Qaeda plotters heats up," *Boston Globe*, p. A1. Retrieved from the World Wide Web on June 12, 2002: www.boston.com/dailyglobe2/163/...hunt_of_Qaeda_plotters_heats-upP.shtml; Michael Elliott, "How the U.S. Missed the Clues," *Time* 159, no. 21, pp. 24–32 (May 27, 2002); Robert Schlesinger, "Renovation of Attack Site Exterior Ends—Under Budget," *Boston Globe*, p. A12. Retrieved from the World Wide Web on June 12, 2002:www.boston.com/dailyglobe2/163/...site_exterior_ends_under_budgetP.shtml.

5. Henley, p. 70.

6. The Associated Press, "Panel of U.S. Bishops Consider a Response to Sexual Abuse," *The New York Times*. Retrieved from the World Wide Web on June 12, 2002: www.nytimes.com; David Van Biema, "Rebels in the Pews," *Time* 159, No. 24: pp. 54–58 (June 17, 2002).

7. Henley, p. 71.

8. Michael B. Katz, *In the Shadow of the Poorhouse*, 10th ed. (New York: BasicBooks, 1996), p. 214.

9. Henley, pp. 71–72.

10. Liane V. Davis and Jan L. Hagen, "The Problem of Wife Abuse: The Interrelationship of Social Policy and Social Work Practice," *Social Work* 37, No. 1: pp. 15–19 (1992).

11. Henley, pp. 72–73.

12. Malcom Spector and John I. Kitsuse, *Constructing Social Problems* (Menlo Park, CA: Cummings Publishing, 1977), p. 75, as quoted in Henley, p. 73.

13. Clayborne Carson, ed., *The Autobiography of Martin Luther King, Jr.* (New York: TimeWarner, 1998), p. 289; Bruce S. Jansson, *The Reluctant Welfare State: American Social Welfare Policies—Past, Present, and Future*, 4th ed. (Belmont, CA: Wadsworth/Thomson Learning, 2001), pp. 52–55, 174, 248.

14. Majchrzak, p. 43.

15. Edith Stokey and Richard Zeckhauser, *A Primer for Policy Analysis* (New York: W. W. Norton & Company, 1978), p. 8.

16. Ibid., pp. 8–21.

17. Ibid., p. 9.

18. Ibid.

19. Beulah Roberts Compton and Burt Galaway, *Social Work Processes*, rev. ed. (Homewood, IL: The Dorsey Press, 1979), pp. 300–309.

20. Stokey and Zeckhauser, p. 11.

21. Erik H. Erikson, *Childhood and Society*, 2nd ed. (New York: Norton, 1963); Calvin S. Hall, *A Primer of Freudian Psychology* (New York: The World Publishing Company, 1954); Charles Brenner, *An Elementary Textbook of Psychoanalysis* (Garden City, NY: Anchor Books, 1974).

22. Stokey and Zeckhauser, pp. 13–15.

23. Marija J. Norusis, *The SPSS Guide to Data Analysis for SPSS* (Chicago, IL: SPSS, 1988), pp. 325–333.

24. Stokey and Zeckhauser, pp. 13–15.

25. Ibid., pp. 134, 137.

26. Ibid., pp. 15–17.

27. Ibid.

28. Allen Rubin and Earl Babbie, *Research Methods for Social Work*, 2nd ed. (Pacific Grove, CA: Brooks/Cole, 1993), pp. 223, 239.

29. Stokey and Zeckhauser, pp. 9–21.

30. Marjorie E. Starrels and Sally Bould, "The Feminization of Poverty in the United States," *Journal of Family Issues* 15, No. 4: pp. 590–607 (December 1994).

31. Ibid.

32. Earl Babbie, *The Practice of Social Research*, 7th ed. (Belmont, CA: Wadsworth, 1995), pp. 70–71.

33. Allen Rubin and Earl Babbie, *Research Methods for Social Work*, 2nd ed. (Pacific Grove, CA: Brooks/Cole, 1993), pp. 25–28.

34. Majchrzak, p. 43.

35. Janet D. Perloff and Kim D. Jaffee, "Late Entry into Prenatal Care: The Neighborhood Context," *Social Work* 44, No. 2: pp. 116–128 (March 1999).

36. Joy Swanson Ernst, "Community-Level Factors and Child Maltreatment in a Suburban County," *Social Work Research* 25, No. 3: pp. 133–142 (September 2001).

14 Researching Technically Feasible Recommendations

President George W. Bush is seen here at work in the White House.

Technical Feasibility and Policy Options

The technical research stage in policy planning is most similar to traditional social science methods.[1] At this stage in policy development, the social work policy analyst is looking for a technically feasible policy alternative for addressing the identified key issue. In other words, will a policy and/or program be effective in solving, or at least mitigating, the key policy issue? Criteria for technical feasibility include effectiveness, that is, does the policy or program help solve the problem? In addition, technical feasibility includes adequacy. In other words, is the policy or program effective enough?[2]

Class Discussion: Evaluating Policy

When policy analysts discuss effectiveness and adequacy, what constitutes success? In other words, how effective does a policy or program have to be in order to be successful? How adequate does a policy or program have to be in order to be considered successful?

Research Designs

In researching technically feasible policy alternatives, the first step is to decide on a research design. The classic experimental design involves independent and dependent variables, experimental and control groups, and pretesting and posttesting. Particularly in research done by social workers, this research research typically starts with a group of recruited volunteers.[3] Individuals within the group are then randomly assigned either to an experimental group or to a control group. Once this is done, both groups are given a pretest of some sort. If we were to use the example of Clozaril and schizophrenia, the pretest could be a measurement of well-being of the individual with schizophrenia before being treated with the drug Clozaril. Next, the experimental group is, in fact, treated with Clozaril. Following this treatment, both the experimental group and the control group are given a posttest to measure well-being. Once the posttest is completed, the difference in well-being in the experimental group is examined by comparing the results of the posttest to the pretest. The difference in well-being of individual members in the control group is also calculated by comparing differences in the results of the posttest and pretest. Finally, differences in well-being between the experimental group and the control group are examined to determine if, in fact, being treated with Clozaril had a significant positive effect on the well-being of individuals with schizophrenia. In this classic experimental design, the independent variable would be the Clozaril treatment; the dependent variable would be the well-being of individuals participating in the experiment.

A second research design used in policy analysis is the **quasi-experimental design.**[4] In this design, some of the conditions required for a classic experiment are relaxed. For instance, there is no equivalent control group in a time-series design, an example of a quasi-experimental design. To illustrate, let us say that the key issue being addressed by the policy analyst is the high number of traffic fatalities among adolescents in a given state. Let us say that to address this issue, a new law is passed to increase by one year the age at which a teen can obtain a driver's license.

To see if this law is, in fact, successful, we could set up a simple inter-rupted time-series design.[5] In this design, the independent variable would be the policy change, in other words, the increase in the driving age of teen-agers. The dependent variable would be the number of teen traffic fatalities per year. Measurements would have been taken, preferably over several years, of the number of teen traffic fatalities per year before the policy change was instituted. After the new law is implemented, the same measure-ments of the number of teen traffic fatalities per year would be taken over several subsequent years to see if there was a significant decrease. That is to say, the number of teen traffic fatalities per year would be observed over sev-eral years to see if, in fact, there was a significant decrease after increasing the age at which teens can drive. In this time series design, the years before the policy change become a baseline by which to compare the success of the new driving age on teen traffic fatalities in future years.

A third research design of interest to policy developers is called a **corre-lational design.** Correlational designs are also referred to as cross sectional studies.[6] Correlational designs usually involve a random sample and multi-variate statistical controls. Like the time-series design, there is no equivalent control group used in the study.

An example of a correlational design would be a study done by me on gender and human service giving.[7] The purpose of the study was to see if there was a relationship between gender and charitable giving to human ser-vices. In other words, was there a significant difference in charitable giving to human services between men and women? To conduct this study, I used a large random sample of Americans done by the Gallup organization for the Independent Sector. While examining the potential relationship between the independent variable, gender, and the dependent variable, human service giving, the effect of other relevant variables on human service giving, such as individual income levels and education levels, were controlled using lo-gistical regression analysis. (In case the reader is interested in this sample, those giving to human services, in contrast to those who did not, were more likely to be women.)

A fourth research design used in policy development is called a **pre-experimental design.**[8] In this type of design, the requirements of the classic experiment are relaxed even further, while at the same time, there are no random samples and multivariate statistics as in the correlational design. An example would be a one-shot case study. In this type of study, a service (perhaps part of a pilot study) might be provided to a group of people. After the intervention, an attribute of the group is measured. Theoretically, the group may suffer from low self-esteem—a group of female victims of domestic violence, for instance. The participants might be asked to attend a women's support group for a period of time, after which the self-esteem of each woman is measured. If the group measures high on self-esteem, further research might be done in anticipation of a policy proposal to fund such women's services throughout a given state.

Case studies, in general, are particularly useful for examining the process by which a policy proposal has been passed. Case studies can utilize both quantitative and qualitative research methods, although they tend to be more qualitative than quantitative in nature. What distinguishes a "case study" is its exclusive focus on a given case. An illustration of a policy case study would be the publication by Theodore Marmor on the development of Medicare, which was discussed earlier in this text.[9]

Data Collection

Once the social work policy analyst has chosen a research design, the next step is to select a method for collecting data. In planning for data collection, there are two types of data: **primary data** and **secondary data.**[10] Primary data is data that policy analysts collect themselves. Secondary data, in contrast, is existing data that someone else has already collected. If sufficient data does not already exist, there are several methods for collecting information.[11] One is the basic literature review in which the policy analyst reviews pertinent books and journal articles on the key policy issue. A second method is the personal interview, in which the policy analyst interviews relevant individuals either in person or over the telephone.

Direct observation is a third method of collecting information. That is, the policy analyst observes, either directly by taking part in some event or indirectly by watching some activity. Either way, the policy analyst will witness pertinent activities firsthand. In addition, questionnaires are a popular data collection method in policy development. Questionnaires can be administered over the phone or face-to-face by a trained interviewer or sent to individuals through the mail (including e-mail).

Another frequently used data collection method is the **focus group.** In a focus group, a selected group of people, typically twelve to fifteen in number, are brought together to explore some topic in depth. The facilitator of the focus group guides the discussion to solicit information regarding beliefs and opinions of individuals on the topic at hand.

Social workers involved in policy development, from Jane Addams to Senator Barbara Mikulski, have also used a data collection technique from the political sector: the public hearing. Whether we are referring to a town meeting or a congressional committee hearing, these forums are a frequently used source of information for social policy.

Finally, as previously stated, policy analysts can take advantage of existing databases to gather information. In addition to government sources, existing data on a variety of topics may be obtained from private organizations as well. Some of these databases can be accessed through libraries such as those at local universities. In other cases, data files can be accessed or purchased directly from the outside organization. In any case, using existing data can save the policy analyst time and money.

Using Agencies on the Internet for Data Collection

Social workers involved in policy research can also collect much pertinent information from reputable agencies on the Internet. A few of these organizations, such as the Library of Congress and the National Association of Social Workers, were discussed in the feasibility study section of this text. Other organizations that maintain excellent web sites, such as The Children's Defense Fund and The Child Welfare League of America, have also been discussed in other sections of this book. Here is a list of additional agencies providing valuable policy information on the Web.

Administration for Children and Families (ACF)—www.acf.dhhs.gov. This agency administers approximately sixty federal programs that serve children and their families.[12] The site includes information on these programs, ACF statistics, research, fact sheets, data, publications, and related links.

American Civil Liberties Union (ACLU)—www.aclu.org/index.html. The ACLU seeks to defend and preserve the individual rights and liberties of all Americans.[13] Its web site contains position papers, message boards, chat rooms, updates on issues before Congress and in the courts, links to other web sites, suggested search terms, and the ability to send free faxes to politicians.

Center for Substance Abuse Prevention (CSAP)—www.samhsa.gov/csap. The CSAP is a federal organization dealing with substance abuse prevention policies, programs, and services, including illegal drug use, and underage alcohol and tobacco use.[14] Its web site includes fact sheets, statistics, reports, databases, model prevention programs, and online courses on prevention.

Department of Health and Human Services (DHHS)—www.os.dhhs.gov. DHHS is the federal government's primary agency responsible for protecting the health of all Americans and providing vital human services.[15]

DHHS's web site contains links to many federal agencies under DHHS, testimony, speeches, fact sheets, and press releases on key issues.

HIV InSite—http://hivinsite.ucsf.edu.   This HIV/AIDS information site is a collaborative effort developed by the University of California, San Francisco.[16] The web page offers fact sheets and a complete textbook on HIV/AIDS in addition to information on prevention, program development and evaluation, and policy analysis.

National Association for the Advancement of Colored People (NAACP) —www.naacp.org.   The NAACP works to protect the civil rights of African Americans and other minorities.[17] The organization's web site includes the history and intent of NAACP-sponsored programs, archives of press releases, and links to related associations and resources.

National Council on Aging (NCOA)—http://www.ncoa.org.   The NCOA promotes the dignity, self-determination, and well-being of older persons.[18] Its web site contains issue briefs, recent published articles, legislative alerts and updates for current congressional legislation, research results, and related links.

National Mental Health Association (NMHA)—www.nmha.org.   NMHA seeks to improve the mental health of all Americans through advocacy, education, research, and service.[19] Its site provides legislative alerts, news releases, position statements, a description and information on NMHA programs, and mental health policy-related links.

National Organization for Women (NOW)—http://now.org.   NOW works to bring about equality for all women through direct mass actions, lobbying, grassroots organization, and litigation.[20] NOW's web page contains position statements, fact sheets, news releases, legislative updates with background information and history, and alerts to upcoming votes.

Urban Institute (UI)—www.urban.org.   The Urban Institute, a nonprofit nonpartisan policy research and educational organization, provides information and analysis to public and private decision-makers.[21] The Urban Institute's web site offers research and reports on key issues, press releases, databases, program evaluations, and book lists related to various key issues.

Data Analysis

Once data is collected in one or more of the ways described previously, the next step is to analyze the collected information. Several **data analysis strat-**

egies are appropriate for policy development. The first and probably most used strategy is to do a **focused synthesis,**[22] also referred to as a quick analysis.[23] In a focused synthesis, the social work policy analyst puts together pertinent information from several existing information sources. These can include traditional books and journals, but may also include the Internet, personal interviews with experts on the policy issue, unpublished documents such as agency files, congressional hearings, and even prior personal experiences with the subject matter.

A focused synthesis or quick analysis is useful for more short-term policy analysis. This is in contrast to long-term policy research projects such as those conducted at universities or so-called think tanks. For example, a social worker volunteering on a political campaign might use a quick analysis to help the candidate write a position paper on a specific policy issue. A social worker employed in a school system might use a quick analysis to help establish a school policy around an issue such as school violence or substance abuse. And finally, social work students enrolled in social welfare policy courses typically synthesize information found in published materials to complete their assignments during the semester.

A more complex data analysis strategy is the use of **benefit-cost analysis.**[24] A benefit–cost analysis (or cost–benefit analysis, depending on the author) consists of five steps. First, the project to be analyzed is identified. Second, all impacts favorable and unfavorable, present and future, on all of society are determined. This process is called impact prediction. By impacts, the policy planner means the impact on society both positive and negative of implementing the new policy. Third, values are assigned to these impacts. Typically, values are presented in terms of total dollars. In any case, favorable impacts are registered as benefits while unfavorable ones are considered costs. This step is called valuation. The fourth step in benefit–cost analysis is calculating the net benefit. The net benefit of implementing the policy is the total benefits minus the total costs. The last step is to make a decision. If net benefits are greater than zero, the policy is implemented; if the policy analyst and decision-makers are choosing among two or more policy options, the policy option with the highest net benefit is selected. In fact, the fundamental rule of benefit–cost analysis states that "in any choice situation select the alternative that produces the greatest net benefit."[25]

Cost-effectiveness is an abbreviated version of benefit–cost analysis.[26] With cost-effectiveness, either the benefits or the costs of two alternative policy options are the same, and, therefore, are considered fixed when comparing the two options. Typically, benefits are fixed so that only the costs of the two competing policy alternatives are compared. In other words, benefits related to each policy alternative are comparable and, therefore, do not have to be examined further; only costs are compared between the two policy options.

An emergency shelter can be used to provide a simple illustration. Let us say you are a social worker on the board of directors of a private nonprofit organization providing emergency shelter to adolescent girls. Hence, part of your responsibility is to set policy for the agency. And, let us say you have a capital expenditure decision to make. The decision is whether to put in a dropped ceiling in the building used as a shelter. The estimated cost of the ceiling is $2,000. The estimated energy saving on heating oil over the next five years, as a result of the new ceiling, is $5,000. Thus, the net benefit to agency of installing the ceiling would be $3,000. A benefit–cost analysis, therefore, would suggest purchasing the new ceiling.

An example of cost-effectiveness analysis is the choice of ceiling contractors. That is, if two contractors are bidding on the job and both are reputable and can do the job, cost-effectiveness would suggest that the board of directors select the contractor with the lowest bid. This would be most cost-effective to the agency. In this way, benefit–cost analysis and cost-effectiveness can be used to produce economic and financial criteria for choosing between or among policy alternatives.[27]

That said, benefit–cost analysis has both strengths and weaknesses.[28] Some of the strengths include the fact that it provides a systematic approach to policy decisions. Benefit–cost analysis also helps to make the rationale for choosing among various policy options more explicit to the public. This is particularly the case when dollar values are assigned to benefits and/or costs. The public understands this unit of measurement.

At the same time, however, benefit–cost analysis has several weaknesses. Complex social problems and policies are difficult to analyze in a benefit–cost framework. For instance, placing a dollar value on all of the benefits to society of a given policy option is difficult, if not impossible, to accomplish. Thus, although benefit–cost analysis lends an image of precision and objectivity to a given policy decision, this can be deceiving. In addition, benefit–cost analysis is not immune to bad assumptions. The preceding shelter ceiling, for example, decision assumes that a dropped ceiling is the best way to save energy. Maybe wall insulation would have yielded a greater net benefit to the agency, but it was never considered. Hence, the assumption that a new ceiling was best for the shelter was, in fact, a bad assumption. In any case, given an awareness of these limitations, benefit–cost analysis can be useful in policy development.

Linear regression is another procedure that can be used for data analysis in policy development.[29] Linear regression uses the equation of a line to predict the values of one variable given values of a second variable. The equation of a line, you will remember, is a model. It is a model that can be used to describe and predict.[30] The equation of a line is $y = mx + b$ where y is the variable plotted on a vertical axis, x is the variable plotted on a horizontal axis, m represents the slope of the line, and b is the y-intercept. In other words, b represents the point at which the line crosses the y axis.[31] (The exact letters used for the slope and y-intercept differ depending on the author.)

Let us say that the policy issue is school violence in a given state. Education policymakers might hypothesize that the more social workers hired to assist in addressing student feelings of anger, alienation, isolation, etc., the less likely violent behavior among students will become. In this case, variable y equals the number of violent acts among students in a given school system per year, and variable x equals the number of full-time social workers employed in the school system. Given values for x and y, linear regression can be used to help examine a policy on the number of social workers hired in each school system throughout the state.

For each school system, the number of full-time social workers and corresponding number of violent acts among students in the past year can be plotted on a graph. Using linear regression analysis, a line closest to all of these data points in the graph can be estimated. Using a method called the method of least squares, a line can be estimated that has the smallest sum of squared vertical distances from the observed points to the line.[32] Once the equation of this regression line is obtained, the policy analyst may be able to predict values of y, the dependent variable, given values for x, the independent variable. In other words, the policy analyst may be able to predict the likelihood of a violent act among school students, given the number of full-time social workers employed at that school system.

The policy analyst can make the analysis more informative by adding other potentially relevant predictor variables in a multiple regression analysis, variables such as median family income in the school system or overall crime rates in the community served by the school system. Based, in part, on an analysis such as this, education policymakers can make decisions on the desired number of social workers in each school system in the state. (Of course, the number desired and the number that can be funded may differ.)

Linear regression analysis contains some of the same strengths that benefit–cost analysis presents. That is, it provides quantitative precision (or the appearance of) to policy decisions and offers a concrete rationale for these decisions to the general public. However, linear regression requires certain assumptions before it can be used legitimately. These include interval or ratio levels of data measurement. In addition, the procedure assumes a linear relationship between the independent and dependent variable.[33] Needless to say, these assumptions cannot always be met in policy analysis.

Needs Analysis

Another tool employed in policy and program development is **needs analysis.**[34] It is used for decision making that involves the identification as well as the evaluation of needs. A need is defined by Jack McKillip, a psychologist and writer on the subject of needs analysis, as the value judgment that some group has a problem that can be solved.[35] Needs analysis, therefore, can be used to select and define major social problems in the feasibility stage of policy development. It can also be used in the technical research stage of policy planning for data collection and data analysis, particularly when the policy proposal is likely to include new or expanded programs and services. Thus, needs analysis is a handy tool for social workers researching programs to better meet the unmet needs of some client population.

Several common techniques are employed in needs analysis, including social indicator analysis, resource inventory, service use analysis, needs assessment models, surveys, and structured groups. As discussed previously, **social indicators** are aggregate statistical measures that depict important aspects of a social situation and of underlying historical trends and developments.[36] Local, state, or federal government statistics on such things as unemployment and crime rates are examples.

Synthetic estimation is used in social indicator analysis to estimate characteristics of smaller geographic populations from larger government geographic data sets.[37] This procedure assumes comparable prevalence rates between the larger and smaller geographic regions. To illustrate, if national statistics reveal a school drop-out rate for pregnant teens of 50 percent, the same proportion of pregnant teens would be expected to drop out of school on a state or county level. **Risk factors** are social indicators used to predict undesirable outcomes. Again, teen pregnancy is a risk factor associated with the undesirable outcome—school drop-out. Risk factors can be indicators of a need for services (for example, school-based child care).

A **resource inventory** is a compilation of the services available to one or more target groups, usually in a specific geographic area.[38] Such an inventory is usually the result of service provider surveys. It can help identify service gaps, utilization rates, and service capacity. Using the teen pregnancy illustration, three approaches to categorizing the inventory are by service typology (child care), client functioning level (dropout), and eligibility requirements (high school mothers).

Service use analysis compares expected service use with actual service use to further define need.[39] Expectations can be based on the presence of at-risk factors or professional standards. Service use analysis includes an examination of barriers such as target population awareness of services and service accessibility to target population. (For example, can a high school mother drop off her child at child care and get to class on time?)

Needs assessment, a term more familiar to social workers, is the process of evaluating the problems and solutions identified for a target population.[40] The discrepancy (or gap) model is the most widely used needs assessment model. The model involves three phases: goal setting (identifying what ought to be); performance measurement (determining what is); and discrepancy identification (the greater gap between goals and actual performance, the greater need).

Surveys and structured groups such as focus groups are also commonly used in needs analysis. Two structured groups not described earlier are the **delphi panel** and the **nominal group**.[41] Both group processes can be used to collect and analyze information. A conventional delphi uses a questionnaire that is sent to a group of experts. After the questionnaire is returned, the policy analyst summarizes the results and develops a new questionnaire. The group of experts is given an opportunity to reevaluate its original answers based on examination of the group response. This process continues until a relative consensus on the issue emerges (or the experts no longer modify their answers).

Participants in a nominal group write down their individual answers to a question from a facilitator. In this case, the facilitator may be soliciting ideas about possible solutions to a key policy issue. At this point in the process, no discussion is allowed among members of the group. Next, each participant is asked to state one idea, which is listed on a flip chart (or blackboard, etc.) where the rest of the group can observe the response. Each participant presents one of his/her ideas in round-robin fashion until all ideas are listed. Again, no group discussion is allowed. Subsequently, each individual is allowed a chance to clarify one or more of their ideas listed on the flip chart. Following this, each participant is asked to rank the top ideas on a piece of paper or card, which is then handed into the facilitator. The facilitator tabulates the responses and presents the overall results to group members and later to other interested people.

Needs analysis has several strengths and weaknesses.[42] As stated previously, it is a useful tool in policy planning in that it helps to guide the development of programs. The numerous techniques available in needs analysis provide flexibility. Social indicators, for instance, require little cost, time, and skill to use. Large-scale surveys, on the other hand, will use more of these resources. In addition, like benefit–cost analysis and linear regression, needs analysis provides credibility when justifying the use of public funding or charitable donations. Furthermore, certain needs analysis techniques such as structured groups allow for the participation of stakeholders in the development of service systems. Participation promotes commitment!

Needs analysis also has its weaknesses, however. Different techniques in needs analysis sometimes produce conflicting results. Some techniques rely on experts and key informants. This may lead to elitist-dominated policy and program planning. Also, resource inventories that rely on program providers may be negatively impacted by agency self-interest. Problems and solutions tend to be defined in existing agency perspectives. What is more, social indicators have a questionable validity at times. This is not an exhaustive list of weaknesses, but you get the idea: needs analysis is a tool with strengths and weaknesses. Social workers in policy development need to be aware of both to effectively conduct needs analysis.

Tentative Policy Recommendations

Once the social work policy analyst has analyzed the pertinent policy information using one or more strategies, he or she should be able to develop a tentative policy recommendation. This recommendation will be based on the previously discussed criterion of technical feasibility.[43] Based on the research, in other words, this policy recommendation should produce policies and/or programs that better address the key policy issue. Thus, the policy proposal is an example of a prescriptive policy analysis in that it provides policy decision-makers with a recommended policy action.[44] However, at this point, it is a tentative recommendation based solely on technical research. In the next chapter, other criteria such as the political and administrative feasibility of the policy proposal will be examined.

C O N T E N T S E L E C T

For more information on related social work topics, use the following search terms:

Benefit-cost analysis	Focused synthesis	Quasi-experimental design
Classic experimental design	Linear regression	Resource inventory
Correlational design	Needs analysis	Risk factors
Cross sectional studies	Needs assessment	Secondary data
Data analysis strategies	Nominal group	Service use analysis
Delphi panel	Pre-experimental design	Social indicators
Focus group	Primary data	Synthetic estimation

N O T E S

1. Ann Majchrzak, *Methods for Policy Research* (Newbury Park, CA: Sage, 1984), p. 55.

2. Carl V. Patton and David S. Sawicki, *Basic Methods of Policy Analysis and Planning,* 2nd ed. (Englewood Cliffs, NJ: Prentice Hall, 1993), pp. 208–210.

3. Allen Rubin and Earl Babbie, *Research Methods for Social Work,* 2nd ed. (Pacific Grove, CA: Brooks/Cole, 1993), pp. 272–275.

4. Ibid., pp. 280–283.

5. Ibid., pp. 281–282.

6. Ibid., pp. 288–289.

7. Jerry D. Marx, "Women and Human Services Giving," *Social Work* 45, No. 1: pp. 27–38 (January 2000).

8. Rubin and Babbie, pp. 269–270; Majchrzak, p. 63.

9. Theodore R. Marmor, *The Politics of Medicare* (New York: Aldine Publishing Company, 1973).

10. Majchrzak, p. 60.

11. Ibid., pp. 59–63; Jack McKillip, *Need Analysis: Tools for the Human Services and Education* (Newbury Park, CA: Sage Publications, 1987), pp. 86–93.

12. Administration for Children and Families, "About ACF." Retrieved from the World Wide Web on May 7, 2002: www.acf.dhhs.gov.

13. American Civil Liberties Union, "About the ACLU." Retrieved from the World Wide Web on April 29, 2002: www.aclu.org/index.html.

14. Center for Substance Abuse Prevention, "About CSAP." Retrieved from the World Wide Web on May 16, 2002: www.samhsa.gov/csap.

15. Department of Health and Human Services, "HHS: What We Do." Retrieved from the World Wide Web on May 16, 2002: www.os.dhhs.gov.

16. HIV InSite, "About HIV InSite." Retrieved from the World Wide Web on May 8, 2002: http://hivinsite.ucsf.edu.

17. National Association for the Advancement of Colored People, "NAACP @ Work." Retrieved from the World Wide Web on May 16, 2002: http://www.naacp.org.

18. National Council on Aging, "Advocacy." Retrieved from the World Wide Web on May 16, 2002: www.ncoa.org.

19. National Mental Health Association, "About Us." Retrieved from the World Wide Web on May 16, 2002: www.nmha.org.

20. National Organization for Women, "What is NOW." Retrieved from the World Wide Web on May 16, 2002: http://now.org.

21. Urban Institute, "Our Mission." Retrieved from the World Wide Web on May 16, 2002: www.urban.org.

22. Majchrzak, pp. 59–60.

23. Carl V. Patton and David S. Sawicki, pp. 2–3.

24. Stokey and Zeckchauser, *A Primer for Policy Analysis* (New York: Norton & Company, 1978) p. 136.

25. Ibid., p. 137.

26. Ibid., pp. 153–155.

27. Patton and Sawicki, p. 208.

28. Stokey and Zechchauser, pp. 135, 147–149; Patton and Sawicki, pp. 280–281.

29. Marija J. Norusis, *The SPSS Guide to Data Analysis for SPSSX* (Chicago: SPSS, 1988), pp. 325–333.

30. Earl Babbie, *The Practice of Social Research,* 6th ed. (Belmont, CA: Wadsworth Publishing, 1992), p. 437; Norusis, pp. 329–332.

31. Norusis, pp. 326–329.

32. Ibid., p. 325.

33. Babbie, p. 440.

34. McKillip, p. 7.

35. Ibid., p. 10.

36. Ibid., p. 43.

37. Ibid., pp. 43, 45.

38. Ibid., pp. 32, 35.

39. Ibid., p. 65.

40. Ibid., pp. 20–21.

41. Ibid., pp. 86, 88–91.

42. Ibid., pp. 19, 105.

43. Patton and Sawicki, pp. 208–210.

44. Ibid., p. 24.

15 Developing Final Recommendations

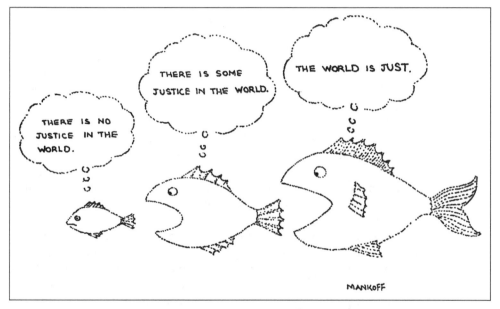

Social workers consider social and economic justice when developing policy recommendations.

Theories of Social and Economic Justice

Let us assume that the social work policy analyst has completed the technical research and, as a result, developed a tentative policy recommendation. As discussed before, the technical feasibility of a policy recommendation in addressing a policy issue is one criterion; however, there are other criteria to consider. Economic and financial criteria have been described in the previous chapter. In this chapter, we will look at other criteria, including political and administrative criteria. At this point, though, policy analysts need to think about the way justice relates to their tentative policy recommendation. Social and economic justice are of fundamental importance to the social work profession; therefore, social workers should consider both criteria when developing policy recommendations. In order to do this, let us examine the theoretical contributions of three leading intellectuals: Adam Smith, Karl Marx, and John Rawls.

Adam Smith and the Market's Invisible Hand

Adam Smith was born in 1723 in Scotland and later became a professor of moral philosophy at the University of Glasgow.[1] In 1776, he published his famous book *The Wealth of Nations.* It is still the greatest description of how a market-based economic system works.[2] Adam Smith's famous concept was the **invisible hand.**[3] By this, he meant that the pressure of competition in the marketplace directs the selfish activities of individuals, as if by an invisible hand, into socially useful outcomes. In other words, the drive for self-betterment through profit-making activity in the market ensures that society gets the goods it demands, and the quantity or supply it wants, at the lowest possible price (and with minimum government intervention).[4]

To examine whether a policy recommendation results in a more just society, the policy planner can use **marginal productivity theory.**[5] (Marginal productivity theory is not directly attributable to Adam Smith, but it is consistent with his writing.) According to this theory, incomes in a market system, by and large, reflect the marginal productivity of different contributors to the economic process. That is, the greater the value of the individual's production, the greater the individual's income. The greater the income, the more goods and services the individual can purchase. Therefore, the distribution of goods and services to each individual is just.

Contributions of Marxist Theory

Karl Marx offers a second way to think about social and economic justice. Marx was born in 1818 in Trier, Germany.[6] His father was a well-known lawyer. After studying law for a time, Marx went on to earn a doctorate in philosophy, though his political views were too liberal for German universities.[7]

After turning to radical journalism, Marx met Friedrich Engels, his famous writing partner. Together they published *The Communist Manifesto* in 1848.[8] After the French Revolution in 1848, Marx moved to London where he stayed for the rest of his life. Marx published the first volume of *Das Kapital* in 1867.[9] He died in 1883.

Did You Know?

Marx spent eighteen years writing *Das Kapital.* In addition to Volume I, three more volumes were published from his writing after his death. Altogether, the four volumes consisted of 2,500 pages[10] (and they were not exactly bedtime reading!).

If Adam Smith was the foremost expert on the adaptive behavior of the market, then Karl Marx was the foremost expert on the maladaptive behavior of the market. *Das Kapital* offered a brilliant critique of the market system. In so doing, Marx described with eloquence and passion how the market can fail to produce well-being. Because of the injustices and other flaws that he believed inherent in capitalism, Marx wrote that, in a higher phase of an alternative (communist) society, the distribution of social goods should conform to the following principle: "from each according to his ability, to each according to his needs."[11]

John Rawls and His Theory of Justice

John Rawls offers a third way to think about social and economic justice. Rawls was an American philosopher born in Baltimore, Maryland, in 1921. He taught at Cornell, MIT, and Harvard. In his 1971 book *A Theory of Justice*, Rawls envisioned a social contract in which social justice is defined by free and rational citizens in an original position of equality.[12] In the original position, people are to decide in advance the principles by which to distribute basic rights, responsibilities, and benefits in society—the principles that will guide social cooperation.[13] In addition, people in this original position will do all of this under a veil of ignorance. That is, "no one knows his place in society, his class position, or social status, nor does anyone know his fortune in the distribution of natural assets and abilities, his intelligence, strength, and the like."[14] Because everyone starts from an original position of equality and no one knows his or her particular condition, the principles of justice so derived will be the result of a fair agreement (under initial conditions of fairness). All social policies and institutions will then be developed or revised in accordance with the principles of justice originally agreed to. Rawls argued that under these conditions people would choose the following general conception of justice: "All social primary goods—[meaning] liberty and opportunity, income and wealth, and the bases of self-respect—are to be distributed equally unless an unequal distribution of any or all of these goods is to the advantage of the least favored."[15] Rawls believed this, in part, because no one would know in advance if they were the least favored in society.

Class Discussion: Social and Economic Justice

Which of the three conceptions of social and economic justice do you prefer personally? Which of the three perspectives on social and economic justice would you adhere to as a professional social worker? Are all three statements realistic in today's society? If not realistic, is each of the three perspectives on social and economic justice still useful in developing social policy today? Are any of the perspectives useful in defining social problems and key issues? Are one or more of the statements useful in developing a policy recommendation?

Diversity and Populations at Risk

I agree with authors Hagan and Davis in their November 1992 *Social Work* article that stated, "All social problems, policies, programs, and practice models must be analyzed in terms of how they differentially affect women and men, as well as people of color and whites."[16] To further social and economic justice, variables such as gender and race need to be important considerations in policy development. Not only must policies and programs be reviewed in terms of how they influence populations at risk, social problems should be critically examined in terms of the different effects of key policy issues on populations at risk. For example, what assumptions does your model of the identified key issue make regarding one or more populations at risk? What are the most influential contributing factors to the issue? Are populations at risk such as women or people of color blamed for their unmet needs? Any definition of a social problem or key issue should be reviewed with these considerations in mind. Before finalizing a policy recommendation, the social work policy analyst can return to the selected key issue to evaluate it in these terms.

Also before making a final recommendation, a tentative policy proposal should be critiqued in terms of its influence on populations at risk. Given the discrimination and oppression of women in America, for instance, any policy proposal should be critiqued regarding its influence on women.

In other words, the needs of women should be considered while developing the policy recommendation. In this case, the gender variable becomes an important variable in the policy analysis.

To illustrate, the following five questions can be considered when developing policy recommendations that may affect women.[17] Does the proposed policy materially improve the lives of women? Does it build the self-respect of women? Does the recommendation empower women? In addition, does the proposed recommendation educate women politically? And finally, will the policy recommendation weaken patriarchal control of institutions, thereby giving women more of a voice in American institutions such as business and government?

Similar questions can be used to critique a tentative policy proposal in terms of its influence on other vulnerable populations, such as people of color. Does the policy recommendation materially empower the lives of people of color? Does it build the self-respect of people of color? Does it empower people of color or educate people of color politically? And, does the recommendation help people of color weaken white control of American institutions, giving people of color more self-determination in America? The major point here is that at this stage in policy development, it is not too late to make revisions in the key issue and policy proposal so that the final policy recommendation maximizes social and economic justice for diverse and vulnerable populations.

Stakeholders and Political Viability

In analyzing the tentative policy recommendation, the criteria of social and economic justice have been considered. Another criterion to consider is the political viability criterion. With this criterion, the policy analyst needs to answer the question: Would a majority of the most powerful and influential stakeholders support the policy recommendation? As defined earlier, a stakeholder is any individual or group that can affect or be affected by the passage of the policy proposal. To analyze the political viability of a tentative policy recommendation, an analysis of the major stakeholders in the policy proposal is important.

One way to conduct a **stakeholder analysis** is as follows.[18] First, revise the stakeholder list that you developed during the feasibility stage of the policy analysis. That is, reexamine your stakeholder list to ensure that you have between eight and twelve of the stakeholder groups most interested in the social issue. Secondly, distinguish between those stakeholders who will be the decision-makers regarding passage of the policy proposal and those stakeholders who will try to influence that decision. With national legislation, the decision-maker is typically Congress and those attempting to influence the decision are special interest groups.

Next assess the support of each major stakeholder regarding the policy proposal. In other words, answer the question: Would each stakeholder group support or oppose the policy recommendation and why? The proposal may represent an opportunity for some groups but a threat to others. The policy proposal may be consistent with the values of some groups but violate those of others. Some stakeholders may have a long history of support or opposition to the proposal or similar proposals. All this information is important in getting a policy proposal passed.

A fourth step in a stakeholder analysis is to evaluate the relative power of the identified stakeholders. Power can be evaluated in several ways. One way is to estimate for each stakeholder group the amount of resources available to it, resources such as money, information (including research on the key issue), volunteers, and political contacts. Money will affect the group's ability to make political contributions and mount a campaign in opposition or support of a policy proposal. Often, the larger the membership size of the group, the greater its ability to recruit volunteers in a campaign to support or oppose the policy proposal. In any case, one way to estimate the power of a stakeholder group is to examine the amount of resources available to the group.

A second and related way to measure power is to estimate the ability of that group to mobilize these resources. In gauging this, the policy analyst should look at the internal cohesion of the group. That is, how much solidarity is there within the membership of the group? Also, is there a virtual consensus within the group on the policy recommendation? Furthermore, just how effective is the leadership of the stakeholder group? Is there a nationally known leader with many political contacts in Congress? Is the leader generally regarded as an expert on the policy issue? Is the leader able to galvanize the group's membership in a campaign in support or opposition to the policy recommendation? All of these questions should be addressed.

Finally, another indicator of the stakeholder group's power is its access to key policy decision-makers. Do the members of the stakeholder group, particularly its leadership, have direct access to key decision-makers? Do they have an opportunity to meet one-on-one with key decision-makers regarding various policy issues? Are they asked regularly for information and opinions on various policy issues by policy decision-makers? All of these dimensions of power should be considered when analyzing the overall power influence of each major stakeholder group.

The important point to remember, though, when considering each stakeholder group is the potential influence of the special interest group on the decision-maker. An individual special interest group may be passionate about the key issue, but have few sources of power, and therefore, little influence with members of Congress, for instance. It is this influence with key decision-makers that is of utmost importance in getting new policies passed.

Modeling the Stakeholder Analysis

The use of models in problem definition was discussed earlier in the text, but models are also useful in completing a stakeholder analysis. In her book *Methods for Policy Research,* Ann Majchrzak suggests doing a diagrammatic model that includes the major special interest groups, an indication of each special interest group's opposition or support to the policy proposal, and an indication of the influence of each special interest group over the key policy decision-maker.[19] To illustrate, let us take the social problem of violence in America. This problem has a number of aspects to it: gun control, domestic violence, school violence, media portrayals of violence, among others. Because of a number of shootings within America's public schools in recent years, let us say that we choose as our key issue the issue of school violence. And, let us say our tentative policy recommendation is a mandate that trigger locks be provided with all guns sold. The decision-maker in this case is Congress. A list of special interest groups on this issue would include the Americans for Gun Safety Foundation, the National Education Association (representing those working at every level of public education), the National Association of Police Organizations, the Brady Center To Prevent Gun Violence, Physicians for Social Responsibility, the Consumer Federation of America, the National Rifle Association, the National Shooting Sports Foundation, the Sporting Arms and Ammunition Manufacturers' Institute, and the National Association of Firearms Retailers.[20]

In building a model for the stakeholder analysis, select symbols to denote the decision-makers, the special interest groups, and the policy recommendation. As seen in Figure 15.1, in this case we have chosen to identify the recommendation with a rectangle, Congress with a diamond, and special interest groups with an oval. Next, go down the list of special interest groups and indicate whether the group is likely to support or oppose the tentative policy recommendation. And, for each group indicate whether that support or opposition would be strong or only moderate. In other words, those likely to support the policy proposal would have a plus sign next to the group's name. If the group is likely to strongly support the proposal, it would receive two plus signs, and if it is only moderately interested in the proposal, it would receive one plus sign. Those likely to oppose the proposal strongly would receive two negative signs. Those interest groups likely to oppose it only moderately would receive one negative sign.

As indicated in Figure 15.1, those likely to oppose the gun trigger lock proposal would include the National Rifle Association, the National Shooting Sports Foundation, the Sporting Arms and Ammunition Manufacturers'

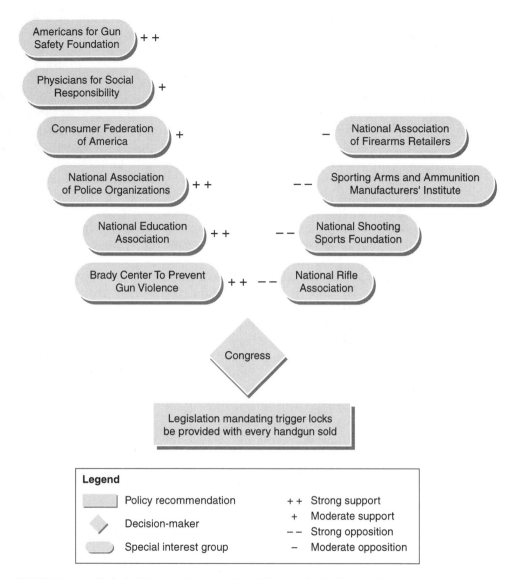

FIGURE 15.1   Stakeholder Analysis of Gun Trigger Lock Proposal

Institute, and the National Association of Firearms Retailers. Those likely to support the proposal would include the Americans for Gun Safety Foundation, the National Education Association, the National Association of Police Organizations, the Brady Center To Prevent Gun Violence, Physicians for Social Responsibility, and the Consumer Federation of America.[21]

In our model, the influence of each special interest group over the decision-maker can be indicated by the distance of each group from the decision-maker in the model. For instance, the NRA with its roughly three million members, state associations, money for campaign contributions (over $3 million in 2000), solidarity, information (including web site with legislative updates and research summaries), and access to members of Congress, would be placed very close to the decision-maker in our model.[22] On the other side, the Brady Center To Prevent Gun Violence (along with its sister organization, the Brady Campaign To Prevent Gun Violence, formerly Handgun Control, Inc.) is the largest national nonpartisan grassroots organization addressing this issue.[23] This stakeholder has nationally known leadership in Jim and Sarah Brady, money for campaign contributions (close to $400,000 in 2000), information (including a web site with legislative updates and research summaries), and political access in Washington. For these reasons, it would be placed closest to Congress in the model.

Did You Know?

Jim Brady of the Brady Center To Prevent Gun Violence was formerly press secretary for President Ronald Reagan. Brady was shot and seriously wounded on March 30, 1981, during an assassination attempt on Reagan. Along with his wife, Sarah, Jim Brady subsequently became the leading national advocate for the reduction of gun violence.[24]

By completing a similar and more detailed (than space permits here) analysis for each group, a model depicting the relative power of each special interest group as well as its position on the key issue can be constructed to help examine the political viability of the tentative policy recommendation. In this way, a social worker involved in policy development can estimate the probability of the policy proposal passing Congress given the present sociopolitical climate. With this information, the policy analyst is ready to develop a specific political strategy for passing the policy proposal.

Note, however, that the policy analyst can make incremental adjustments to the policy proposal at this stage in the policy development process. In other words, although a policy recommendation may be the best technical solution to a social problem or issue, it may not have much political viability, and, consequently, may not be implemented. Therefore, in a legislative setting, the policy developer may want to make adjustments to the proposal in order to make it more politically viable before approaching individual lawmakers to sponsor the bill and other major stakeholders for support.

Political Strategy

Once the initial stakeholder analysis is completed and bill sponsors recruited (if dealing with proposed legislation), the social work policy analyst may assist the sponsors in developing a political advocacy strategy for passing the policy proposal. The target of the strategy would be the policy decision-maker, such as Congress on the national level or a state legislature on the state level. In terms of advocacy goals, the most fundamental goal would be to have the decision-maker pass the policy recommendation. To do this, policy advocates frequently need to develop a political strategy involving partnerships with other policy proposal supporters. In this instance, the partnership may take the form of a coalition of major stakeholders identified as supportive in the preceding stakeholder analysis. It is vital to remember that the stakeholder analysis will identify potential coalition partners! **Coalitions,** by definition, are usually temporary partnerships organized for a specific and time-limited purpose.[25] Such would be the case in organizing solely for the purpose of passing a piece of legislation. Some groups, becoming more of an association, continue to work together indefinitely under the name of a coalition. Once organized, the coalition members can employ numerous advocacy tactics to influence policy decision-makers. More specific and detailed information on advocacy roles and tactics are provided in Chapter 16.

Illustration of Successful Coalitions

An example of an ongoing national coalition is the National Coalition for the Homeless, which maintains a web site at www.nationalhomeless.org. This coalition works to end homelessness through grassroots organizing, public education, policy advocacy, ethical assistance, and partnerships. Its web site offers fact sheets, alerts to upcoming legislative activities, tips on communicating with Congress, forums, and personal stories of homelessness. One of the coalition's major advocacy successes was the Stewart B. McKinney Homeless Assistance Act of 1987.

A second illustration of partnering through coalitions involves the Mental Health Parity Act of 1996. This legislation was passed thanks to the successful advocacy efforts of The Coalition for Fairness in Mental Illness Coverage. The act mandates that health insurance plans offering mental health benefits not designate an annual or lifetime dollar limit different from those pertaining to medical services. The Coalition for Fairness in Mental Illness Coverage—comprised of the American Psychological Association, the American Psychiatric Association, the National Mental Health Association, the National Alliance for the Mentally Ill, and other organizations—prevailed over groups that tried to defeat the bill, such as the National Association of Manufacturers and the Association of Private Pension and Welfare Plans.[26]

Furthermore, developing a political strategy usually involves the need for funding. In building a campaign to pass a piece of legislation, a coalition may elect to hire staff for the period of the campaign. This will cost money. The coalition may also need to purchase time or space in the media in order to educate the public about the benefits of the policy change. Funds for additional information, such as brochures, posters, or direct mailings may also be needed. In any case, funds for this type of campaign may come from private donations, such as individual donations or grants from foundations. Funds may also be raised through grass-roots fundraisers such as dinners, auctions, or athletic events (such as road races).

Program Planning

If the tentative policy recommendation will include new or expanding programming, a program description should be included in the final proposal. The social problem and target population need to be clearly defined, program goals need to be established, treatment methodology should be explained, program evaluation should be designed, the level of staffing required in the program is typically described, and finally, the amount of required funding for such programming needs to be projected.

To illustrate, let us say that the social work policy analyst is working on the social problem of child abuse and neglect. The key aspect of this problem chosen for further action is the shortage of effective counseling programs for adolescents with a history of child abuse and neglect. Further, let us say research indicates that adventure-based counseling programs appear to be effective with this population.[27] If this policy development is taking place on the state level, then the target population of the program might be adolescents in a given state's child welfare system, in other words, teens with a history of child abuse and neglect. Program goals could include the promotion of adolescent development in the areas of self-esteem, communication skills, self-image, problem-solving skills, and physical health.

The treatment methodology in this type of programming would involve activities in the outdoors, such as canoeing, hiking, white water rafting, skiing, and rope courses. In addition to these outdoor activities, an adventure-based program might include individual and group counseling, family counseling, and follow-up in the community. The counseling may use behavioral contracts with teenagers to focus on the previously listed developmental goals. Be that as it may, a design for program evaluation would depend on the precise program goals and methodology selected. Staffing in such a program might include a mixture of staff with outdoor education degrees and staff with undergraduate and graduate social work degrees.

Finally, program planning should include a projection of the number of programs to be funded around the state and the total cost of such programming in a given year. In so doing, program planning may also include a description of projected funding channels for the program. Several funding channels could be considered (although this is not an exhaustive list).[28] One is the situation where federal funds are provided directly to local service providers, such as when funding is distributed through project grants. A second scenario is when federal funds are distributed through state government and then to local service providers, as with federal block grants to states. A third option is where the federal government provides funding directly to consumers, such as childcare vouchers to working parents. Another possibility is the case where states provide funding from their general revenues to local service providers. And, of course, public funds can be combined with private donations. In any case, the policy analyst needs to review likely funding channels for the proposed program when developing final policy recommendations.

Organizational Parameters and Implementation

In developing final policy proposals, future implementation of the policy must be considered. That is, certain **administrative criteria** need to be examined when looking at the potential organizations that will implement the new legislation.[29] Three administrative criteria to examine are authority, capability, and commitment. First, does the agency most likely to implement the new policy recommendation, in fact, have the authority to do so? Does it have the required policy mechanisms, including potential sanctions to adequately implement and enforce the new legislation? Has the organization implemented and monitored similar legislation in the past?

Second, particularly in the case where new legislation produces new programming, does the implementing organization have the capability to do the job? In other words, does it have the resources needed for implementation? These would include finances, personnel, capital needs such as building space, and possibly items such as materials and supplies needed for administration. In this case, the policy analyst needs to compare what is required by the new program to what is currently available in organizations likely to implement the new policy and programming.

A third and related administrative criterion to consider is commitment. Will the potential implementing organization be committed to the policy and programming? Most importantly, will its leaders be committed to the new policy and programming? Will they believe that the new policy and programming fit the mission of the organization? Will they believe that the new policy and programming are technically the most feasible way of addressing the social problem and key policy issue? And, will they believe that their organization and staff are the most competent to implement the new policy and programming? These are all factors when assessing the probable commitment of an agency in implementing a new policy and program. If the agency is, in fact, not committed, then implementation is not likely to be adequate. In such cases, organizational leaders and staff may sabotage, or at least significantly change, the original intent of the policy and related programming. Policy analysts working on final policy recommendations, therefore, need to think ahead to the requirements for adequate implementation.

Case Study: Implementation of the Adoption Assistance and Child Welfare Act of 1980

A study done by Kaye Samantri during 1985–1986 shows the importance of implementation in policy development.[30] The study dealt with the implementation of the Adoption Assistance and Child Welfare Act of 1980. The act addressed the social problem of child abuse and neglect in the United States. More specifically, the act dealt with the key issue of foster care drift. This was because children were drifting from one foster home or residential program to another without plans for permanent placement of the child. The act mandated that state caseworkers develop plans for a permanent placement of the child within specific time periods. Thus, a major goal of the Adoption Assistance and Child Welfare Act was to ensure permanency planning for children in state child welfare systems.

Samantri's study looked specifically at the implementation of the legislation. The act was implemented using a block grant approach that contained minimum federal regulations. This was part of the Reagan Administration's devolution of federal responsibility for social welfare to individual states across the country. The block grant approach was intended to give states not only more responsibility but more independence in implementing federal legislation. However, the study discovered negative ramifications for implementation. For instance, the Adoption Assistance and Child Welfare Act of 1980, according to the research, contained no public input into regulations for implementation. It also contained no mechanisms for enforcement in the regulations. There were also only minimum standards for service in the legislation. The result was great variation in the quality of permanency programs from one state to another. One moral of this policy story is that planning for program implementation needs to be done while developing final policy recommendations and not after the policy has been passed by policy decision-makers.

Case Study: Implementation and Welfare-to-Work Programs

A 1996 study by two UCLA researchers of California welfare-to-work programs shows the importance of implementation in policy planning.[31] The

Job Opportunities and Basic Skills Training Program, which is part of the Family Support Act of 1988, required all AFDC recipients with children three and over to take part in a welfare-to-work program. The researchers examined four different county administered welfare-to-work programs in California. Based on individual socioeconomic demographic data from each county, the counties were labeled rural, urban, suburban, and agribusiness. The suburban county consisted primarily of high-technology industries. The urban had a combination of high-technology and service industries. The rural county was primarily agricultural, and the agribusiness county contained a combination of related manufacturing industries.

Case managers and program participants from each county were surveyed. In total, 133 case managers and 167 clients participated. All the data was collected in 1992. The researchers described the study as exploratory because the sample of program participants was not a representative sample. Consistent with the trend of devolution of federal responsibility for social welfare, the jobs program left it up to individual state welfare bureaucracies to develop their own compliance programs for the mandatory welfare-to-work requirements. The researchers were interested in the relationship between various organizational factors and client compliance in these programs.

The authors found that counties which implemented their compliance programs with the following characteristics were more likely to achieve high compliance and participant satisfaction. These program characteristics included an ideology that did not stigmatize welfare recipients as well as goals that stressed education and skill training for program participants. In addition, programs that stressed a service technology that relied on counseling, persuasion, and trusting relationships in contrast to simply following bureaucratic rules were more successful. Finally, programs that settled disputes with clients using professional treatment and leniency regarding bureaucratic rules were more successful in achieving compliance in their welfare-to-work components. That is to say, counties that were more likely to bargain and compromise when settling client disputes were generally more successful than those counties that relied strictly on bureaucratic rules and sanctions. The lesson is that the manner in which policy was implemented ultimately influenced the success of the welfare-to-work program.

CONTENTSELECT

For more information on related social work topics, use the following search terms:

Administrative criteria	Marginal productivity theory	Program evaluation
Coalitions	Marxist theory	Program planning
Funding channels	Political strategy	Stakeholder analysis
Invisible hand	Political viability	

NOTES

1. Robert L. Heilbroner, *The Worldly Philosophers: The Lives, Times, and Ideas of the Great Economic Thinkers,* 6th ed. (New York: Simon & Schuster), pp. 42, 45–46.

2. Robert Heilbroner and Lester Thurow, *Economics Explained: Everything You Need to Know About How the Economic Works and Where It's Going* (New York: Simon & Schuster, 1994), pp. 26–27.

3. Ibid., p. 29.

4. Ibid., p. 27.

5. Ibid., pp. 207–208.

6. Heilbroner, p. 142.

7. Heilbroner and Thurow, p. 34; Heilbroner, p. 143.

8. Heilbroner and Thurow, p. 34.

9. Michael Curtis, ed., *The Great Political Theories: Volume 2* (New York: Avon Books, 1981), p. 155.

10. Heilbroner, p. 155.

11. Karl Marx, as quoted in Terrel Carver, ed., *The Cambridge Companion to Marx* (Cambridge, United Kingdom: Cambridge University Press, 1999), p. 151.

12. John Rawls, *A Theory of Justice* (Cambridge, MA: Belknap Press, 1971), p. 12.

13. Ibid., p. 11.

14. Ibid., p. 12.

15. Ibid., p. 303.

16. Jan. L. Hagan and Liane V. Davis, "Working with Women: Building a Policy and Practice Agenda," *Social Work* 37, No. 6: pp. 495–502 (1992). Retrieved from EBSCOhost, Academic Search Premier, page 8 of 15, on July 3, 2002: http://ehostvgw12.epnet.com/ fulltext.asp?resultSetId=R00000000&hitNum=8 &booleanTerm=%...

17. Jacqueline Leavitt, "Feminist Advocacy Planning in the 1980s," in Barry Checkoway, ed., *Strategic Perspectives on Planning Practice* (Lexington, MA: D.C. Heath and Company, 1986), pp. 184–185.

18. Ann Majchrzak, *Methods for Policy Research* (Newbury Park, CA: Sage, 1984) pp. 76–80.

19. Ibid., p. 80.

20. Lisa Kimbrough, Deputy Director of Policy and Research, the Americans for Gun Safety Foundation, personal communication, July 8, 2002.

21. Ibid.

22. National Rifle Association, "A Brief History of the NRA." Retrieved from the World Wide Web on August 7, 2002: www.nrahq.org/ history.asp.

23. The Brady Center To Prevent Gun Violence, "About Us: Mission Statement." Retrieved from the World Wide Web on August 7, 2002: www.bradycenter.org/about/mission.asp.

24. The Brady Center To Prevent Gun Violence, "About Us." Retrieved from the World Wide Web on August 7, 2002: www.bradycenter.org/about/index.asp.

25. Karen S. Haynes and James S. Mickelson, *Affecting Change: Social Workers in the Political Arena* (Boston: Allyn & Bacon, 2003), pp. 122–123.

26. National Coalition for the Homeless, "About NCH." Retrieved from the World Wide Web on May 16, 2002: www.nationalhomeless.org; Peter Newbould, "Federal Purity Law Takes Effect." Retrieved from the World Wide Web on January 16, 2003: www.apa.org/practice/pf/feb98/parity.html.

27. Jerry D. Marx, "An Outdoor Adventure Counseling Program for Adolescents," *Social Work,* 33, No. 6: pp. 517–520 (1988).

28. Bruce Jansson, *Becoming an Effective Policy Advocate: From Policy Practice to Social Justice* (Pacific Grove, CA: Brooks/Cole, 1999), pp. 184–185.

29. Carl V. Patton and David S. Sawicki, *Basic Methods of Policy Analysis and Planning,* 2nd ed. (Englewood Cliffs, NJ: Prentice Hall, 1993), pp. 218–219.

30. Kaye Samantri "To Prevent Unnecessary Separation of Children and Families: Public Law 96-272—Policy and Practice," *Social Work* 37, No. 4: 295–302 (1992).

31. Yeheskel Hasenfeld and Dale Weaver, "Enforcement, Compliance, and Disputes in Welfare-to-Work Programs," *Social Service* Review 70, No. 2: pp. 235–256 (1996).

16 Advocating Policy Recommendations

American socialist and labor advocate Eugene Debs speaks to a crowd.

The Social Worker as Advocate

A social worker, as suggested in earlier chapters, may also be an advocate in the policy development process. In fact, there are various ways that social workers can advocate for a specific policy recommendation. Perhaps the policy recommendation focuses on a certain client population. Perhaps the policy recommendation pertains to an organizational policy that needs changing. In any case, a social worker may not only present facts and information regarding policy alternatives to policy decision-makers but also be in a position to advocate for a specific recommendation.

Social work author Margaret Dietz Domanski outlines several (somewhat overlapping) advocacy roles that social workers can play.[1] One is simply a **communicator.** While developing and presenting final policy proposals, the social worker involved in policy advocacy may communicate the details of the recommendation to policy decision-makers. Some ideas for effective communication will be presented later in this chapter.

Second, particularly as part of an association's lobbying campaign, social workers may play the role of a **lobbyist.** That is, they may contact government officials regarding the specific policy issue and recommendation. Telephone calls, fax messages, e-mail, and letters to elected politicians are typical means of communication.

A third role is that of a **persuader.** To provide one illustration, social workers advocating for specific policy recommendations can influence the opinion of the general public on a policy issue using their professional position and expertise. Letters written to the editors of major newspapers informing readers about the policy issue and recommendation, for example, are a way to educate and persuade the community.

In addition, social workers often serve as **witnesses** in advocating for specific policy recommendations. They may take part in a congressional or other public hearing on the key policy issue. The setting may be a hearing on welfare reform before a congressional committee in Washington, a state appropriations hearing regarding annual health and human service spending, or a hearing before a city or town council on its health and human service budget. In any of these settings, social workers can bring to the public forum their knowledge of the specific needs of various populations at risk.

Social workers can also play the role of **activist** in advocating for a policy recommendation. In so doing, the social worker may participate in an organized demonstration, march, sit-in, or boycott to draw attention to the key policy issue and policy recommendation.

Furthermore, social workers can take an active role as a political **campaigner,** whether working for a political party or candidate or running for office themselves. Social workers often work behind the scenes gathering information to help candidates develop positions and recommendations on specific policy issues. However, there is no reason why a professional social worker cannot be elected president of the United States!

And finally, there is my favorite advocacy role, because it precisely fits the theme of this book. As part of a political strategy to get a specific policy recommendation passed, social workers may play the part of a collaborator. In performing this role, social workers can organize or participate in a coalition to address a specific policy issue and promote specific policy recommendations. As the previous chapters in this book illustrate, U.S. history contains many examples of advocates, including social workers, networking through various voluntary associations to promote social reform, whether it was abolition, women's suffrage, civil rights, or mental health parity.

Effectively Communicating Policy Recommendations

As stated at the beginning of this chapter, social workers engaged in policy development often need to communicate directly with policy decision-makers. In addition to direct correspondence, communication with decision-makers can be done through their staff members, the media, and special interest groups.[2] Be that as it may, know the right time and place to communicate with policymakers, particularly in presenting final policy recommendations. If a big vote is coming up in Congress on a crime bill, it may not be the best time to talk to members of Congress about child welfare legislation, for example.

When communicating with policymakers, the social worker should use a multimedia approach.[3] For instance, the social worker could use one or more of the following: slides, charts, handouts, videos, and the Internet. In doing so, keep the presentation simple; some of the new graphics can be confusing. Remember that all tables and graphs should be self-explanatory. Also, when communicating to policy decision-makers, a combination of oral and written, detailed and summarized methods is preferable. For example, the communicator may want to use an oral presentation combined with a written report. Another option is to use a detailed report combined with a summary report. Some presenters prefer to provide a written summary report and an appendix for more detailed information. Others even use a summary report along with a data book for a detailed presentation of statistics.

If communicating verbally and in writing, it may be helpful to provide a summary at the beginning of both the written and verbal statements. A one-page summary at the beginning of a written report is usually effective. In terms of an oral presentation, a written agenda handed out at the beginning of the meeting may suffice to provide the audience with a summary of topics to be addressed.

What is more, using quotable terms and phrases in this era of sound bite politics is often advantageous. Remember the use of terms such as *voodoo economics* and *Reaganomics* to describe Ronald Reagan's economic policy, and the phrase "three strikes and you're out," which was part of the communication on Bill Clinton's crime bill.[4] They were all created or picked up by the media and communicated to the general public.

Illustration: The Maine Chapter of the National Association of Social Workers

The following illustration is taken from the January 2003 newsletter of the Maine Chapter of the NASW. Notice how these social work advocates work through collaboration and partnerships.

Our top six legislative priorities are:

- **Mental Health Parity.** As in the past, NASW will work with our legislative coalition partners at NAMI-Maine and the Maine Psychological Association to obtain parity in insurance coverage for mental health.
- **Expansion of Mental Health Services.** We are working with marriage and family therapists, and professional counselors to obtain direct reimbursement from Medicaid for LCSWs, LMFTs, and LCPCs practitioners. Based on initial figures, this would allow twice as many persons to receive mental health services without an increase in cost to the state.
- **Child and Family Services.** We will work with our legislative coalition partners at the Maine Children's Alliance to improve the way that the State of Maine provides services to Maine children and families.
- **Violence Against Women.** We will work with our legislative partners at the Maine Coalition Against Sexual Assault and the Maine Coalition to End Domestic Violence to preserve and/or restore funding for violence against women.
- **Anti-Poverty Legislation.** As TANF is reauthorized, we will work with our legislative coalition partners at the Maine Equal Justice Project to do what is necessary to maintain a safety net for Maine families. Additionally, we will work with the Maine Women's Lobby on the issue of PAID family leave and with the AFL-CIO toward unemployment insurance for part-time and temporary employees.
- **Licensure.** We will continue to work to protect legislation passed in previous sessions that limits the future LSW licensure to persons who have a Bachelor degree in Social Work. To help ease the possibility of employee shortages for agencies like DHS, we are working with Representative Marie Lavierrer-Boucher to create a new licensure, Licensed Human Service Worker, for persons who have a bachelor's degree in a related field.

Source: Lacey Sloan, "Legislative Action Committee News," *NASW-Maine Chapter Newsletter,* Jan. 2003, p. 15.

Another effective communication technique is to use lots of examples and anecdotes when communicating a policy recommendation. Again, Ronald Reagan is a good illustration. Known as the "Great Communicator," Reagan was famous for his stories when communicating with policymakers and the general public.[5] Although it is important not to rely too heavily on anecdotes, and Reagan was criticized for this, his short stories and concrete examples made him a more effective communicator with politicians and the public alike.

Clearly, one thing to avoid when communicating with decision-makers is professional jargon.[6] Although it is a term commonly used in the social work profession, for instance, elected officials in government may have no idea what the "strengths perspective" is.[7] The objective is not to impress policy leaders with the theories and concepts of your profession; rather, the intent is to communicate in a way that leads to the passage of your policy recommendation.

Furthermore, be prepared to be brief when communicating either verbally or in writing to policymakers. Generally, oral presentations should be kept to ten to fifteen minutes. And remember that some policy decision-makers want more details, some want just major findings, and others only want information for a sound bite. As in all communication, therefore, the communicator needs to know their audience.

It cannot be stressed enough, though, that the choice of the person to communicate policy recommendations to decision-makers is extremely important.[8] Sometimes a person who is great at gathering pertinent policy information is not the one most suited to communicate a final recommendation. Again, the aim is to motivate and inspire decision-makers to pass the policy recommendation. This being the case, some characteristics to consider in addition to speaking ability are the charisma of the speaker, the personality of the speaker, job titles and past professional accomplishments of the speaker, organizational affiliations, personal appearance, and overall credibility of the policy communicator. In short, find a speaker with charisma and credibility.

In preparing to communicate policy, it is wise to anticipate those areas where the credibility of the communicator may be questioned, particularly by those known to be opposed to the policy recommendation.[9] For instance, when presenting the results of a policy analysis, the presenter needs to be prepared to explain the methodology by which results were obtained. In such a case, it is important not to lose credibility if other policy experts or special interest groups challenge the research findings. If verbal communication will be an important part of the communication process, it is wise to find speakers who can think quickly on their feet, anticipate questions, read an audience, and speak without notes. That said, it is better to be prepared than have to think on one's feet! It is also better, when a communicator does not have an answer, to offer to provide the information later. Do not jeopardize the credibility of the speaker with a weak, uninformed answer.

With respect to reading an audience, those trained in social work should be generally proficient at recognizing nonverbal communication and asking for feedback when appropriate. Regarding the use of notes, there is nothing wrong with using notes as an outline, but don't read a prepared text word-for-word. Otherwise, the policy communicator risks making their presentation a bedtime story for the audience!

Social Workers and Policy Debate

Some social work policy advocates may find themselves not only in the role of communicator but also in the roles of lobbyist and persuader. In such cases, knowledge of debate tactics as they relate to policy communication may be helpful.[10] In the case of competing policy proposals, the policy advocates need to offer their policy recommendation as an alternative to other less desirable policy options. To achieve this, the communicators need to point out important distinctions between their recommendation and competing recommendations. The strengths of the policy proposal should be highlighted, whereas the weaknesses of other policy alternatives identified.

Potential weaknesses in alternative policy options include those pertaining to problem definition. Does the alternative policy recommendation, for instance, clearly define the values, assumptions, and factors associated with the problem? Second, are there flaws in the research methodology of alternative policy proposals? For example, are there biases in survey instruments used to collect information in alternative policy proposals? Should a random sample have been used in collecting information? Do competing proposals rely too heavily on anecdotal evidence? These and other potential flaws can be pointed out when advocating for a specific proposal and against other competing policy proposals.

Third, the choice of criteria used in competing policy proposals can be critiqued. Perhaps competing proposals rely too heavily on financial criteria. Perhaps they do not rely enough on more technical criteria such as program effectiveness. Maybe competing policy proposals fail to examine potential unanticipated consequences of the proposal on certain populations at risk. Maybe alternative proposals are vague in terms of their implementation planning. In these and other ways, social workers advocating for a specific policy recommendation may make the strongest case when communicating to policy decision-makers and the public in general.

Advocacy Illustration: The Problem of Wife Abuse

Davis and Hagen illustrate one style of advocacy in their 1992 journal article on the problem of wife abuse.[11] Davis and Hagen use a feminist perspective in their policy recommendations concerning the problem of wife abuse. To start, the authors present two theoretical models of the social problem. The first is referred to as the women-centered model. This model maintains that the problem of wife abuse is caused by such factors as women's lack of power, women's concern for family preservation, patriarchal social systems, and the sexist socialization of women. This sexist socialization promotes economic and psychological dependence of women on men. Policy recommendations derived from this model would include social and economic policies and programs that promote independence for women, such as higher education opportunities, more jobs for women, affordable housing, and transportation.

The second model presented by the authors is referred to as the family-focused model. This model sees the causes of wife abuse in terms of dysfunctional families, violent role models, external stress, and escalating interpersonal conflict between people, the abused and the abuser. Policy and program recommendations associated with this model would include family preservation; education around nonviolent problem solving and role modeling; as well as various treatment including marital counseling, family counseling, and behavior modification.

Davis and Hagen promote and defend the women-centered model of the social problem. The authors' analysis of the problem and recommended solutions give first priorities to the needs of women in contrast to those of men, children, or families in general. In other words, the authors view the problem of wife abuse through a narrow lens focused on women. They choose not to use a broader lens that might focus on the family as a whole. Their advocacy approach is not broad-minded, nor is it supposed to be; it is single-minded. This single-mindedness produces an intensity of focus that can make policy decision-makers and the general public notice. As the old saying goes: Not only may they see the light, they may also feel the heat! Some may even say the authors' approach to policy advocacy is extremist. Be that as it may, their total focus on the needs of women in contrast to the needs of other groups is a way to move policy from the status quo. Others may choose to be advocates for men or families. Davis and Hagen are clearly advocates for the needs of women.

Internet Advocacy

Internet advocacy is another political strategy that every social worker can employ. Today, organizations, including health and human service organizations, are able to develop web sites that provide crucial information about the mission and programs of the agency to the public. Visitors to the web site can be informed in much greater detail about the services, client populations, finances, leaders, and staff of an agency than through typical agency brochures. Interested Internet visitors can find out the latest news about an organization, upcoming events, and past accomplishments.

Once informed and interested in the mission of the organization, an Internet user may decide to get more involved in the activities of the organization, including those dealing with policy advocacy.[12] If a health and human service organization is mounting a campaign to get a policy recommendation passed, the agency can provide Internet supporters with contact information for crucial decision-makers and other stakeholders involved with the policy recommendation. This contact information may include e-mail addresses, phone numbers, and regular mailing addresses of key stakeholders in the decision-making process. In addition, agencies can provide chat areas and links with like-minded agencies (perhaps part of a coalition) right on their web site.

Another communication vehicle for supporters is the use of a list serve that allows supporters to exchange e-mail regarding the policy proposal, the decision-making process, and other related activities.[13] Furthermore, the web site of the agency can be used to allow policy advocates a chance to ask questions and provide feedback to agency leaders and staff regarding the policy recommendation and advocacy campaign. Some agencies today even allow policy supporters an opportunity to send e-mail or faxes from the agency's web site directly to policy decision-makers.[14] Printed copies of such faxes or e-mails can be collected by the agency and presented in hard copy later to policy decision-makers to emphasize support for the policy proposal.

Agencies may also choose to provide campaign material on their web site that can be printed by supporters in trying to get a policy recommendation passed. Such material may be used for posters, fliers, brochures, or fact sheets during the advocacy process.[15] Agencies in support of a policy proposal can also add some pizzazz to their Internet campaign by using the latest in Internet animation, sound, and video.

Some agencies even provide an on-line tool kit for supporters wanting to start state or local chapters of a national organization.[16] In the case of a campaign to support a policy recommendation, the tool kit may be used to help organize efforts at the state and local level. Tool kits can show supporters how to raise money, write press releases, set up phone trees, and lobby state and local policymakers. This would include, of course, ways to use the Internet in such lobbying efforts. Environmental and human rights activists have used Internet advocacy successfully in the past. These agencies include The Rain Forest Activist Network and Amnesty International. Health and human service agencies and various political campaigns will increasingly do the same in the future.

> **Did You Know?**
>
> In 2002, the National Association of Social Workers (NASW) used the Internet to advocate for policy recommendations regarding welfare reform reauthorization and mental health parity legislation. The web site on welfare reform, for example, provided information on the Personal Responsibility and Work Opportunity Reconciliation Act, fact sheets on NASW's reauthorization priorities, a "toolkit" (as described earlier), sample letters to the editor, sample op-ed columns, citations from welfare research by social workers, and anecdotal stories about the outcome of previous welfare reform efforts.[17]

Partnership and Advocacy Success

> Justice is the first virtue of social institutions, as truth is of systems of thought. A theory however elegant and economical must be rejected or revised if it is untrue; likewise laws and institutions no matter how efficient and well-arranged must be reformed or abolished if they are unjust.[18]
>
> John Rawls

The American market economy produces a relatively high standard of living. Yet, when change is needed, government and voluntary associations often play leading roles in the effort. In fact, the history of American social welfare is filled with successful collaborative efforts at social reform. Social workers at times have been leaders in these reform movements. At other times, they have been called to implement programs and services as a result of new social legislation. Whatever the case, do not let the cynicism of contemporary American culture fool you.

The foremothers of social work were successful in many advocacy efforts. Dorothea Dix, one of the first great lobbyists, was certainly a success in establishing state services for the mentally ill.[19] Using their excellent communication skills, women such as Lucretia Mott, Lucy Stone, Susan B. Anthony, and Elizabeth Cady Stanton during the 1800s contributed significantly to the abolition movement.[20] Many of the same women fought for women's suffrage and were ultimately successful in gaining the right to vote.

The driving force behind much social reform during the Progressive Era was the grassroots advocacy of women. The General Federation of Women's Clubs was a national advocacy network, starting at the local community level, which was very influential in passing many of the reforms of the Progressive Era. The National Congress of Mothers was another advocacy organization heavily involved in reform efforts during the Progressive Era.[21] Depending on the specific issue, at various times, these organizations partnered in coalitions with other reform groups, including progressive business associations, trade unions, farm groups, urban political machines, and the emerging social work profession.

Social workers Jane Addams, Grace Abbott, Edith Abbott, and other settlement house workers were successful in their efforts to improve the quality of life for immigrants in inner-city neighborhoods.[22] And they did so by personally witnessing the growing social need and stressing social cooperation among business, government, and voluntary associations to address this need.

Like the settlement houses, charity organization societies also stressed community collaboration in addressing social problems. Led by professionals such as social worker Mary Richmond, many of these organizations later evolved into community chests, and ultimately, the United Way system, a nationwide partnership between business and nonprofit health and human service organizations.[23]

Worker's compensation, which was established in most states before the end of the Progressive Era, has been a success. Social Security and unemployment compensation established during the New Deal are successful poverty prevention programs.[24] Former settlement house workers, Eleanor Roosevelt, Harry Hopkins, and Frances Perkins, were top advisors to President Franklin Roosevelt during the creation of the New Deal programs.[25] Eleanor Roosevelt was one of the great campaigners and advocates in American history.

The programs of the Great Society, despite continuing criticism, have been successful in many ways. The Food Stamp Program has helped the poor obtain critical food supplies.[26] Medicare, despite the issues of cost control, has provided many older Americans with needed health care while keeping them from falling into poverty.[27] Community health centers, also established during the Great Society, provide accessible services in low-income communities.[28] Poor children have benefited from the early educational support of Head Start, a Great Society program that increases the likelihood of future high school graduation and employment.[29] And, the Civil Rights Acts of 1964 and 1965 ended segregation in the South.[30]

The point is, many social programs, although perhaps not perfect, perhaps not completely solving the various problems they address, have, in fact, been successful, providing needed services and support to millions of Americans. Contemporary social workers and students studying to be social workers should be proud of these successes and not give in to cynical comments that would suggest social legislation has been a waste of money. American social welfare is the result of a cooperative effort, a partnership among various institutions, groups, and individuals to further national well-being. To the extent that this collaboration at times has needed to be coerced, American social welfare reflects a rich heritage of advocacy that can be built upon by today's social workers. The next successful social reform movement involving social workers might address current issues involving social security, welfare reform, managed health care or homelessness. It might address issues related to globalization. It might address any number of issues. One thing is for sure, it will happen, and hopefully, social workers will play a lead role in the effort.

Therefore, let a vision of social justice guide the profession of social work, a vision based on respect for diversity, individual dignity, self-determination, and empowerment. Every graduate on leaving social work education should have a personal and professional vision of social justice to guide their future activities as social workers. Without this social vision, social work becomes a profession without passion, a profession without power.

CONTENTSELECT

For more information on related social work topics, use the following search terms:

Activist	Communicator	Persuader
Campaigner	Lobbyist	Witness

NOTES

1. Margaret Dietz Domanski, "Prototypes of Social Work Political Participation: An Empirical Model," *Social Work* 43, No. 2: pp. 156–167 (1998).

2. Ann Majchrzak, *Methods for Policy Research* (Newbury Park, CA: Sage Publications, 1984) p. 93.

3. Ibid., pp. 97–99.

4. Jeffrey H. Birnbaum and Alan S. Murray, *Showdown at Gucci Gulch: Lawmakers, Lobbyists, and the Unlikely Triumph of Tax Reform* (New York: Vintage, 1988), p. 25; Lou Cannon, *President Reagan: The Role of a Lifetime* (New York: Public Affairs, 2000), p. 223; Bruce S. Jansson, *The Reluctant Welfare State: American Social Welfare Policies—Past, Present, and Future*, 4th ed. (Belmont, CA: Wadsworth/Thomson Learning, 2001), pp. 368–369.

5. Cannon, pp. 84; Jansson, *The Reluctant Welfare State: American Social Welfare Policies—Past, Present, and Future*, 4th ed., p. 314.

6. Majchrzak, p. 98.

7. Rosemary Kennedy Chapin, "Social Policy Development: The Strengths Perspective," *Social Work* 40, No. 4: pp. 506–513 (1995).

8. Majchrzak, pp. 99–100.

9. Ibid., pp. 100–101.

10. Bruce Jansson, *Becoming an Effective Policy Advocate: From Policy Practice to Social Justice* (Pacific Grove, CA: Brooks/Cole, 1999), pp. 248–250; Paul Davidoff, "The Advocate Relationship: Advocacy and Pluralism in Planning," in Neil Gilbert and Harry Specht, eds., *Planning for Social Welfare: Issues, Models, and Tasks* (Englewood Cliffs, NJ: Prentice-Hall, 1977), pp. 191–203.

11. Liane V. Davis and Jan L Hagen, "The Problem of Wife Abuse: The Interrelationship of Social Policy and Social Work Practice," *Social Work* 37, No. 1: pp. 15–19 (1992).

12. Michael Johnston, "Inviting People to Action: Campaigning," *The Fundraiser's Guide to the Internet* (New York: Wiley), pp. 165, 169.

13. Ibid., p. 169.

14. Ibid., p. 178.

15. Ibid., pp. 181, 185.

16. Ibid., p. 184.

17. John O'Neill, "Web Site on Welfare is Launched," *NASW NEWS*, June 2002, p. 10; John O'Neill, "Party Prospects Bright," *NASW NEWS*, May 2002, p. 7.

18. John Rawls, *A Theory of Justice* (Cambridge, MA: Belknap Press, 1971), p. 3.

19. Helen E. Marshall, *Dorothea Dix: Forgotten Samaritan* (Chapel Hill, NC: University of North Carolina Press, 1937), p. 245.

20. Alice Stone Blackwell, *Lucy Stone: Pioneer of Woman's Rights* (Norwood, MA: The Plimpton Press, 1930), p. 76; Harriet Sigerman, *Biographical Supplement and Index*, ed. Nancy F. Cott, *The Young Oxford History of Women in the United States*, vol. 2 (New York: Oxford University Press, 1995), p. 150.

21. Robert D. Putnam, *Bowling Alone: The Collapse and Revival of American Community* (New York: Simon & Schuster, 2000), p. 386; Theda Skocpol, *Protecting Soldiers and Mothers: The Political Origins Of Social Policy in the United States* (Cambridge, MA: Harvard University), pp. 265–266, 318, 329, 332–333.

22. Walter I. Trattner, *From Poor Law to Welfare State: A History of Social Welfare in America*, 6th ed. (New York: The Free Press, 1999), p. 171.

23. Eleanor Brilliant, *The United Way: Dilemmas of Organized Charity* (New York: Columbia, 1990), p. 19.

24. Sar A. Levitan, Garth L. Mangum, and Stephen L. Mangum, *Programs in Aid of the Poor*, 7th ed. (Baltimore, MD: The Johns Hopkins University Press, 1998), pp. 63, 95–96.

25. James Leiby, *A History of Social Welfare and Social Work in the United States* (New York: Columbia University Press, 1978), p. 224, Doris Kearns Goodwin, *No Ordinary Time* (New York: Touchstone, 1995), p. 87, George Martin, *Madam Secretary Frances Perkins* (Boston: Houghton Mifflin, 1976), pp. 60–63, 72–74; John H. Ehrenreich, *The Altruistic Imagination: A History of Social Work and Social Policy in the United States* (Ithaca, NY: Cornell University Press, 1985), p. 104.

26. Levitan, p. 135.

27. Ibid., p. 110.

28. Ibid., p. 117.

29. Ibid., p. 163.

30. Jansson, *The Reluctant Welfare State: American Social Welfare Policies—Past, Present, and Future*, 4th ed., p. 248; Joseph A. Califano, Jr., *The Triumph & Tragedy of Lyndon Johnson: The White House Years* (College Station: Texas A&M University Press, 2000), p. 58.

GLOSSARY

Able-bodied Poor parish members thought to be less deserving of relief than children and the impotent.

Abolition Movement Groups, including women, business, and religious leaders, who believed slavery was immoral and who sought to end this institution.

Activist Refers to one of several policy advocacy roles that social workers can play.

Administrative criteria Criteria that need to be examined when looking at the potential organizations that will implement new legislation. Three administrative criteria to examine are the authority, capability, and commitment of the agencies.

Administrative oversight The third major function of Congress and is partly the result of the American public's feeling that citizens should not only be served by government, but protected from it as well. Often bureaucratic agencies make expert decisions; Congress then reviews those decisions. Techniques for oversight include special investigations by congressional committees, budget hearings, Senate confirmation of presidential appointments, and impeachment.

AmeriCorps A national volunteer program of the Clinton administration.

Apprentice system Those wanting to learn a trade apprenticed to master craftsmen, typically for a period of seven years. The master craftsman was expected to provide on-the-job training in exchange for the youth's labor.

Artisan The term used for skilled craftsmen who made candles, barrels, silver items, and so forth.

Benefit–cost analysis A data analysis strategy used to determine the impacts of policy proposals. Favorable impacts are registered as benefits while unfavorable ones are considered costs.

Bicameral Composed of two legislative bodies.

Black Codes After the Civil War, these laws surfaced to subjugate and segregate African Americans.

Boycott To join together in abstaining from dealing with another as a means of protest or coercion.

Calvinism Based on the writings of John Calvin, the Protestant Reformer, whose work represented God's calling on earth, and was therefore sacred. If one was apparently able-bodied yet poverty-stricken, this was an indication that he or she was immoral and not destined for salvation.

Campaigner Refers to one of several policy advocacy roles that social workers can play.

Capitalism Is a market economic system stressing individual pursuit of profits through the use of private property.

Causation To establish causation, the independent and dependent variables must be empirically related, independent variable must occur before the dependent variable; and the observed relationship between the independent and dependent variable is not the result of the influence of some third variable that causes them both.

Charitable choice Refers to a clause in the 1996 welfare reform legislation promoting government funding of social services by faith-based organizations.

Charity organization societies Based on scientific philanthropy, these organizations emerged to better coordinate and deliver services to the needy. They aimed to be more scientific, professional, and business-like and emphasized individual needs assessment, case histories, case conferences, service referrals, interviewing skills as well as community service coordination.

Charters Issued by English monarchs to companies of adventurers who risked their own money to establish colonies in America. These individuals invested their cash in joint stock to finance the expedition.

Chattel slaves Treated as the legal property of their owners; like livestock commodities to be bought and sold. The slave's service was perpetual.

Children's Aid Society Established in 1853 by Charles Loring Brace, this mission provided education, lodging, and homes to vagrant children.

Children's Bureau Established in 1912, this organization conducted research and disseminated information on women's health and child development.

City mission movement A voluntary effort to help the needy following the Second Great Awakening. It was dependent upon philanthropy and often inspired by religious beliefs. The city missions provided religious education, food, shelter, employment referrals, and child care.

Civil Rights Act of 1964 This act promoted African American voting rights by outlawing poll taxes and literacy tests. It also called for desegregation of public facilities and prohibited employment discrimination in organizations receiving federal money.

Civil Rights Act of 1965 This act gave the federal government the right to presume discrimination in any state (or its subdivisions) where less than 50% of minorities voted in the latest federal election. The act also presumed discrimination in any area using screening tests such as literacy tests. In these cases, federal authorities could directly administer elections.

Civilian Conservation Corps (CCC)   A New Deal program which provided jobs for youth in various parks.

Civilian Works Administration (CWA)   A New Deal program which created jobs in public works during the Great Depression.

Claims-making approach   An approach to problem definition utilizes social construction theory to emphasize the process of constructing social problems.

Classic experimental design   A research design that uses random assignment in experimental and control groups along with pretests and posttests in relation to a treatment administered to the experimental group.

Coalitions   Temporary partnerships organized for a specific and time-limited purpose.

Collaborator   Refers to one of several policy advocacy roles that social workers can play.

Committee system   Most congressional work is done in committees. Committees initiate and prioritize specific policy proposals, hold public hearings on various policy issues and conduct investigations, initiate studies and publish reports, and perform administrative oversight such as reviewing budget requests and passing judgment on presidential appointees.

Commons   Pastures where animals grazed during the feudal period.

Communicator   Refers to one of several policy advocacy roles that social workers can play.

Community Action Programs   Referred to as "CAP" agencies, these local advocacy agencies were started during the Johnson administration's War On Poverty in the 1960s.

Community chests   Centrally organized fund-raising for several community charities which used a single, yearly, community-wide drive as an efficient, well-organized method of raising funds to support health and human services.

Conceptual model   A category of model used to make predictions about human or organizational behavior. Conceptual models familiar to social workers include Sigmund Freud's psychodynamic model as well as Erik Erikson's lifespan model.

Conservatives   Believe that individual profit is the great motivator and that individuals left free to pursue their own self-interest in a capitalist system work for the betterment of all. To this end, the role of government should be limited to defending private property rights and maintaining social order.

Consumer Price Index   This index measures the prices of a fixed market basket of some 300 goods typically purchased by an urban consumer.

Corporate strategic philanthropy   Integration of contributions management into the overall strategic planning of the corporation; in so doing, corporations target charitable contributions to serve their business interests while also meeting the needs of recipient organizations.

Correlational design   A type of research design, often referred to as a "cross sectional study," usually involving a random sample and multivariate statistical controls. Similar to the time-series design, there is no equivalent control group used in the study.

Cost-effectiveness   A data analysis strategy in which benefits related to each policy alternative are comparable and, therefore, don't have to be examined further. Only costs are compared between the two policy options.

Criterion   Information that allows the policy analyst to evaluate policy alternatives.

Data analysis strategies   Methods used to analyze collected information.

Data collection   Process of gathering information from various sources through a variety of techniques, including literature reviews, personal interviews, direct observations, questionnaires, focus groups, and existing databases.

Daughters of Liberty   During the Revolutionary War these politically active women's groups were formed in opposition to certain British policies such as the British tax on tea. The groups encouraged colonial women to boycott British goods, "buy American" products, and make their own goods when possible.

Decision agenda   Contains problems and solutions ready to be voted on by policy decision-makers.

Delphi panel   A structured group used in needs analysis to collect and analyze information. A traditional Delphi panel uses a mailed questionnaire to collect information from a group of experts.

Descriptive/predictive models   Policy models that describe alternatives and predict outcomes.

Deserving poor   Those who were too sick, too young, or too old to do substantial work and who were treated more humanely by society.

Deterministic model   Model in which the outcomes are assumed to be certain.

Diagrammatic model   Model that provides the essential features of a subject, but is generally two-dimensional in form.

District visitors   Were encouraged to visit and advise poor families in each district of the city in the 1800s by private nonprofit agencies organized to help the needy.

Elite theory   Elite theory maintains that the society is divided into a tiny elite with power and the masses with relatively little power. It is the elite who define the ideology and values used to construct society's major institutions, and who have the most influence on policy.

Elizabethan Poor Law Act   Consolidation of various laws dealing with the poor as English society dealt not only with periodic crises such as the bubonic plague, war, and famine, but also with the social disorder resulting from the breakdown of medieval institutions and the rise of capitalism.

Emancipation Proclamation of 1863   The act in which Abraham Lincoln emancipated slaves in those southern states still fighting against the Union.

Employee stock ownership plan   An employee invests some of their wages or salary in their company's stock and receives dividends regularly like other company investors. Upon retirement, the employee can either take the company stock from the fund or sell the shares back to the corporation.

Enclosure   Fields enclosed with fences and hedges.

Evaluative policy analysis   Often takes the form of program evaluation. That is, policies many times produce programs to achieve their goals. If the programs are implemented and conducted successfully, the policy is a success. Therefore, evaluative policy analysis seeks to answer the question: Did the program achieve its goals?

Feasibility study   Refers to the first stage in the policy development process. In this information-gathering stage, we want to answer the following questions: Can the policy analysis be done? Is there sufficient support for the analysis? And is it likely that its final recommendations will be passed by policymakers?

Federal Emergency Relief Administration (FERA)   Created by the Federal Emergency Relief Act in 1932. As its name suggests, FERA was given primary responsibility for managing the effort to distribute federal relief funds to individual states. The relief funds were used to sustain unemployed families during the Great Depression.

Federal Trade Commission   Legislation passed in 1915 to further regulate anticompetitive practices by corporations.

Fief   During the feudal period, the king and higher lords granted this control over land to lesser lords in exchange for military service.

Fifteenth Amendment   In 1870 gave African American males the right to vote.

First Amendment   Provides for freedom of religion, freedom of assembly, freedom of speech, and the right to petition government over grievances.

First Great Awakening   Essentially, a religious revival movement which began in the late 1720s emphasizing faith, repentance, and regeneration. As such, it featured a conversion experience, commonly referred to as being "born again."

Focus group   A frequently used data collection method in which a selected group of people, typically twelve to fifteen in number, are brought together to explore some topic in depth. The facilitator of the focus group guides the discussion to solicit information regarding beliefs and opinions of individuals on the topic at hand.

Focused synthesis   Also known as a quick analysis, the policy analyst puts together pertinent information from several existing information sources.

401(k) retirement plans   Plans in which employees typically contribute a small percentage of their before-tax income to their 401(k) fund. These plans often include an employer contribution as well.

Food stamps   A federal program in which participants receive a monthly allotment of stamps. These stamps can then be used to purchase food at most retail stores.

Fourteenth Amendment   In 1868 granted African Americans citizenship.

Founding Fathers   After the American Revolutionary War ended, a relatively small and elite group of men who completed the institutional structure for the new nation.

Freedmen Bureau Act   Established the Bureau of Refugees, Freedmen, and Abandoned Lands. Authorized to establish courts in southern states, the Freedmen's Bureau provided legal assistance to freed slaves.

Freedmen's Camps   Camps run by the Union Army that provided former slaves with food, clothing, health care, and work details.

Friendly visitors   Primarily female volunteers from the business and professional classes who did home visits to investigate and document family needs. This was to cut down on indiscriminate giving, which was thought to promote idleness, destroy character, and lead to poverty.

Functional approach   This approach to problem definition claims that a social problem is any condition that upsets the smooth functioning of society.

Funding channels   Refers to the various ways that funding is distributed to service providers. One scenario is when federal funds are provided directly to local service providers, such as when funding is distributed through project grants. A second scenario is when federal funds are distributed through state government and then to local service providers, as with federal block grants to states.

General Assistance   A program for the needy who do not qualify for other federal assistance; benefits include cash and/or in-kind payments.

Globalization   The term used for the process by which corporations create a global market for their goods and services, a market that increasingly reaches across national borders, defense systems, and cultures.

Goal   An action-oriented phrase, meant to direct and motivate someone or some group regarding an identified issue.

Great Society   The term Lyndon Johnson called his legislative agenda to greatly expand the role of the federal government in addressing social welfare throughout the country.

Gross Domestic Product (GDP)   Measures the dollar value of total output of all goods and services produced within the United States by both domestic and foreign entities.

Gross National Product (GNP)   Is the dollar value of the total output of all goods and services produced in the private and public sectors. The GNP includes the value of all production of U.S. entities even if they are located in foreign nations.

Group theory model   Model through which to view policy analysis. This model sees politics as a struggle among competing groups to influence policy.

Habitat for Humanity International   An international voluntary housing development program.

Health maintenance organizations or "HMOs"   Organizations in which health care consumers select a "primary care physician" who serves as a gatekeeper in managing health care services and costs.

Homestead Act of 1862   Offered farmers 160 acres of public land at $1.50 an acre or for free after five years of residence.

Ideology   A set of values.

Incremental policy development   A fundamental approach to policy planning in which a limited number of policy options and possible outcomes are analyzed. In this approach, policy proposals tend to vary only marginally from each other and from existing policy.

Indentured servants   Immigrants who were nonfree servants obligated to provide their labor for a period of four to seven years before they became free.

Independent Sector   Another name for the social sector in America. It is also referred to as the private nonprofit sector or voluntary sector. This sector is not a part of government or business.

Indian Removal   The policy American political leaders supported for the forced removal of Native Americans to the western frontier in order to clear the land for agriculture and manufacturing.

Indoor relief   Services provided to the poor in an institution such as a workhouse.

In-kind services   Programs where no cash support is given directly to the individual.

International Monetary Fund (IMF)   Established after World War II, the International Monetary Fund is charged with the responsibility for facilitating world trade by maintaining stability and liquidity in national currencies around the globe.

Individual Retirement Accounts (IRAs)   A private retirement option.

Institutional model   Examines policy as a product of institutions and emphasizes a description of the characteristics of policy-making organizations.

Invisible hand   Adam Smith's famous concept referring to his belief that the pressure of competition in the marketplace directs the selfish activities of individuals, as if by an "invisible hand," into socially useful outcomes.

Key issues   The various dimensions that constitute a social problem.

Ku Klux Klan   A secret organization that aims to discriminate and oppress African Americans, Jews, Catholics, and other groups.

Knights   Part of a military force a king maintained for protection against outside invasion during the feudal period.

Laissez-faire   The belief that government should not interfere with the operations of the marketplace.

Labor   Those working for wages.

Laws of Settlement   Stated that the poor could only receive assistance if they resided in the parish of their birth. These laws helped to decrease the number of poor peasants wandering the countryside, spreading disease, increasing local relief costs, and at the very least, causing fear among local residents.

League of Iroquois   One of the most powerful Native American tribes in U.S. history. The League consisted of the Mohawks, Oneidas, Onondagas, Cayugas, and Senecas. All shared the Iroquois language. The Iroquois lived in what is now Pennsylvania and upper New York.

Legislation   An enacted law or body of laws.

Legislative history (review) A step in a feasibility study for policy development in which past legislation related to the selected key issue is examined.

Less eligible The poor in this category received relief funds only after the needs of the more worthy poor were met.

Liberals Believe that the market economy has certain negative tendencies that should be monitored and regulated by government to maximize social welfare.

Life cycles In terms of policy analysis, this term refers to the process in which a social problem initially sees much investigative activity by government and other interested institutions. The problem starts to warrant research grants and the development of task forces. Subsequently, programs are developed to alleviate or solve the social problem. Later, funding and interest start to dry up. The problem may have been solved or perhaps it is considered unsolvable. In any case, the condition does not receive public attention any longer.

Linear regression Uses the equation of a line to predict the values of one variable given values of a second variable.

Lobbyist Refers to one of several policy advocacy roles that social workers can play.

Louisiana Purchase An agreement in 1803 with France that allowed the United States to roughly double its geographic size for about $11 million.

Majority Leader In the U.S. Congress, this elected official performs numerous duties, including organizing the work of the Senate, scheduling debate on policy issues, and helping to gather enough votes to pass specific pieces of legislation.

Manifest Destiny Term coined by John L. O'Sullivan in an 1845 magazine article related to the U.S. social policy of westward expansion, claiming it was "our manifest destiny to overspread the continent allotted by Providence for the free development of our yearly multiplying millions."

Manor A social and economic organization comprising the lord and his serfs during the feudal period.

March of the Mill Children A march organized by Mother Jones in 1903 to protest the exploitation of children in the workplace.

Marginal productivity theory Maintains that incomes in a market system, by and large, reflect the marginal productivity of different contributors to the economic process; thus, the greater the value of your production, the greater the income you will receive.

Market system An economic system in which the "factors of production" are commodities for sale. These factors of production are land, labor, and capital.

Mass marches   Marches involving many participants, often for the purpose of social protest and reform.

Matching funding formulas   Typically formulas in which for every dollar of state funding, the federal government contributes a specified percentage of funding.

Maximum feasible participation   A concept encouraging empowerment of the poor through participation in social services and social change activities.

Medicaid   (Title 19 of the Social Security Act) Passed during the Johnson administration, this legislation assists the poor with health care.

Medicare   (Title 18 of the Social Security Act) Also passed during the Johnson administration, this legislation made health care more affordable for older Americans.

Mercantile policy   Policies that were in place during the transition from feudalism to capitalism, the wealth of a nation-state was measured by the amount of gold and silver obtained through a favorable balance of trade. The basic economic unit was the state in contrast to the individual under capitalism.

Middle Ages   The period in European history from 600 A.D. through 1500. Society in this period is often referred to as medieval or feudal society.

Minority leader   In U.S. politics, this elected official works with (or against) the majority party on legislation.

Missouri Compromise   Maintained a sensitive balance between free and slave states.

Model   As defined by Stokey and Zeckhauser, a "simplified representation of some aspect of the real world."

Mother's pensions   A forerunner of Aid to Dependent Children, this legislation provided money to poor, single mothers to help them in caring for their children.

Mutual benefit organizations   Nonprofit organizations which focus on aid to their members—in contrast to a "public good."

National Association for the Advancement of Colored People (NAACP)   Civil rights advocacy organization founded in 1909.

National Congress of Mothers   Started in 1897, this was another advocacy organization heavily involved in reform efforts during the Progressive Era. The organization later became the well-known Parent-Teacher Association or "P.T.A."

National Consumers League   Founded in 1899, this organization used consumer pressure in advocating for child labor laws, minimum wages, and shorter work days for women, as well as for safer consumer products.

National Labor Relations Board   Created by the 1936 Wagner Act, the board enforced the right of workers to start their own unions.

National Recovery Administration   This controversial program, which was declared unconstitutional by the Supreme Court in 1935, sought to stabilize the economy by establishing wage and price agreements to curb the slashing of prices and wages during the Great Depression.

National Youth Administration.   A forerunner of modern student financial assistance, this New Deal program allowed high school and college students to finish their education by providing part-time public sector jobs. It also established rural camps where youth could learn trade skills.

Need   The value judgment that some group has a problem that can be solved.

Needs analysis   A tool employed in policy and program development used for decision making that involves the identification as well as the evaluation of needs.

Needs assessment   Is the process of evaluating the problems and solutions identified for a target population.

Noblesse oblige   During the feudal period, the moral obligation for the lords to treat peasants with generosity.

Nominal group   A structured group used in needs analysis to collect and analyze information. A nominal group ranks individual participant answers to questions posed by a group facilitator.

Nonviolent resistance   Martin Luther King's coalition used this strategy to fight racial segregation, employing peaceful mass marches, sit-ins, and business boycotts to achieve its objectives.

Normative approach   This approach to problem definition claims a social problem is any condition that deviates from accepted societal norms.

Objective approach   Another approach to problem definition, the objective approach claims that a social problem is recognized when the quantitative indicators of a problem become indisputably large over time.

Objectives   Time-limited and measurable indicators of goal achievement.

Outdoor relief   Services provided to the poor in the home. Such services might include assistance with health care, food, clothing, and fuel (i.e., wood).

Overseerers of the Poor   In England within each parish, these public officials were nominated by justices of the peace to carry out such duties as collecting taxes for poor relief and making sure that the poor received care. This system was adopted in colonial America.

Parish   In England this term referred to a political subdivision of a county, to the church in that subdivision, and to the people of that church.

Partnership   An association or collaboration between, or among, individuals, groups, or institutions to pursue some endeavor, in this case, social welfare.

Party System   In the U.S. Congress, the majority political party has the primary responsibility for organizing the legislative agenda, controls the selection of the Speaker of the House, and its members constitute a majority on each committee.

Past research (review)   A step in a feasibility study for policy development in which past research related to the selected key issue is examined.

Pauper   One who is extremely poor, especially one dependent on public assistance or charity.

Persuader   Refers to one of several policy advocacy roles that social workers can play.

Physical model   Usually a three-dimensional form that represents some real object.

Placing out   An 1800s version of foster care that Charles Loring Brace began where homeless children lived with farmers and other families in western states while Brace typically retained guardianship of the children to deter possible abuse or neglect.

Policy analysis (also "policy research")   A form of applied research carried out to acquire a deeper understanding of social problems and to bring about better solutions to those problems.

Policy development (or "policy planning")   The process by which policies are proposed, enacted, and implemented.

Political machines   Sophisticated political organizations that aggressively pursued the support of new immigrants.

Political patronage   A distributive system where political parties provided jobs and services to individuals in return for the individual's political support.

Political stream   A policy metaphor for describing the socio-political environment in which policy is developed. The political stream is made up of various types of institutions, organizations, and events. For Congress and state legislatures, the political stream consists of public opinion, constituent support, campaign donors, advocacy groups, lobbyists, the media, and powerful political leaders (committee chairs, etc.).

Poorhouses   Dwellings erected to house one or more poor individuals or families and supported by taxes from each household in a parish.

Predictive policy analysis   Requires the projection of future outcomes resulting from implementing individual alternatives.

Pre-experimental design   In this type of design, the requirements of the classic experiment are relaxed even further, while at the same time, there are no random samples and multivariate statistics as in the correlational design. An example would be a one-shot case study.

Prescriptive model   A type of model that describes options and predicts outcomes for the policy analyst; it also provides a rule for choosing among alternatives and making recommendations. For instance, the cost-benefit analysis framework is a prescriptive model.

Prescriptive policy analysis   Includes specific recommendations for the decision-maker, given projected outcomes for each policy alternative.

Primary data   Data that policy planners collect themselves.

Private-investment accounts   An option supported by President George W. Bush to address the sustainability of Social Security; these accounts would be managed by private pension and investment companies, with part of the social security tax currently paid by workers.

Private nonprofit sector   Also referred to as the voluntary sector, this sector of U.S. society is comprised of private nonprofit organizations, which are not a part of government and business. These organizations are often characterized as philanthropic, charitable, or public benefit organizations. They usually exist to provide a service or promote a cause. For the most part, they are private organizations serving a public purpose and are exempt from federal income tax.

Probabilistic model   Models where outcomes are assigned a probability.

Problem definition   A step in policy development in which the policy analyst attempts to obtain a thorough understanding of the social problem and key issue before researching possible solutions to the problem.

Problem stream   A policy metaphor used to illustrate the many conditions generally problematic in society. Specific examples include problems such as crime, inadequate health care, racism, and unemployment. The problem stream contains the social problems of interest in the government policy agenda.

Process model   Examines policy analysis as a developmental process with underlying theory and methodology.

Process streams   A policy metaphor used by author John Kingdon to illustrate the policy development process.

Progressive Era   The period in American history from about 1900 to 1920 which was a time of major reforms in the economic, political, and social institutions of the nation.

Public-private partnerships   Collaborations among public and private (for profit and/or nonprofit) entities.

Public assistance programs   Selective programs based on individual need.

Public Works Administration (PWA)   Created in 1933, this New Deal program focused on complex public works such as dams and airports.

Puritans   A group of religious nonconformists who were followers of Calvin in England. The group first landed on the coast of present-day Massachusetts in 1620. They brought their version of the English poor relief system to America.

Quasi-experimental design   A type of research design used in policy analysis in which some of the conditions required for a classic experiment are relaxed. For instance, there is no equivalent control group in a time-series design, an example of a quasi-experimental design.

Quick analysis   An approach to policy analysis in which the policy analyst collects and synthesizes pertinent information from several existing information sources.

Radical left   Typically supports a major reorganization of the three major institutional sectors in the U.S., one that would result in a greatly reduced role for capitalist in the economic and political sectors.

Rational policy development (rational-comprehensive)   An approach to policy planning in which all possible courses of action need to be identified before a decision is made.

Reconstruction   The period in U.S. history from the end of the Civil War to about 1876 during which the Confederate States were reintegrated into the Union.

Representation   A second major function of Congress; each member of Congress represents two groups of citizens, their own congressional representation district or state and the nation as a whole.

Residency requirements   Established in colonial America; similar to those in England for receiving public assistance. One reason for residency requirements was public concern regarding the cost of providing relief to the poor in any one community.

Resource inventory   A compilation of the services available to one or more target groups, usually in a specific geographic area.

Retrospective policy analysis   The description and interpretation of past events in policy development.

Risk factors   Social indicators used to predict undesirable outcomes.

Sanction   A mechanism for promoting a collective's standards. Sanctions can be regulatory such as fines, copyrights, building codes, zoning, certification, and licensing. They can also be financial in nature. For example, taxes, grants, contracts, loans, and rewards are examples of sanctions.

Sanctions can be positive, such as a bonus or negative, such as employment termination.

Scientific management Refers to a process by which industrial work projects were reduced to simple, repetitive tasks that any unskilled immigrant could learn quickly.

Scientific philanthropy Refers to a more professional approach to health and human services predicated on the latest scientific information.

Second Great Awakening Began in America in the late 1780s, lasting into the 1830s. This second great Protestant religious revival, once again, rejected the Calvinist notion of predestination, the belief that personal salvation is gained only through the grace of God. In contrast, the Second Great Awakening preached that all people could be saved and that all Christians should practice benevolence.

Secondary data Existing data that someone else has already collected.

Selective programs Programs in which benefits are based on individual need.

Serfs A term in the Middle Ages for peasants.

Service use analysis Compares expected service use with actual service use to further define need.

Settlement houses Private nonprofit organizations, established in poor, inner-city neighborhoods to promote the social welfare of community residents.

Sherman Antitrust Act To counter the growing power of corporations in America, the federal government passed this legislation in 1890 to regulate business monopoly and promote free competition.

Sit-down strike A labor stoppage in which workers occupy their workplace and refuse to work until the strike is settled.

Sit-in An organized protest in which demonstrators occupy a public place and refuse to leave; used often in the Civil Rights Movement to protest racial segregation.

Social indicators Aggregate statistical measures that depict important aspects of a social situation and of underlying historical trends and developments.

Social policy Collective course of action, set by policymakers, involving the use of sanctions, to address the needs of some group of people.

Social problem An unmet need of some group of people.

Social security Old Age, Survivors, and Disability Insurance.

Social Security Act of 1935 New Deal legislation that constituted a package of social program consisting of both insurance and poor relief.

Social Service Block Grant   A federal block grant that funds a broad array of social services.

Social welfare   A policy outcome referring to collective well-being.

Society for the Prevention of Pauperism   Organizations established by business and professional leaders in cities such as New York (1817), Philadelphia (1817), Baltimore (1820), and Boston (1835) during the early 1800s. These organizations were noteworthy for their attempt to analyze the causes of pauperism and possible ways to prevent it.

Solution stream   A policy metaphor used to illustrate the various policy mechanisms (like sanctions), administrative strategies, program designs, and treatment methodologies currently in use. If they are not in use, they are at least known to academics, and possibly, practitioners and policymakers. Solution streams, therefore, include those potential problem-solving initiatives currently receiving attention by policymakers as part of the general government policy agenda.

Speaker of the House   The presiding officer of Congress, who along with the other party leaders called "whips," determines the issues that will get top priority during the session.

Spoils system   After his landslide victory in 1828, Andrew Jackson instituted this system whereby the new administration replaces as many government employees as possible from the previous administration.

Stakeholder   In the case of policy proposals, any individual or group that can affect or be affected by the proposed legislation.

Stakeholder analysis   A step in the policy development process done to analyze the political viability of a tentative policy recommendation by examining the major stakeholders involved in the policy proposal.

Subjective approach   An approach to social problem definition that claims the quantitative evidence has been available for a considerable amount of time; it is the public's perception of the data that changes.

Supplemental Security Income (SSI)   A program that assists poor people aged 65 or older as well as blind people and people with disabilities.

Supply-side economics   The essence of Reagan's economic recovery plan, supply-side economics maintains that tax cuts for the wealthy will be reinvested in business expansion. Business expansion will create more jobs and consumer goods. More jobs, in turn, will create the income needed to buy those consumer goods. In short, increased production will create increased demand for the goods produced. This is the premise underlying the supply-side economics promise that "supply will create its own demand."

Survivors insurance   Part of social security that covers children under 18 years of age, dependent parents, and dependent widowers or widows.

These categories of recipients receive benefits when an insured worker dies.

Synthetic estimation   Used in social indicator analysis to estimate characteristics of smaller geographic populations from larger government geographic data sets. This procedure assumes comparable prevalence rates between the larger and smaller geographic regions.

Systems theory   With respect to policy analysis, systems theory views government as a system that receives "inputs" from its environment in the form of constituent demands and support, while government's "output" is public policy.

Tammany Hall   The famous New York political organization.

Temporary Assistance to Needy Families (TANF)   A block grant program that ended Aid to Families with Dependent Children (AFDC) as an entitlement.

Tennessee Valley Authority (TVA)   Established in 1933, the goal of the TVA was to facilitate economic development in that region of the country during the Great Depression. To this end, dams and generating plants were constructed, providing inexpensive electric power to the region.

Thirteenth Amendment   Outlawed slavery in 1865.

Thousand Points of Light   A national volunteer program of the administration of President George H. W. Bush.

Title XX   Passed during the Nixon administration, this amendment to the Social Security Act contributes federal funds to states for a range of social services.

Trail of Tears   The forced march of Cherokees for relocation in 1838, during which an estimated 4,000 of the 17,000 Cherokee people perished.

Underground Railroad   A secret network of supporters to assist slaves in escaping to free states in the north.

Undeserving poor   Those considered "less eligible" for poor relief.

Unemployment insurance   A major social insurance program benefiting unemployed workers in the United States.

United Way   A private nonprofit organization, United Way was formerly known as the "Community Chest," and for a time, the "United Fund." With the help of the business sector, United Way raises and allocates funds for voluntary health and human services.

Universal program   Citizens are entitled to participate in the program as a social right, meaning program participation is not based on financial need.

Value   A principle or quality that is considered desirable.

Value conflict   This approach to problem definition argues that social problems are created when groups have conflicting values.

Vendor system   Payments are made directly to the service provider.

Voluntary sector   Another name for the social sector in America. It is also referred to as the private nonprofit sector and independent sector.

Warn away   A technique colonial towns used to keep their relief costs down from strangers looking for public assistance. Those not heeding the town's warning could be punished, including flogging, tarring and feathering.

Windows of opportunity   Policy windows of opportunity occur when problems, solutions, and political support converge at some point in time.

Witness   Refers to one of several policy advocacy roles that social workers can play.

Workhouses   Institutions where able-bodied, but idle poor were likely to be put to work in exchange for their support. These institutions were often prison-like in that their goal was more to prevent public disorder and serve as a deterrent to public relief than to provide human charity.

Worker's compensation   Provides victims of work-related injuries with cash, medical care, and to a limited extent, rehabilitation services. It also compensates survivors if an injury is fatal. Workers' compensation does not cover all workers; farm and domestic workers are not covered in many states.

Works Progress Administration (WPA)   This program, which replaced the Federal Emergency Relief Administration created at the start of the New Deal, employed two million people a month building libraries, schools, hospitals, parks, and sidewalks.

World Bank   Established after World War II, this international organization is charged with the mission of promoting capital investments in developing countries.

World Trade Organization   This organization's purpose is to facilitate world trade, in large part, by serving as an arbitrator in trade disputes between various nations around the world.

Yeomen   Small farmers in colonial America.

INDEX